CONTENTS

1998

TAKE AN EXCITING VOYAGE THROUGH THE ZODIAC—AND DISCOVER A WONDROUS YEAR AHEAD!

Enter Sydney Omarr's star-studded world of accurate day-by-day predictions for every aspect of your life. With expert readings and forecasts, you can chart a course to romance, adventure, good health, or career opportunities while gaining valuable insight into yourself and others. Offering a daily outlook for 18 full months, this fascinating guide shows you:

- The important dates in your life
- What to expect from an astrological reading
- The initials of people who will be influential in your life
- How the stars can help you stay healthy and fit
- Your lucky lottery numbers
- And more!

Let this expert's sound advice guide you through a year of heavenly possibilities—for today and for every day of 1998!

SYDNEY OMARR DAY-BY-DAY ASTROLOGICAL GUIDE FOR

ARIES—March 21–April 19
TAURUS—April 20–May 20
GEMINI—May 21–June 20
CANCER—June 21–July 22
LEO—July 23–August 22
VIRGO—August 23–September 22
LIBRA—September 23–October 22
SCORPIO—October 23–November 21
SAGITTARIUS—November 22–December 21
CAPRICORN—December 22–January 19
AQUARIUS—January 20–February 18
PISCES—February 19–March 20

IN 1998

SYDNEY OMARR'S DAY-BY-DAY ASTROLOGICAL GUIDES
18 Months of Daily Horoscopes From
July 1997 to December 1998

Let America's most accurate astrologer show you what the signs of the zodiac will mean for you in the coming year! Sydney Omarr gives you invaluable tips on your love life, your career, your health—and your all-round good fortune.

☐	**Aquarius**—January 20–February 18	(193067—$5.50)
☐	**Pisces**—February 19–March 20	(193148—$5.50)
☐	**Aries**—March 21–April 19	(193075—$5.50)
☐	**Taurus**—April 20–May 20	(193172—$5.50)
☐	**Gemini**—May 21–June 20	(193105—$5.50)
☐	**Cancer**—June 21–July 22	(190083—$5.50)
☐	**Leo**—July 23–August 22	(193113—$5.50)
☐	**Virgo**—August 23–September 22	(193180—$5.50)
☐	**Libra**—September 23–October 22	(193121—$5.50)
☐	**Scorpio**—October 23–November 21	(193164—$5.50)
☐	**Sagittarius**—November 22–December 21	(193156—$5.50)
☐	**Capricorn**—December 22–January 19	(193091—$5.50)

Buy them at your local bookstore or use this convenient coupon for ordering.

PENGUIN USA
P.O. Box 999 — Dept. #17109
Bergenfield, New Jersey 07621

Please send me the books I have checked above.
I am enclosing $_____ (please add $2.00 to cover postage and handling). Send check or money order (no cash or C.O.D.'s) or charge by Mastercard or VISA (with a $15.00 minimum). Prices and numbers are subject to change without notice.

Card #_____ Exp. Date _____
Signature_____
Name_____
Address_____
City _____ State _____ Zip Code _____

For faster service when ordering by credit card call **1-800-253-6476**

Allow a minimum of 4-6 weeks for delivery. This offer is subject to change without notice.

SYDNEY OMARR'S

DAY-BY-DAY ASTROLOGICAL GUIDE FOR

SAGITTARIUS

November 22 — December 21

1998

A SIGNET BOOK

SIGNET
Published by the Penguin Group
Penguin Books USA Inc., 375 Hudson Street,
New York, New York 10014, U.S.A.
Penguin Books Ltd, 27 Wrights Lane,
London W8 5TZ, England
Penguin Books Australia Ltd, Ringwood,
Victoria, Australia
Penguin Books Canada Ltd, 10 Alcorn Avenue,
Toronto, Ontario, Canada M4V 3B2
Penguin Books (N.Z.) Ltd, 182–190 Wairau Road,
Auckland 10, New Zealand

Penguin Books Ltd, Registered Offices:
Harmondsworth, Middlesex, England

First published by Signet, an imprint of Dutton Signet,
a division of Penguin Books USA Inc.

First Printing, July, 1997
10 9 8 7 6 5 4 3 2 1

Sydney Omarr is syndicated worldwide by *Los Angeles Times* Syndicate.
Cover art by Faranak

 REGISTERED TRADEMARK—MARCA REGISTRADA

Printed in the United States of America

INTRODUCTION

Astrology
Your Link to the Millennium

We're now in an exciting time of transition between this century and the next, as our personal universe opens up with possibilities we never imagined. Thanks to the Internet, our favorite comfortable chair can be a command control center from which we can travel the globe at warp speed. Information from a distant library can be at our fingertips in moments. New friends and new lovers can meet in cyberspace. But though our lifestyle is changing, our longings haven't. We are still searching for the same things that have always made life worth living—love, meaningful work, and fulfilling personal relationships.

Astrology is an age-old tool that can guide us in our search, one that works as well today as it has for several millennia. Like "links" in the Internet, astrological clues can speed you from where you are now to where you'd like to be. But if you're new to astrology, you may feel just as bewildered as you did when you got a new PC. Though you have a marvelous tool available, it takes some practice and familiarity to operate effectively in your life. Fortunately, a little knowledge can get you up and running quickly. We give you basic information to help you understand the scope of astrology. We tell you what you need to know about your sun sign. Then you can look up other planets in your horoscope, to find out how each contributes to your total personality.

Many readers are fascinated by astrology's insights into relationships. This year, we give you ways to rate your relationship, to find out who you're most likely to get along with and why. You'll learn the upsides and downsides of possible partners, and how to handle each sign.

For those who are connected to the Internet, we've added a special chapter this year, so you can surf the many astrology sites to download programs, connect with other astrology fans, even find someone who is born on your birthday—your astro-twin.

It's fitting that Jupiter, the planet of expansion, will be moving into the astrology-friendly sign of Pisces this year. What better portent for using this ancient art every day. Let our daily forecasts guide you to having the happiest, most successful year ever!

CHAPTER 1

What's Hot for '98!

*This year's picks and predictions—
the worldwide trends that
can influence your life.*

The Year of Interactivity

Welcome to the world of cyberspace, where you can reinvent yourself. Who's to know if you have the dazzling form of Cindy Crawford or you're fifty pounds overweight? It makes no difference if you're a beauty or a beast, a grandma or a teenager. In the electronic world of Neptune and Uranus in 1998, you can be who you want to be with no one the wiser! Expect this year's high-tech innovations to play a new theme that could send you dashing through cyberspace as wild, wonderful, or wacky as you want to be. You create your own character, then interact with others in whatever way you choose. It's all in the mind, aided and abetted by the imagination.

The action starts in late February, when Neptune makes its big move into Aquarius. Get ready for a new kind of fun and games. You'll have your choice between watching TV or "doing" TV, actively participating in shows by offering your instant opinion via the phone or a special gadget connected to your TV. Or you'll interact through a tiny screen popping up on your computer. If you've been a couch potato, you'll now be jockeying new kinds of remote controls that can propel you right into the action.

Neptune, the planet of illusion, dissolves boundaries

between reality and fantasy. Uranus, the planet of high tech, has already been setting the stage in Aquarius, its natural home space. So when these two planets get together again in the same sign, watch out!

Spiritual Revival

The slow-moving planet Pluto is our guide to the hottest trends. Pluto is the planet of transformation, and while traveling through a sign, it brings about a heightened consciousness and the transformation of matters related to that sign. While traveling through Scorpio in the Eighties, we saw Scorpio-type "hotness" everywhere—black clothing, radical kinds of sexual issues, tattoos, transvestites, police dramas. Now traveling through Sagittarius, Pluto's task is to eliminate outworn belief systems to prepare us philosophically for the future. All that is ruled by Sagittarius is sure to be emphasized and transformed—religion, advertising, banking, higher education, the travel industry, the legal professions, publishing, gambling, outdoor sports, pets. At this writing, we've become a pet-happy nation, with pigs, Dalmatians, and St. Bernards playing leading roles in hit films. Color has come back into fashion, pushing black to the sidelines. Rugged, sporty four-wheel drive vehicles are in, as are pick-up trucks. Legs (Sagittarius-ruled) are exposed in fashion, emphasized by eye-catching hosiery.

The old, intrusive commercials and print ads are being replaced by a more subtle, well-disguised motivational message. Books, magazines, and newspapers are experimenting with new electronic publishing methods.

Along with an emphasis on spirituality, look for new insights and interpretations of ancient manuscripts, such as the Dead Sea Scrolls. We astrologers are reclaiming our own roots, by retranslating ancient manuscripts in a more astrology-friendly way. These writings are now published and circulating in professional astrology circles and they're eye-openers.

The Sagittarius bow and arrow now greets visitors to one of the gambling casinos on Native American reservations. Because Sagittarius rules gambling and sporting events, expect these to translate into the electronic Aquarian world. By the time this is published, gambling via your PC may be a reality.

Pisces Is Lucky

Good fortune and big money are always associated with Jupiter, the planet that embodies the principle of expansion. Jupiter has a 12-year cycle, staying in each sign for approximately one year. When Jupiter enters a sign, the fields governed by that sign usually provide excellent investment opportunities. Areas of speculation governed by the sign Jupiter is passing through will have the hottest market potential—they're the ones that currently arouse excitement and enthusiasm.

This year, Jupiter is traveling through Pisces, so sun-sign Pisceans, or those with strong Pisces influence in their horoscopes, will have abundant growth opportunities. On the other hand, those born under Virgo, the sign opposite Pisces, will need to make adjustments because this particular Pisces expansive atmosphere is opposed to their natural tendencies. For example, Virgo prospers in an atmosphere of order, efficiency, and precision, where skills and techniques are emphasized. While Jupiter is in Pisces, the expansive emphasis is ongoing with the flow, breaking rules and boundaries, appreciating chaos, imagination, escape. Though these qualities promote creativity and are excellent for artistic expansion, those who prefer a regimented atmosphere might feel uncomfortable and out of sync.

Some of the Pisces-blessed areas that should prosper this year are the oil industry, fishing and ocean-related industries, shipping, perfume, cosmetics, theater, poetry, dance, pharmaceuticals, alcohol, hospitals, prisons, monastic life (wherever we escape the world), footwear, and spiritual counseling. It's a great year for dancers and those involved with theatrical arts and filmmaking of all kinds. Expect a revival of all kinds of issues related to the petroleum industry.

If you're planning a vacation, consider a Pisces place: Portugal, Scandinavia, Vermont, north Africa, southern Asia, Normandy, Polynesia, Florida, or Chicago.

Pisceans are especially lucky this year. However, the principle of expansion also applies to your waistline. This is one of your most difficult times to diet! So focus on providing yourself with an abundance of fruits and vegetables and avoid fats and sugar.

Tests for Taurus, Unfinished Business for Aries

The emphasis so far has been on the idealistic, spiritual, philosophical areas governed by Aquarius, Sagittarius, and Pisces. It is interesting that, when there is so much emphasis on the idealistic, there is always some force in astrology that brings us back to earth and makes us face reality. This year, and for the next two years, it will be Saturn passing through the earth sign of Taurus.

Saturn keywords are focus, time, commitment, accomplishment, discipline, restriction. If Jupiter steps on the gas, Saturn applies the brakes. It's always a good idea to find the houses of your horoscope where Saturn and Jupiter are passing at any given time. It should help you to focus your time and energy on what is of value. But in Saturn areas, be sure to finish what you start. Saturn rewards responsible actions, hard work, and persistence.

Talk to an Aries and chances are, you'll be hearing about the trials and tribulations of the past two years, when Saturn was transiting this sign. Aries is a sign that facilitates fast action, rather than the slow, methodical, thorough approach, which Saturn demands. Most Aries will be heaving a sigh of relief when Saturn leaves their sign in June. However, "it's not over 'til it's over." Saturn retrogrades back to Aries to clear up unfinished business until March 1999, so Aries, as well as the other cardinal signs (Cancer, Libra, Capricorn) will still be feeling the restrictive, disciplinary influence of Saturn.

The brief stay of Saturn in Taurus from June to October should give the fixed signs (Taurus, Leo, Scorpio, Aquarius) a preview of challenges ahead. Saturn is quite powerful in the fixed signs, which are more focused and methodical by nature. It will facilitate the more stubborn, tyrannical forces over the next two years, building up to a meeting of Saturn and Jupiter in Taurus in the year 2000. The last time this conjunction happened in Taurus was in 1941, with ominous results. We can only hope that the wisdom and maturity of Saturn will be manifested this time around.

Taurus rules financial matters, the earning and spending of money, possessions of all kinds, and our attitude toward them. Retailing, land development, the territorial attitudes of nations, and wealth and poverty issues are areas to watch for Saturn's restrictive influence.

CHAPTER 2

Your Astro-Agenda
Plan Ahead for Perfect Timing

From the stacks of best-selling books on how to become more effective, gain control of our time, and set goals and priorities, we could say that the Nineties have become the Decade of the Agenda. Whether you use a computer program to schedule your activities or simply pencil activities in your calendar, chances are, you're more conscious of how you spend your time than ever before. Astrology has a different perspective on time management, as you become more sensitive to the cycles of the moon and planets and relate these celestial movements to your own life. If you become attuned to the natural rhythms of these cycles, you may find that certain activities go more smoothly if done at the most advantageous time.

The next step is to harmonize your schedule with the astrological cycles. If you know that three times a year, the tricky planet Mercury will be creating havoc with communications, you'll back up that vital fax with a duplicate by Express Mail; you'll read between the lines of contracts and put off closing that deal until Mercury is in a better mood.

Why not find out for yourself if there's truth to the saying "timing is everything," by marking your own calendar for love, career moves, vacations, and important events, using the following information and lists in this chapter and the one titled "Look Up Your Planets," as well as the moon sign listings under your daily forecast.

Here are some special times to note on your calendar:
• Dates of your sun sign (high-energy period)

- The month previous to your sun sign (low-energy period)
- Dates of planets in your sign this year
- Full and new moons (pay special attention when these fall in your sun sign)
- Eclipses
- Moon in your sun sign every month, as well as moon in the opposite sign (listed in your daily forecast)
- Mercury retrogrades

Check Your Vital Sign

Each birthdate recharges your energy with a powerful surge of vitality as the sun enters your sign. Take advantage of this time, when the predominant energies are most favorable to you to start new projects and make your big moves. You're more likely to get support and recognition now, when everyone is naturally attuned to your sun sign. Look in the tables in this book to see if other planets will also be passing through your sun sign at this time. Venus will activate your social and love life, making you the flavor of the month. Mars fuels your energy and drive, while Mercury turns on your brain power and helps you communicate, and Jupiter signals an especially lucky period of expansion.

There are two "down" times related to the sun. During the month before your birthday period, when you are completing your annual cycle, you could be feeling more vulnerable and depleted. It's a time when you may need extra rest and an especially nutritious diet. Cut back on stressful activities while you prepare for a big push when the sun enters your sign.

Another "down" time is when the sun is passing through the opposite sign (six months from your birthday) and the prevailing energies are very different from yours. You may feel at odds with the world, and things might not come easily. You'll have to work harder for recognition, because people are not on your wavelength. However, this could be a good time to work on a team, in cooperation with others or behind the scenes.

15

Phasing In and Out
With the Moon

Working with the phases of the moon is as easy as looking up at the night sky. At the new moon, when both
sun and moon are in the same sign, it's the best time to
begin new ventures, especially the activities that are favored by that sign. You'll have powerful energies pulling
you in the same direction. You'll be focused outward,
toward action. Postpone breaking off, terminating, delib-
erating, or reflecting activities that require introspection
and passive work.

Get your project under way during the first quarter, then
go public at the full moon, a time of high intensity, when
feelings come out into the open. This is your time to shine,
so express yourself. Be aware, however, that because pressures are being released, other people are also letting off
steam and confrontations are possible. So try to avoid arguments. Traditionally, astrologers often advise against surgery at this time, which could produce heavier bleeding.

During the last quarter until the next new moon,
you'll be most controlled. This is a winding-down phase,
a time to cut off unproductive relationships and to do
serious thinking and inward-directed activities.

You'll feel some new and full moons more strongly
than others, especially those new moons that fall in your
sun sign and full moons in your opposite sign. Because
that full moon happens at your low-energy time of year,
it is likely to be an especially stressful time in a relationship, when any hidden problems or unexpressed emotions could surface.

1998 Full and New Moons

January 12   Full Moon in Cancer
January 28   New Moon in Aquarius

February 11   Full Moon in Leo
February 26   New Moon/Solar Eclipse in Pisces

March 12	Lunar Eclipse/Full Moon in Virgo
March 27	New Moon in Aries
April 11	Full Moon in Libra
April 26	New Moon in Taurus
May 11	Full Moon in Scorpio
May 25	New Moon in Gemini
June 10	Full Moon in Sagittarius
June 23	New Moon in Cancer
July 9	Full Moon in Capricorn
July 23	New Moon in Leo
August 7	Full Moon/Lunar Eclipse in Aquarius
August 21	New Moon/Solar Eclipse in Leo
September 6	Full Moon/Lunar Eclipse in Pisces
September 20	New Moon in Virgo
October 5	Full Moon in Aries
October 20	New Moon in Libra
November 4	Full Moon in Taurus
November 19	Full Moon in Scorpio
December 3	Full Moon in Gemini
December 18	New Moon in Sagittarius

Forecasting With the Daily Moon Sign

The daily moon sign listed under your forecast in this book can be a powerful tool when scheduling your activities. To forecast the daily emotional weather, to determine your monthly high and low days, or to prioritize your time, note the activities favored and the moods you are likely to encounter as the moon passes through each sign.

Moon in Aries

Get moving! The new moon in Aries is an ideal time to start new projects. Everyone is pushy, raring to go, impatient, and short tempered. Leave the details and the follow-up for later. Competitive sports or martial arts are great ways to let off steam. Quiet types could use some assertiveness, but it's a great day for dynamos. Be careful not to step on too many toes.

Moon in Taurus

Stick to solid, methodical tasks, and tackle follow-through or backup work, laying the foundations for later success. Make investments, buy real estate, do appraisals, bargain hard. Attend to your property or get out in the country and spend some time in your garden. Enjoy creature comforts—your favorite music, a delicious dinner, sensual lovemaking. Forget about starting a diet at this time.

Moon in Gemini

Talk means action today, so telephone, write letters, fax! Make new contacts, and stay in touch with steady customers. you can handle lots of tasks at once. It's a great day for mental activity of any kind. Don't try to pin people down, for they too are feeling restless, so it helps to keep it light. Flirtations and socializing are good, but watch the gossip—and don't give away secrets.

Moon in Cancer

This is a moody, sensitive, emotional time. People respond to personal attention and mothering, and some may feel insecure and in need of extra TLC. Stay at home, have a family dinner, call your mother at a time when nostalgia, memories, and psychic powers are heightened. You'll want to hang on to people and things (don't clean out your closets now). You could have some insights into what others really need and want, so pay attention to dreams, intuition, and your own gut reactions.

Moon in Leo

Everybody is in a much more confident, warm, generous mood. It's a good day to ask for a raise, show what you can do, and dress up for your audience. People will respond to flattery and even enjoy a bit of drama. You may be more extravagant, so treat yourself royally and show off a bit—but don't break the bank! Be careful not to promise more than you can deliver!

Moon in Virgo

Do practical, down-to-earth chores—review your budget, make repairs, be an efficiency expert. This is not a day to ask for a raise. Have a health checkup, revamp your diet, or buy vitamins or health food. Be a demon house cleaner, taking care of details and piled-up chores. Reorganize your work and life so they run more smoothly and efficiently and save money too. Be prepared for others to be in a critical, fault-finding mood.

Moon in Libra

Attend to legal matters, negotiating contracts and arbitrating disputes. Do things with your favorite partner, socializing and being very romantic. Buy a special gift or a beautiful object and decorate yourself or your surroundings. Buy new clothes and then throw a party—make it an elegant, romantic evening. Smooth over any ruffled feathers. Avoid confrontations by sticking to civilized discussions.

Moon in Scorpio

This is a day to do things with passion, for you'll have excellent concentration and focus. Try not to get too intense emotionally, however, and avoid sharp exchanges with your loved ones. Others may tend to go to extremes, getting jealous and overreacting. Today is great for troubleshooting, problem-solving, research, scientific work—and making love. Pay attention to psychic vibes.

Moon in Sagittarius

It's a great time for travel and philosophical discussions. Set long-range career goals. Work out, do sports, or buy athletic equipment. Others will be feeling upbeat, exuberant, and adventurous. Risk taking is favored—you may feel like taking a gamble, betting on the horses, visiting a local casino, or just buying a lottery ticket. Teaching, writing, and spiritual activities also get the green light. Relax outdoors, taking care of animals.

Moon in Capricorn

You can accomplish a lot today, so get on the ball! Issues concerning your basic responsibilities and duties, and those involving your family and parents could crop up. You'll be expected to deliver on promises now. Weed out the dead wood from your life. Get a dental checkup.

Moon in Aquarius

It's a great day for doing thing with groups—clubs, meetings, outings, politics, parties. Campaign for your candidate or work for a worthy cause, dealing with larger issues that affect humanity, such as the environment or metaphysical questions. Buy a computer or electronic gadget. Watch TV. Wear something outrageous. Try something you've never done before—present an original idea and refuse to stick to a rigid schedule. Go with the flow. Take a class in meditation, mind control, or yoga.

Moon in Pisces

This can be a very creative day, so let your imagination work overtime. Film, theater, music, or ballet could inspire you. Spend some time alone, resting and reflecting, reading or writing poetry. Daydreams can also be profitable. Help those less fortunate or lend a listening ear to someone who may be feeling blue. Don't overindulge in self-pity or escapism, however. People are especially vulnerable to substance abuse now. Turn your thoughts to romance and someone special.

How to Handle Eclipses

One of the most amazing phenomena in the cosmos, which many of us take for granted, is the spatial relationship between the sun and the moon. How many of us have ever noticed or marveled that, relative to our viewpoint here on earth, both the largest source of energy (the sun) and the smallest (the moon) appear to be almost exactly the same size. This is most evident to us at the time of the solar eclipse, when the moon is directly aligned with the sun and so nearly covers it that scientists use the moment of eclipse to study solar flares.

When the two most powerful forces in astrology—the sun and the moon—are lined up, we're sure to feel the effects, both in world events and in our personal lives. It might help us to learn how best to cope with the periods around eclipses. Both solar and lunar eclipses are times when our natural rhythms are changed, depending on where the eclipse falls in your horoscope. If it falls on or close to your birthday, you're going to have important changes in your life, and perhaps even come to a turning point.

Lunar eclipses happen when the earth is on a level plane with the sun and moon and lines up exactly between them during the time of the full moon, breaking the opposition of these two forces. We might say the earth short-circuits the connection between them. The effect can be either confusion or clarity, as our subconscious energies, which normally react to the pull of opposing sun and moon, are turned off. As we are temporarily freed from the subconscious attachments, we might have objective insights that could help us change any destructive emotional patterns, such as addictions, which normally occur at this time. This momentary turn-off could help us turn our lives around. On the other hand, this break in the normal cycle could cause a bewildering disorientation that intensifies our insecurities.

The solar eclipse occurs during the new moon, when the moon blocks the sun's energies as it passes exactly between the sun and the earth. Symbolically, this means the objective, conscious force, represented by the sun, will be temporarily darkened and subconscious lunar forces, activating our deepest emotions, will now dominate, putting us in a highly subjective state. Emotional truths can be revealed or emotions can run wild, as our objectivity is cut off and hidden patterns surface. If your sign is affected, you may find yourself beginning a period of work on a deep inner level; you may have psychic experiences or a surfacing of deep feelings.

You'll start feeling the energies of an upcoming eclipse a few days after the previous new or full moon. The energy continues to intensify until the actual eclipse, then disperses for three or four days. So plan ahead at least a week or more before an eclipse, and allow several days afterward for the natural rhythms to return. Try not to make major moves during this period—it's not a great time to get married, change jobs, or buy a home.

Eclipses in 1998:

February 26	Solar Eclipse in Pisces
March 12	Lunar Eclipse in Virgo
August 7	Lunar Eclipse in Aquarius
August 21	Solar Eclipse in Leo
September 6	Lunar Eclipse in Pisces

When the Planets Go Backward

All the planets, except for the sun and moon, have times when they appear to move backward—or retrograde—in the sky, or so it seems from our point of view on earth. At these times, planets do not work as they usually do, so it's best to take a break from that planet's energies in our life and do some work on an inner level.

Mercury Retrograde

Mercury goes retrograde most often, and its effects can be especially irritating. When it reaches a short distance ahead of the sun three times a year, it seems to move backward from our point of view. Astrologers often compare retrograde motion to the optical illusion that occurs when we ride on a train that passes another train traveling at a different speed—the second train appears to be moving in reverse.

What this means to you is that the Mercury-ruled areas of your life—analytical thought processes, communications, scheduling, and such—are subject to all kinds of confusion. So be prepared for people to change their minds and renege on commitments. Communications equipment can break down; schedules must be changed on short notice; people are late for appointments or don't show up at all. Traffic is terrible. Major purchases malfunction or don't work out in some way, or they get delivered in the wrong color. Letters don't arrive or might be delivered to the wrong address. Employees tend to make errors that have to be corrected later, and contracts might not work out or must be renegotiated.

Since most of us can't put our lives on hold for nine weeks every year (three Mercury retrograde periods), we should learn to tame the trickster and make it work for us. The key is in the prefix "re." This is the time to go back over things in your life, reflecting on what you've done during the previous months and looking for deeper insights. Try to spot errors you may have missed and then take time to review and reevaluate what has happened. This time is very good for inner spiritual work and meditations. REst and REward yourself—it's a good time to take a vacation, especially if you revisit a favorite place. REorganize your work and finish up projects that are backed up. Clean out your desk and closets. Throw away what you can't REcycle. If you must sign contracts or agreements, do so with a contingency clause that lets you reevaluate the terms later.

Postpone major purchases or commitments. Don't get married—unless you're re-marrying the same person. Try not to rely on other people keeping appointments, contracts, or agreements to the letter—have several alternatives. Double-check and read between the lines, and don't buy anything connected with communications or transportation (if you must, be sure to cover yourself). Mercury retrograding through your sun sign will intensify its effect on your life.

If Mercury was retrograde when you were born, you may be one of the lucky people who don't suffer the frustrations of this period. If so, your mind probably works in a very intuitive, insightful way.

The sign that Mercury is retrograding through can give you an idea of what's in store—as well as the sun signs that will be especially challenged.

Mercury Retrograde Periods in 1998

Mercury Retrograde in Aries	March 27–April 20
Mercury Retrograde in Leo	July 30th–August 23
Mercury Retrograde in Sagittarius	November 21–December 11

CHAPTER 3

Have Mouse . . . Will Travel!
An Astrologer's Guide to Surfing the Internet

If you have a personal computer and access to the Internet, you're connected to a global community of astrologers. This brings you instant access to atlases, programs, charts, databases, and personal contacts that could only be dreamed about just a few years ago. Since the Internet is buzzing with new astrology sites, its astrology resources will probably be much more extensive when this guide is published.

Here are some of the things you can do on the Internet: Find a pen pal who's interested in astrology at your level; get a hard-to-find book on any aspect of astrology; get information on your moon sign or the exact location and time zone of your birthplace from an online atlas; find your astro-twin, someone who shares your birthday; look for the perfectly compatible romantic partner in an astro-dating area. So click your mouse and travel the worldwide astrology community. Here are our picks from the hundreds of sites now open to "surfers."

Newsgroups:

Of the many newsgroups, there are several devoted to astrology. The most popular is "alt.astrology." Here's your chance to connect with astrologers worldwide, exchange information, and answer some of the skeptics who frequent this newsgroup.

Mailing Lists

Want to fill your e-mail box with astrology-related notes? Subscribe to a list and get e-mail sent directly to your address. The following lists are especially for astrology fans.

Festival

To subscribe, send e-mail to: srozhon@cybergate.net with the message: "Subscribe festival," plus your e-mail address, and you will receive further instructions.

Oracle-a

To subscribe, send e-mail to: oracle-a-request@idirect.com, with the message: "subscribe," and you will receive all details.

AAmail

This is the mailing list of the Astrological Association of Great Britain. To subscribe, send e-mail to: listserver @astrologer.com with the message: "subscribe AAmail end."

Online Services

The top online services offer areas devoted to astrology that include chat rooms, daily forecasts, special interest groups, articles, lectures, and links to other interesting astrology sites. They're an easy place to begin surfing.

America Online

This huge service offers ASTRONET, with an Astrology Newsstand, software reviews, horoscopes, featured guests, and a shopping area for books, reports, and software. A popular feature is "Astromates," where you can browse profiles of prospective partners under their zodiac sign. There are lots of links to other sites.

An Astrological Calendar

Download a calendar for each month, with Moon sign changes and important aspects.
  Address: http://users.aol.com/zodiactime

Dates of Important Events

Find out what important events happened on any date in history.
  Address: http://www.scopsys.com/today

Great Places to Visit

Metalog Yellow Pages

This offers an extensive list of international sites, as well as an agenda of astrology conferences and seminars all over the world. If you'll be traveling and you'd like to take in an astrology conference in, say, England or New Zealand, check out this site.
  Address: http://www.astrologer.com/

The Urania Trust Guide

Here's another great list of astrologers, from Kansas to Kazakstan.
  Address: http://www.astrologer.com/utguide/index

Internet Atlas

Get the geographic longitude and latitude and the correct time zone for cities worldwide.
Address: http://www.astro.ch/atlas/

The Zodiacal Zephyr

This is a great place to start out. It has a U.S. and World Atlas, Celebrity Birthdata, an Ephemeris, and information on conferences, software, and tapes. There is also a link to an Astrology Compatibility Service, where you can meet potential soulmates from around the world.
Address: http://metro.turnpike.net/S/SRozhon/index.html

TMA Communications

Here you'll find articles and astroweather.
Address: http://www.lightworks.com

Astrology Alive

This site features Barbara Schermer's creative approach to astrology, along with a great list of links.
Address: http://www.lightworks.com/Astrology/Alive/

National Council for Geocosmic Research (NCGR)

This site contains information on membership and testing programs, and updates on conferences. Order conference tapes and get complete lists of conference topics. There's also a list of astrology Websites to visit and links to resources. This is an easy place to find chapters and conferences near you.
Address: http://www.geocosmic.org/

Astrology Software: Freeware and Shareware

Magitech

Download *Astrolog,* a terrific astrology program, here.
   Address: http://www.magitech.com/pub/astrology/software/pc

The Widening Gyre

This is a good source for software.
   Address: http://www.prairienet.org/rec/gyre/widegyre.html

Software Search Engine: Shareware.Com

Select DOS or Windows and type "astrol" in the search input.
   Address: http://www.shareware.com

Best General Search Engine: Yahoo!

This is an excellent search engine that enters your input into other popular search engines.
   Address: http://www.yahoo.com

Astrolabe

Preview some of Astrolabe's terrific astrology programs. You can download a demo version of their top-rated Solar Fire III at this site.
   Address: http://www.alabe.com

Astrolog

Walter Pullen's freeware program has fascinating graphics and lots of features used by professional astrologers. An excellent program for serious students. You'll enjoy it most if you have a basic knowledge of astrology and can read astrology symbols. Get a preview before you download.

Address: http://www.speakeasy.org/~cruiser1/astrolog.htm

Matrix Software

Connect here to Matrix Software's innovative programs. Check out the easy-to-learn Winstar and the colorful fun-to-use Kaleidoscope.

Address: http://www.theNewAge.com

ACS Software and Services

Here is the online headquarters of Astro Computing Services, with a bookstore, software demos, chart services, and lots of features.

Address: http://www/astrocom.com

Astrology Books

National Clearinghouse for Astrology Books

Here is a wide selection of books on all aspects of astrology, from basics to advanced, and including many hard-to-find books.

Address: http://www.astroamerica.com

Your Astrology Questions Answered

ASTROLOGY FAQ (Frequently Asked Questions)
  Address: http://magitech.com/pub/astrology/info/faq.txt

Who was born on your Birthday?

Find out who was born on any day you specify. You can also get biographies of your choice at this site.
   Address: http://www.eb.som/bio.html

Online Astrology Magazines:

Welcome to Planet Earth

Get the astrology slant on fast-breaking news and the latest trends. A great site for links, articles, celebrity profiles.
   Address: http://alive.mcn.org/greatbear/tofc.html

The Mountain Astrologer

Read articles by top astrologers. Good material for beginning students.
   Address: http://www.jadesun.com/tma

A Terrific Link to the Astrology Community:

Web First

A comprehensive astrology site well worth a visit. Features a list of teachers, a link to homepages of professional astrologers on the "Festival" mailing list, plus lots of interesting links.
   Address: http://hudson.idt.net/~motive/

CHAPTER 4

Sydney Omarr's Yellow Pages
The Top Astrological Clubs, Conferences, Organizations, and More

Ever wondered where the astrologers are in your area, where you can get a basic astrology program for your new computer, or where to take a class with a professional astrologer? Look no further. In this chapter we'll give you the information you need to locate the latest products and services available.

There are very well-organized groups of astrologers all over the country who are dedicated to promoting the image of astrology in the most positive way. The National Council for Geocosmic Research (NCGR) is one nationwide group that is dedicated to bringing astrologers together, promoting fellowship and high-quality education. They have an accredited course system, with a systematized study of all the facets of astrology. Whether you'd like to know more about such specialties as financial astrology or techniques for timing events, or if you'd prefer a psychological or mythological approach, you'll find the leading experts at NCGR conferences.

Your computer can be a terrific tool for connecting with other astrology fans at all levels of expertise. If you do not yet own a computer and are thinking about buying a new or used one, have no fear. In spite of the breakneck pace of technology, there will still be plenty of software available for your computer. Even if you are using a "dinosaur" from the early Eighties, there are still calculation and interpretation programs available. They may not have all the bells and whistles or exciting graphics, but they'll still get the job done!

If you are a newcomer to astrology, it is a good idea to learn the glyphs (astrology's special shorthand language) before you purchase a computer program. Use Chapter 7 to help you learn the symbols easily. That way, you'll be able to read the charts without consulting a book. One program, however, Astrolabe's Solar Fire for Windows, has pop-up definitions—just click your mouse on the glyph and a definition appears.

Astrology programs are available at all price levels, from under $20 CD's in your local software chain, to more sophisticated and expensive astrology programs from specialized dealers (approximately $200–250 at this writing). But before you make a serious investment, download or order some demo disks from the company. If you just want to have fun, investigate some of the lower-priced programs—there are many available for under $100. Most of the companies on our list will be happy to help you find the right program for your needs.

If you live in an out-of-the-way place or are unable to fit classes into your schedule, study-by-mail courses are available from several astrological computing services. Some courses will send you a series of tapes; others use workbooks or computer printouts.

Nationwide Astrology Organizations and Conferences

The astrology world has been buzzing this year in preparation for one of its most exciting events, the United Astrology Conference, to take place May 21–26, 1998 at the Hyatt Regency Hotel in Atlanta, GA. Get updated on the latest conference news via the NCGR Website listed below. If you are visiting the Atlanta area, plan to attend and meet astrologers from around the world. The trade show is sure to be a treasure trove of all the latest astrological tools. If you can't attend the conference, you can purchase tapes of the lectures from Bulldog Audio, P.O. Box 127, Coeur D'Alene, Idaho 83814; (208)664–9885. They also have tapes available from previous UAC conferences.

Contact these organizations for information on conferences, workshops, local meetings, conference tapes, referrals:

National Council for Geocosmic Research
Educational workshops, tapes, and conferences; a directory of professional astrologers is available. For questions about NCGR membership, contact:
Pamela Huang
102 Deborah Dr.
Lynchburg, VA 24501–5112
(804)239–8643
http://www.geocosmic.org

American Federation of Astrologers (A.F.A.)
One of the oldest astrological organizations in the U.S., the A.F.A. was established 1938, and it offers conferences and conventions. The federation will refer you to an accredited astrologer.
P.O. Box 22040
Tempe, AZ 85382
(602)838–1751
Fax (602)838–8293

Association for Astrological Networking (A.F.A.N.)
They offer networking and legal issues. Did you know that astrologers are still being arrested for practicing in some states? AFAN provides support and legal information, and works toward improving the public image of astrology.
8306 Wilshire Blvd
Berkeley Hills, CA 90211

ARC Directory
This provides a listing of astrologers worldwide.
2920 E. Monte Vista
Tucson, AZ 85716
(602)321–1114

Conference and Lecture Tapes

National Council for Geocosmic Research
Class, lecture, and conference tapes are available.
Margie Herskovitz
5826 Greenspring Ave.
Baltimore, MD 20754–9998
(410)257–2824

Pegasus Tapes
Lectures and conference tapes are available.
P.O. Box 419
Santa Ysabel, CA 92070

International Society for Astrological Research
Lectures, workshops, and seminars are provided.
P.O. Box 38613
Los Angeles, CA 90038

ISIS Institute
P.O. Box 21222
El Sobrante, CA 94820–1222

Astrol-Analytics Productions
P.O. Box 16927
Encino, CA 91411–6927

Computer Programs

Astrolabe
Check out their powerful Solar Fire Windows software—
it's a breeze to use. This company also markets a variety

of programs for all levels of expertise, as well as a wide selection of computer astrology readings and MAC programs. It's also a good resource for innovative software and programs for older computers.
P.O. Box 1750–R
Brewster, MA 02631
(800)843–6682

Matrix Software
Find a wide variety of software in all price ranges and demo disks at student and advanced level, with lots of interesting readings.
315 Marion Ave.
Big Rapids, MI 49307
(800)PLANETS

Astro Communications Services
They offer books, software for MAC and IBM compatibles, individual charts, and telephone readings. It's a good resource for those who do not have computers, as they will calculate charts for you.
Dept. AF693, P.O. Box 34487
San Diego, CA 92163–4487
(800)888–9983

Air Software
115 Caya Avenue
West Hartford, CT 06110
(800)659–1247
http://www.alphee.com
A free program is available to download at Website.

Time Cycles Research
Beautiful graphic IO Series programs are available for the MAC.
375 Willets Avenue
Waterford, CT 06385
Fax (869)442–0625
astrology@timecycles.com
http://www.timecycles.com

Astro-Cartography
Charts for location changes are available.
Astro-Numeric Service Box 336-B
Ashland, OR 97520
(800)MAPPING

Microcycles
The "world's largest astrological software dealer," they
offer catalogs, demo diskettes, and professional help in
choosing software.
P.O. Box 2175
Culver City, CA 90231
(800)829-2537

Astrology Magazines

Most have listings of conferences, events, and local happenings.

American Astrology
475 Park Avenue South
New York, NY 10016

Dell Horoscope
P.O. Box 53352
Boulder, CO 89321-3342

Planet Earth
The Great Bear
P.O. Box 5164
Eugene, OR 97405

Mountain Astrologer
P.O. Box 11292
Berkeley, CA 94701

Aspects
Aquarius Workshops
P.O. Box 260556
Encino, CA 91426

CHAPTER 5

Clueless About Astrology?
Here's the Least You Need to Know

Want to know how astrology really works, but you're clueless when it comes to knowing the difference between a sign and a constellation or deciphering those strange looking symbols all over the horoscope? Not to mention sorting out zodiacs, planets, houses, and aspects.

You've come to the right place. Here's a user-friendly guide to help you find your way around the fascinating world of astrology.

The Basics—Signs, Houses, Charts

Where the Signs Are

First, let's get our sign language straight, because for most readers, that's the starting point of astrology.

Signs are located on the *zodiac,* an imaginary 360-degree belt circling Earth. This belt is divided into 12 equal 30-degree portions, which define the boundaries of the *signs*. There's a lot of confusion about the difference between the signs and the *constellations* of the zodiac, patterns of stars that originally marked the twelve divisions, like signposts. Though a sign is named after the constellation that once marked the same area, the constellations are no longer in the same place relative to the Earth that they were centuries ago. Over hundreds of years, Earth's orbit has shifted, so that from our point of view here on Earth, the constellations moved, but the signs remain in place. (Most Western astrologers use the 12-equal-part division of the zodiac; however, there are some methods of astrology that still do use the constellations instead of the signs.)

Most people think of themselves in terms of their sun sign. A *sun sign* refers to the sign the sun is orbiting through at a given moment, from our point of view here on Earth. For instance, "I'm an Aries" means that the sun was passing through Aries when that person was born. However, there are nine other planets (plus asteroids, fixed stars, and sensitive points) that also form our total astrological personality, and some or many of these will be located in other signs. No one is completely "Aries," with all their astrological components in one sign! (Please note that, in astrology, the sun and moon are usually referred to as "planets," though of course they're not.)

What Makes a Sign Special?

What makes Aries the sign of go-getters and Taureans savvy with money? And Geminis talk a blue streak and Sagittarians footloose? Definitions of the signs are not accidental; they are derived from different combinations of four concepts—a sign's element, quality, polarity, and place on the zodiac.

Take the element of *fire:* It's hot, passionate. Then add the active cardinal mode. Give it a jolt of positive energy and place it first in line. And doesn't that sound like the active, me-first, driving, hot-headed, energetic Aries?

Then take the element of *earth,* practical and sensual. Add the fixed, stable mode. Give it energy that reacts to its surroundings and settles in. Put it after Aries. Now you've got a good idea of how sensual, earthy Taurus operates.

Another way to grasp the idea is to pretend you're doing a magical puzzle based on the numbers that can divide into twelve (the number of signs)—4, 3, and 2.

There are four building blocks or *elements*, three ways a sign operates *(qualities)*, and two *polarities*. These alternate in turn around the zodiac, with a different combination coming up for each sign.

The four elements. Here's how they add up. The *four elements* describe the physical concept of the sign. Is it fiery (dynamic), earthy (practical), airy (mental), watery (emotional)? There are three zodiac signs of each of the four elements: fire (Aries, Leo, Sagittarius), earth (Taurus, Virgo, Capricorn), air (Gemini, Libra, Aquarius), water (Cancer, Scorpio, Pisces). These are the same elements that make up our planet: earth, air, fire, and water. But astrology uses the elements as *symbols* that link our body and psyche to the rhythms of the planets. Fire signs spread warmth and enthusiasm. They are able to fire up or motivate others, and they have hot tempers. These are the people who make ideas catch fire and spring into existence. Earth signs are the builders of the zodiac, who follow through after the initiative of fire signs to make things happen. These people are solid, practical realists who enjoy material things and sensual pleasures. They are interested in ideas that can be used to achieve concrete results. Air signs are mental people, great communicators. Following the consolidating earth signs, they'll reach out to inspire others through the use of words, social contacts, discussion, and debate. Water signs complete each four-sign series, adding the ingredients of emotion, compassion, and imagination. Water-sign people are nonverbal communicators who attune themselves to their surroundings and react through the medium of feelings.

Quality. The second consideration when defining a sign is how it will operate. Will it take the initiative, or move slowly and deliberately? Will it adapt easily? Its *quality* (or modality) will tell. There are three qualities and four signs of each quality: cardinal, fixed, and mutable.

Cardinal signs are the start-up signs that begin each season (Aries, Cancer, Libra, Capricorn). These people love to be active and involved in projects. They are usually on the fast track to success, impatient to get things under way. *Fixed signs* (Taurus, Leo, Scorpio, Aquarius) move steadily, always in control. They happen in the middle of a season, after the initial character of the season is established. Fixed signs are naturally more centered, tending to move more deliberately and do things more slowly but more thoroughly. They govern parts of your horoscope where you take root and integrate your experiences. *Mutable signs* (Gemini, Virgo, Sagittarius, Pisces) embody the principle of distribution. These are the signs that break up the cycle, preparing the way for a change by distributing the energy to the next group. Mutables are flexible, adaptable, and communicative. They can move in many directions easily, darting around obstacles.

Polarity. In addition to an element and a quality, each sign has a polarity, either a positive or a negative electrical charge that generates energy around the zodiac, like a giant battery. Polarity refers to opposites, which you could also define as masculine/feminine, yin/yang, or active/reactive. Alternating around the zodiac, the six fire and air signs are positive, active, masculine, and yang in polarity. These signs are open, expanding outward. The six earth and water signs are reactive, negative and yin— they are nurturing and receptive in polarity, which allows the energy to develop and take shape. All positive energy would be like a car without brakes. All negative energy would be like a stalled vehicle, going nowhere. Both polarities are needed in balanced proportion.

Order. Finally we must consider the order of the signs. This is vital to the balance of the zodiac and the transmission of energy throughout the zodiac. Each sign is quite different from its neighbors on either side. Yet each seems to grow out of its predecessor like links in a chain, transmitting a synthesis of energy gathered along the chain to the following sign, beginning with the fire-powered active, positive, cardinal sign of Aries and ending with watery, mutable, reactive Pisces.

The Layout of a Horoscope Chart

A horoscope chart is a map of the heavens at a given moment in time. It looks somewhat like a wheel divided with twelve spokes. In between each of the "spokes" is a section called a "house." Each house deals with a different area of life and is influenced (or "ruled") by a special sign and a planet. In addition, the house is governed by the sign passing over the spoke (or cusp) at that particular moment. The houses start at the left-center spoke (or the 9 position if you were reading a clock) and are read counter-clockwise around the chart.

The first house, home of Aries and the planet Mars. This is the house of "firsts"—the first impression you make, how you initiate matters, the image you choose to project. This is where you advertise yourself. Planets that fall here will intensify the way you come across to others. Often the first house will project an entirely different type of personality than the sun sign. For instance, a Capricorn with Leo in the first house will come across as much more flamboyant than the average Capricorn. The sign passing over this house at the time of your birth is known as your ascendant, or rising sign.

The second house, home of Taurus and Venus. This refers to how you experience the material world and what you value. Here is your contact with the material world—your attitudes about money, possessions, finances, whatever belongs to you, as well as your earning and spending capacity. On a deeper level, this house reveals your sense of self-worth, the inner values that draw wealth in various forms.

The third house, home of Gemini and Mars. This concerns how well you communicate with others. Are you understood? This house shows how you reach out to others nearby and interact with the immediate environment. Here is how your thinking process works; here is the way you communicate. Here are your first relationships, your experiences with brothers and sisters, as well as the ways you deal with people close to you, such as neighbors or pals. It's also where you take short trips, write letters, or use the telephone. It shows how your mind works in terms of left-brain logical and analytical functions.

The fourth house, home of Cancer and the moon. This house relates to how you are nurtured and made to feel secure—your roots! At the bottom of the chart, the fourth house, like the home, shows the foundation of your life, your psychological underpinnings. Here is where you have the deepest confrontations with who you are, and how you make yourself feel secure. It shows your early home environment and the circumstances at the end of your life—your final home—as well as the place you call home now. Astrologers look here for information about the primary nurturers in your life.

The fifth house, home of Leo and the sun. This refers to how you express yourself creatively and to your idea of play. The Leo house is where the creative potential develops. Here you express yourself and procreate, in the sense that children are outgrowths of your creative ability. But this house most represents your inner child-like self, who delights in play. If inner security has been established by the time you reach this house, you are now free to enjoy fun, romance, and love affairs—to give of yourself. This is also the place astrologers look for playful love affairs, flirtations, and brief romantic encounters (rather than long-term commitments).

The sixth house, home of Virgo and Mercury. This shows how you function in daily life. The sixth house has been called the "repair and maintenance" department. Here is where you get things done and where you determine how you will look after others and fulfill service duties, such as taking care of pets. Here is your daily survival, your job (as opposed to your career, which is the domain of the tenth house), your diet, and your health and fitness regimens. This house shows how well you take care of your body and organize yourself so you can perform efficiently in the world.

The seventh house, home of Libra and Venus. This house has to do with how you form a partnership. Here is the way you relate to others, including close, intimate, one-on-one relationships (even open enemies—those you face off with). This house shows your attitude toward partners and those with whom you enter commitments, contracts, or agreements. Open hostilities, lawsuits, divorces, and marriages happen here. If the first house is the "I," the seventh or opposite house is the "Not-I," the complementary partner you attract by the way you come across. If you are having trouble with relationships, consider what you are attracting by the interaction of your first and seventh houses.

The eighth house, home of Scorpio, Pluto, and Mars. This refers to how you merge with something, or handle power and control. This is one of the most mysterious and powerful houses, where your energy transforms itself from "I" to "we." As you give up your personal power and control by uniting with something or someone else, these two kinds of energies merge and become something greater, leading to a regeneration of the self on a higher level. Here are your attitudes toward sex, shared resources, and taxes (what you share with the government). Because this house involves what belongs to others, you face issues of control and power struggles, or undergo a deep psychological transformation as you bond with another. Here you transcend yourself with the occult, dreams, drugs, or psychic experiences that reflect the collective unconscious.

The ninth house, home of Sagittarius and Jupiter. This house rules how you search for wisdom and higher knowledge—your belief system. While the third house represents the lower mind, its opposite on the wheel, the ninth house is the higher mind—the abstract, intuitive, spiritual mind that asks big questions like "Why are we here?" The ninth house shows what you believe in. After the third house explored what was close at hand, the ninth stretches out to expand horizons with higher education and travel, or to stretch spiritually with religious activity. Here is where you write a book or an extensive thesis, where you pontificate, philosophize, or preach.

The tenth house, home of Capricorn and Saturn. This house rules your public image and how you handle authority. This house is located directly overhead at the high noon position. This is the most visible house in the chart, the one where the world sees you. It deals with your public image, your career (but not your routine job), and your reputation. Here is where you go public and take on responsibilities (as opposed to the fourth house, where you stay home). This will affect the career you choose and your public relations. This house is also associated with your father figure or whoever else was the authority figure in your life.

The eleventh house, home of Aquarius and Uranus. This refers to your support system, how you relate to society and your goals. Here you extend yourself to a group, a goal, or a belief system. This house is where you define what you really want, the kinds of friends you have, your political affiliations, and the kind of groups you identify with as an equal. Here is where you could become a socially conscious humanitarian—or a partygoing social butterfly. It's where you look to others to stimulate you and discover your kinship to the rest of humanity. The sign on this house can help you understand what you gain and lose from friendships.

The twelfth house, home of Pisces and Neptune. This determines how you become selfless. Here is where the boundaries between yourself and others become blurred. In your trip around the zodiac, you've gone from the "I" of self-assertion in the first house to the final house symbolizing the dissolution of the self that happens before rebirth; it's where accumulated experiences are processed in the unconscious. Spiritually oriented astrologers look to this house for your past lives and karma. Places where we go to be alone and do spiritual or reparatory work belong here, such as retreats, religious institutions, hospitals. Here is also where we withdraw from society—or are forced to withdraw because of antisocial activity. Selfless giving through charitable acts is part of this house. In your daily life, the twelfth house reveals your deepest intimacies and your best-kept secrets, especially those you hide from yourself and keep repressed deep in the unconscious. It is where we surrender the sense of a separate self to a deep feeling of wholeness, such as selfless service in religion or any activity that involves merging with the greater whole. Many sports stars have important planets in the twelfth house that enable them to find an inner, almost mystical, strength that transcends their limits.

Who's Home in Your Houses?

Houses are stronger or weaker depending on how many planets are inhabiting them. If there are many planets in a given house, it follows that the activities of that house will be especially important in your life. If the planet that rules the house is also located there, this too adds power to the house.

CHAPTER 6

The Planets in Your Life and What They Mean

The ten planets in your chart will play starring or supporting roles, depending on their position in your horoscope. A planet in the first house, particularly one that's close to your rising sign, is sure to be a featured player. Planets that are grouped together usually operate together like a team, playing off each other, rather than expressing their energy singularly. A planet that stands alone, away from the others, is usually outstanding and sometimes steals the show.

Each planet has two signs where it is especially at home. These are called its *dignities*. The most favorable place for a planet is in the sign or signs it rules; the next best place is in a sign where it is *exalted,* or especially harmonious. On the other hand, there are places in the horoscope where a planet has to work harder to play its role. These places are called the planet's detriment and fall. The sign opposite a planet's rulership, which embodies the opposite area of life, is its *detriment*. The sign opposite its exaltation is its *fall*. Though the terms may suggest unfortunate circumstances for the planet, that is not always the case. In fact, a planet that is debilitated can actually be more complete, because it must stretch itself to meet the challenges of living in a more difficult sign. Like world leaders who've had to struggle for greatness, this planet may actually develop great strength and character.

The Planets and the Signs They Rule

Here's a list of the best places for each planet to be, in the signs they rule. Note that as new planets were discovered in this century, they replaced the traditional rulers of signs that best complimented their energies.

Aries	Mars
Taurus	Venus in its most sensual form
Gemini	Mercury in its communicative role
Cancer	the Moon
Leo	the Sun
Virgo	Mercury in its critical capacity
Libra	Venus in its aesthetic, judgmental form
Scorpio	Pluto, replacing its original ruler, Mars
Sagittarius	Jupiter
Capricorn	Saturn
Aquarius	Uranus, replacing its original ruler, Saturn
Pisces	Neptune, replacing its original ruler, Jupiter

Exalted Signs

A person who has many planets in exalted signs is lucky indeed, for here is where the planet can accomplish the most, be its most influential and creative

Sun	exalted in Aries, where its energy creates action
Moon	exalted in Taurus, where instincts and reactions operate on a creative level
Mercury	exalted in Virgo, which it also rules, where it reaches analytical heights
Venus	exalted in Pisces, whose sensitivity encourages love and creativity
Mars	exalted in Capricorn, which puts energy to work
Jupiter	exalted in Cancer, where it encourages nurturing and growth
Saturn	at home in Libra, where it steadies the scales of justice and promotes balanced, responsible judgment
Uranus	powerful in Scorpio, where it promotes transformation
Neptune	favored in Cancer, where it gains the security

| | to transcend to a higher state |
| Pluto | exalted in Pisces, where it dissolves the old cycle to make way for transition to the new. |

The Sun Is Always Top of the List

Your sun sign is the part of you that shines brightest. But the other planets add special coloration that make you different from other members of your sign. When you know a person's sun sign, you already know some very useful generic qualities. But when you know all a person's planets, you have a much more accurate profile of that person and you'll be much more able to predict how that individual will act in a given situation. The sun's just one card in your hand—when you know the other planets, you can really play to win!

Since the sun is always the first consideration, it is important to treat it as the star of the show. It is your conscious ego and it is always center stage, even when sharing a house or a sign with several other planets. This is why sun-sign astrology works for so many people. In chart interpretations, the sun can also play the parental role.

The sun rules the sign of Leo, gaining strength through the pride, dignity, and confidence of the fixed-fire personality. It is exalted in "me-first" Aries. In its detriment, Aquarius, the sun-ego is strengthened through group participation and social consciousness, rather than through self-centeredness. Note how many Aquarius people are involved in politics, social work, and public life, following the demands of their sun sign to be spokesperson for a group. In its fall, Libra, the sun needs the strength of a partner—and "other"—to enhance balance and self-expression.

Like your sun sign, each of the other nine planets' personalities are colored by the sign it is passing through at the time. For example, Mercury, the planet that rules the way you communicate, will express itself in a dynamic, headstrong Aries way if it was passing through the sign of Aries when you were born. You would communicate in a much different way if it were passing through the slower, more patient sign of Taurus. And so on through the list. Here's a rundown of the planets and how they behave in every sign.

The Moon—The Inner You

The moon can teach you about the inner side of yourself and about your needs and secrets, as well as those of others. It is your most personal planet, the receptive, reflective, female, nurturing side of you. And it reflects who you were nurtured by—the "Mother" or mother figure in your chart. In a man's chart, the moon position also describes his female, receptive, emotional side, as well as the woman in his life who will have the deepest effect. (Venus reveals the kind of woman who attracts him physically.)

The sign the moon was passing through at your birth reflects your instinctive emotional nature and what appeals to you subconsciously. Since accurate moon tables are too extensive for this book, check through these descriptions to find the moon sign that feels most familiar—or, better yet, have your chart calculated by a computer service to get your accurate moon placement.

The moon rules maternal Cancer and is exalted in Taurus, both comforting, home-loving signs where the natural emotional energies of the moon are easily and productively expressed. But when the moon is in the opposite signs—in its Capricorn detriment and its Scorpio fall—it leaves the comfortable nest and deals with emotional issues of power and achievement in the outside world. Those of you with the moon in these signs will find your emotional role more challenging in life.

Moon in Aries

You are an idealistic, impetuous person who falls in and out of love easily. This placement makes you both independent and ardent. You love a challenge, but could cool once your quarry is captured. You should cultivate patience and tolerance—or you might tend to gravitate toward those who treat you rough, just for the sake of challenge and excitement.

Moon in Taurus

You are a sentimental soul who is very fond of the good life and gravitates toward solid, secure relationships. You like displays of affection and creature comforts— all the tangible trappings of a cozy, safe, calm atmosphere. You are sensual and steady emotionally, but very stubborn and determined. You can't be pushed and tend to dislike changes. You should make an effort to broaden your horizons and to take a risk sometimes.

Moon in Gemini

You crave mental stimulation and variety in life, which you usually get through either an ever-varied social life, the excitement of flirtation, or multiple professional involvements. You may marry more than once and have a rather chaotic emotional life due to your difficulty with commitment and settling down. Be sure to find a partner who is as outgoing as you are. You will have to learn at some point to focus your energies because you tend to be somewhat fragmented. You do two things at once and you may have two homes or even two lovers. If you can find a creative way to express your many-faceted nature, you'll be ahead of the game.

Moon in Cancer

This is the most powerful lunar position, which is sure to have a deep imprint on your character. Your needs are very much associated with your reaction to the needs of others. You are very sensitive and self-protective, though some of you may mask this with a hard shell. This placement also gives an excellent memory and an uncanny ability to psych out the needs of others. All of the lunar phases will affect you, especially full moons and eclipses, so you would do well to mark them on your calendar. You are happiest at home and may work at home or turn your office into a second home, where you can nurture and comfort people; you may tend to mother the world. This psychic, intuitive moon might draw you to occult work in some way, or you may get professionally involved with providing food and shelter to the needy.

Moon in Leo

This is a warm, passionate moon that takes everything to heart. You are attracted to all that is noble, generous, and aristocratic in life, and you may be a bit of a snob. You have an innate ability to take command emotionally, but you do need strong support, loyalty, and loud applause from those you love. You are possessive of your loved ones and your turf and will roar if anyone threatens to take over your territory.

Moon in Virgo

You are rather cool until you decide if others measure up. But once someone or something meets your ideal standards, you hold up your end of the arrangement perfectly. You may, in fact, drive yourself too hard to attain some notion of perfection. Try to be a bit easier on yourself and others. Don't always act the censor! You love to be the teacher and are drawn to situations where you can change others for the better. But sometimes you must learn to accept others for what they are and enjoy what you have.

Moon in Libra

This is a partnership-oriented placement, and you may find it difficult to be alone or to do things alone. But you must learn to lean on yourself first. When you have learned emotional balance, you can have excellent relationships. It is best for you to avoid extremes or your love life can be precarious. You thrive in a rather conservative, traditional, romantic relationship, where you receive attention and flattery—but not possessiveness—from your partner. You'll be your most charming in an elegant, harmonious atmosphere.

Moon in Scorpio

This is a moon that enjoys and responds to intense, passionate feelings. You may go to extremes and have a very dramatic emotional life, full of ardor, suspicion, jealousy, and obsession. It would be much healthier to channel your need for power and control into meaningful work. This is a good position for anyone in the fields of medicine, police work, research, the occult, psychoanalysis, or intuitive work, because life-and-death situations don't faze you. However, you do take personal disappointments very hard.

Moon in Sagittarius

You take life's ups and downs with good humor and a grain of salt. You'll love 'em and leave 'em, and take off on a great adventure at a moment's notice. "Born free" could be your slogan. You can't stand to be possessed emotionally by anyone. Attracted by the exotic, you have wanderlust mentally and physically. You may be too much in search of new mental and spiritual stimulation to ever settle down.

Moon in Capricorn

Are you ever accused of being too cool and calculating? You have an earthy side, but you take prestige and position very seriously. Your strong drive to succeed extends to your romantic life, where you will be devoted to improving your lifestyle and rising to the top. A structured situation, where you can advance methodically, makes you feel wonderfully secure. You may be attracted to someone older or very much younger or from a different social world. It may be difficult to look at the lighter side of emotional relationships, but the upside of this moon in its detriment is that you tend to be very dutiful and responsible to those you care for.

Moon in Aquarius

You are a people collector with many friends of all backgrounds. You are happiest surrounded by people and are uneasy when left alone. You usually stay friends with those with whom you get involved, but intense emotions could turn you off. Though tolerant and understanding, you can be emotionally unpredictable. You don't like anything to be too rigid—you may resist working on schedule or you may have a very unconventional love life. With plenty of space, you will be able to sustain relationships, but you'll blow away from possessive types.

Moon in Pisces

You are very responsive and empathetic to others, especially if they have problems. (You may have to be on guard against attracting too many people with sob stories.) You'll be happiest if you can find ways to express your creative imagination in the arts or in the spiritual or healing professions. You may tend to escape to a fantasy world or be attracted to exotic places or people. You need an emotional anchor, as you are very sensitive to the moods of others. You are happiest near water, working in a field that gives you emotional variety. But steer clear of too much escapism, especially in alcohol, or reclusiveness. Keep a firm foothold in reality.

Close and Personal—Mercury, Venus, and Mars

These are the planets that work in your immediate personal life. Mercury affects how you communicate and how your mental processes work. Are you a quick study who grasps information rapidly, or do you learn more slowly and thoroughly? How is your concentration? Can you express yourself easily? Are you a good writer? All these questions can be answered by your Mercury placement.

Venus shows what you react to. What turns you on? What appeals to you aesthetically? Are you charming to others? Are you attractive to look at? Your taste, your refinement, your sense of balance and proportion are all Venus ruled.

Mars is your outgoing energy, your drive and ambition. Do you reach out for new adventures? Are you assertive? Are you motivated? Self-confident? Hot-tempered? How you channel your energy and drive is revealed by your Mars placement.

Mercury—The Great Communicator

Mercury shows how you think and speak and how logically your mind works. It stays close to the sun, never more than a sign away, and very often shares the same sign, reinforcing the sun's communicative talents. Mercury functions easily in Gemini and Virgo, the natural analytical signs it rules. Yet Mercury in Sagittarius and Pisces, signs where logic often takes second place to visionary ideas and where Mercury is debilitated, can provide great visionary thinking and poetic expression when the planet is properly used.

Since Mercury never travels far from the sun, read Mercury in your sun sign, the sign preceding and following it. Then decide which most reflects the way your mind works.

Mercury in Aries

Your mind is very active and assertive. You never hesitate to say exactly what you think or shy away from a battle. In fact, you may relish a verbal confrontation.

Mercury in Taurus

You may be a slow learner, but you have good concentration and mental stamina. You want to make your ideas really happen. You'll attack a problem methodically and consider every angle thoroughly, never jumping to conclusions. You'll stick with a subject until you master it.

Mercury in Gemini

You are a wonderful communicator, with a great facility for expressing yourself verbally and in writing. Though you learn fast, you may lack focus and discipline. Watch a tendency to jump from subject to subject.

Mercury in Cancer

You are very intuitive, rather than logical. Your mental processes are usually colored by your emotions. This gives you the advantage of great imagination and empathy for others.

Mercury in Leo

You are enthusiastic and very dramatic in the way you express yourself. You like to hold the attention of groups and could be a great public speaker. Your mind thinks big and likes to deal with the overall picture rather than with details.

Mercury in Virgo

This is one of the best places for Mercury. It should give you critical ability, attention to details, and thorough analysis. Your mind focuses on the practical side of things. You are an excellent teacher and editor.

Mercury in Libra

You are a born diplomat who smoothes over ruffled feathers; you may be a talented debater or lawyer. However, you might vacillate when it comes to taking a stand or making decisions; you're forever weighing the pros and cons.

Mercury in Scorpio

This is the investigative mind, which stops at nothing to get the answer. You may have a sarcastic, stinging wit—a gift for the cutting remark. There's always a grain of truth to your verbal sallies, thanks to your penetrating insight.

Mercury in Sagittarius

You are a super salesman with a tendency to expound. You are very broad minded, but you could be dogmatic when it comes to telling others what's good for them. You won't hesitate to tell the truth as you see it, so watch a tendency toward tactlessness. On the plus side, you have a great sense of humor.

Mercury in Capricorn

This placement endows good mental discipline. You have a love of learning and a very orderly approach to your subjects. You will patiently plod through facts and figures until you master your tasks. You grasp structured situations easily, but may be short on creativity.

Mercury in Aquarius

You are an independent thinker who won't hesitate to break the rules to find the most original, innovative approach to problems. But once your mind is made up, it is difficult to change.

Mercury in Pisces

You have the psychic, intuitive mind of a natural poet. You should learn to make use of your creative imagination. You also think in terms of helping others, but check a tendency to be vague and forgetful of details.

Venus—Your Love Planet

Venus is the planet of romantic love, pleasure, and industry. It shows what you react to, your tastes, and what (or who) turns you on. It is naturally at home in the planets it rules—Libra, the sign of partnerships, or Taurus, the sign of physical pleasure. Yet in Aries, its detriment, Venus is daring, full of energy, and negatively self-serving. In Pisces, where Venus is exalted, this planet can go overboard, loving to the point of self-sacrifice. While Venus in Virgo, its fall, can be the perfectionist in love, it can also offer affectionate service and true support.

Venus in Aries

Oh, do you love excitement! You can't stand to be bored, confined, or ordered around. But a good challenge, maybe even a rousing row turns you on. Confess—don't you pick a fight now and then just to get everyone stirred up? You're attracted by the chase, not the catch, which could create problems in your love life if the object of your affection becomes too attainable. You like to wear red and to be first with the very latest fashion. You'll spot a trend before anyone else.

Venus in Taurus

All your senses work in high gear. You love to be surrounded by glorious tastes, smells, textures, sounds, and visuals—austerity is not for you. Neither is being rushed. You like time to enjoy your pleasures. Soothing surroundings with plenty of creature comforts are your cup of tea. You like to feel secure in your nest, with no sudden jolts or surprises. You like familiar objects—in fact, you may hate to let anything or anyone go.

Venus in Gemini

You are a lively, sparkling personality who thrives in a situation that affords a constant variety and a frequent change of scenery. A varied social life is important to you, with plenty of stimulation and a chance to engage in some light flirtation. Commitment may be difficult, when playing the field is so much more fun.

Venus in Cancer

An atmosphere where you feel protected, coddled, and mothered is best for you. You love to be surrounded by children in a cozy, homelike situation. You are attracted to those who are tender and nurturing, who make you feel secure and well provided for. You may be quite secretive about your emotional life or attracted to clandestine relationships.

Venus in Leo

First-class attention in large doses turns you on, and so does the glitter of real gold and the flash of mirrors. You like to feel like a star at all times, surrounded by your admiring audience. The side effect is that you may be attracted to flatterers and tinsel, while the real gold requires some digging.

Venus in Virgo

Everything neatly in its place? On the surface, you are attracted to an atmosphere where everything is in perfect order, but underneath are some basic, earthy urges. You are attracted to those who appeal to your need to teach, be of service, or play out a Pygmalion fantasy.

You're at your best when you are busy doing something useful.

Venus in Libra

Elegance and harmony are your key words. You can't abide an atmosphere of contention. Your taste tends toward the classic, with light harmonies of color—nothing clashing, trendy, or outrageous. You love doing things with a partner and should be careful to pick one who is decisive but patient enough to let you weigh the pros and cons. And steer clear of argumentative types.

Venus in Scorpio

Hidden mysteries intrigue you—in fact, anything that is too open and aboveboard is a bit of a bore. You surely have a stack of whodunits by the bed, along with an erotic magazine or two. You may also be fascinated with the occult, crime, or scientific research. Intense, all-or-nothing situations add spice to your life, but you could get burned by your flair for living dangerously. The color black, spicy food, dark wood furniture, and heady perfume all get you in the right mood.

Venus in Sagittarius

If you are not actually a world traveler, your surroundings are sure to reflect your love of faraway places. You like a casual outdoor atmosphere and a dog or two to pet. There should be plenty of room for athletic equipment and suitcases. You're attracted to kindred souls who love to travel and who share your freedom-loving philosophy of life. Athletics, spiritual, or New-Age pursuits could be other interests.

Venus in Capricorn

No fly-by-night relationships for you! You want substance in life and you are attracted to whatever will help you get where you are going. Status objects turn you on. So do those who have a serious responsible, businesslike approach, or who remind you of a beloved parent. It is characteristic of this placement to be attracted to someone of a different generation. Antiques, traditional clothing, and dignified behavior favor you.

Venus in Aquarius

This Venus wants to make friends more than to make love. You like to be in a group, particularly one pushing a worthy cause. You feel quite at home surrounded by people, remaining detached from any intense commitment. Original ideas and unpredictable people fascinate you. You don't like everything to be planned out in advance, preferring spontaneity and delightful surprises.

Venus in Pisces

This Venus is attracted to being of service. You love to give of yourself and you find plenty of takers. Stray animals and people appeal to your heart and your pocketbook, but be careful to look at their motives realistically once in a while. Fantasy, theater, and psychic or spiritual activities also speak to you.

Mars—How You Go for it

Mars is the mover and shaker in your life. It shows how you pursue your goals and whether you have energy to burn or proceed in a slow, steady pace. Or are you nervous, restless, and unable to sit still? It will also show how you get angry: Do you explode, or do a slow burn, or hold everything inside—then get revenge later?

In Aries, which it rules, and Scorpio, which it corules, Mars is at its most powerful. Yet this drive can be self-serving and impetuous. In Libra, the sign of its detriment, Mars demands cooperation in a relationship. In Capricorn, where it is exalted, Mars becomes an ambitious achiever, headed for the top. But in Cancer, the sign of its fall, Mars aggression becomes tempered by feelings, especially those involving self-protection and security, which are always considered first. The end can never justify the means for Mars in Cancer.

To find your Mars, refer to the Mars chart in this book. If the following description of your Mars sign doesn't ring true, you may have been born on a day when Mars was changing signs, so check the adjacent sign descriptions.

Mars in Aries

In the sign it rules, Mars shows its brilliant fiery nature. You have an explosive temper and can be quite impatient, but on the other hand, you have tremendous courage, energy, and drive. You'll let nothing stand in your way as you race to be first! Obstacles are met head-on and broken through by force. However, those that require patience and persistence can have you exploding in rage. You're a great starter, but not necessarily around for the finish.

Mars in Taurus

Slow, steady, concentrated energy gives you the power. You have great stamina and you never give up. Your tactic is to wear away obstacles with your persistence. Often you come out a winner because you've had the patience to hang in there. When angered, you do a slow burn.

Mars in Gemini

You can't sit still for long. This Mars craves variety. You often have two or more things going on at once—it's all an amusing game to you. Your life can get very complicated, but that only adds spice and stimulation. What drives you into a nervous, hyper state? Boredom, sameness, routine, and confinement. You can do wonderful things with your hands and you have a way with words.

Mars in Cancer

Your rarely attack head-on—instead, you'll keep things to yourself, make plans in secret, and always cover your actions. This might be interpreted by some as manipulative, but you are only being self-protective. You get furious when anyone knows too much about you. But you do like to know all about others. Your mothering and feeding instincts can be put to good use in your work in food, hotel, or child-care related businesses. You may have to overcome your fragile sense of security, which prompts you not to take risks and to get physically upset when criticized. Don't take things so personally!

Mars in Leo

You have a very dominant personality that takes center stage—modesty is not one of your traits, nor is taking a backseat. You prefer giving the orders and have been known to make a dramatic scene if they are not obeyed. Properly used, this Mars confers leadership ability, endurance, and courage.

Mars in Virgo

You are the fault-finder of the zodiac, who notices every detail. Mistakes of any kind make you very nervous. You may worry even if everything is going smoothly. You may not express your anger directly, but you sure can nag. You have definite likes and dislikes and you are sure you can do the job better than anyone else. You are certainly more industrious than most other signs. Why don't you express your Mars energy by teaching instead of by criticizing?

Mars in Libra

This Mars will have a passion for beauty, justice, and art. Generally, you will avoid confrontations at all costs. You prefer to spend your energy finding a diplomatic solution or weighing pros and cons. Your other techniques are passive aggression, or exercising your well-known charm to get people to do what you want.

Mars in Scorpio

This is a powerful placement, so intense that it demands careful channeling into worthwhile activities. Otherwise, you could become obsessed with your sexuality or might use your need for power and control to manipulate others. You are strong-willed, shrewd, and very private about your affairs, and you'll usually have a secret agenda behind your actions. Your great stamina, focus, and discipline would be excellent assets for careers in the military or medical fields, especially research or surgery. When angry, you don't get mad—you get even!

Mars in Sagittarius

This expansive Mars often propels people into sales, travel, athletics, or philosophy. Your energies function well when you are on the move. You have a hot temper and are inclined to say what you think before you consider the consequences. You shoot for high goals—and talk endlessly about them—but you may be weak on groundwork. This Mars needs a solid foundation. Watch a tendency to take unnecessary risks.

Mars in Capricorn

This is an ambitious Mars with an excellent sense of timing. You have an eye for those who can be of use to you, and you may dismiss people ruthlessly when you're angry. But you drive yourself hard and deliver full value. This is a good placement for an executive. You'll aim for status and a high material position in life, and keep climbing despite the odds.

Mars in Aquarius

This is the most rebellious Mars. You seem to have a drive to assert yourself against the status quo. You may enjoy provoking people, shocking them out of traditional views. Or this placement could express itself in an off-beat sex life. Others could find you a bit eccentric—somehow, you often find yourself in unconventional situations. You enjoy being a leader of an active group, which pursues forward-looking studies or goals.

Mars in Pisces

This Mars is a good actor who knows just how to appeal to the sympathies of others. You create and project wonderful fantasies or use your sensitive antennae to crusade for those less fortunate. You get what you want through creating a veil of illusion and glamour. This is a good Mars for a dancer, performer, or photographer, or for someone in motion pictures. Many famous film stars have this placement. Watch a tendency to manipulate by making others feel sorry for you.

Jupiter—Expansion, Luck, Optimism

Jupiter is the planet in your horoscope that makes you want more. This big, bright, swirling mass of gases is associated with abundance, prosperity, and the kind of windfall you get without too much hard work. You're optimistic under Jupiter's influence—anything seems possible. You'll travel, expand your mind with higher education, and publish to share your knowledge widely. But a strong Jupiter has its downside, too. Jupiter's influence is neither discriminating nor disciplined, representing the principle of growth without judgement and resulting in extravagance, weight gain, laziness, and carelessness.

Jupiter also embodies the functions of the higher

mind, where you do complex, expansive thinking and deal with the big overall picture, rather than the specifics (the province of Mercury). Jupiter functions naturally in Sagittarius, the sign of the philosopher, or Pisces, which it corules with Neptune. In Gemini, its detriment, Jupiter can be scattered, a jack-of-all-trades. On the other hand, it can also be a lighthearted, effective communicator. In Cancer, where it is exalted, Jupiter becomes the protective big brother. In Capricorn, its fall, Jupiter is brought down to earth, its vision harnessed to practical goals.

Be sure to look up your Jupiter in the tables in this book. When the current position of Jupiter is favorable, you may get that lucky break. At any rate, it's a great time to try new things, take risks, travel, or get more education. Opportunities seem to open up at this time, so take advantage of them. Once a year, Jupiter changes signs. That means you are due for an expansive time every twelve years, when Jupiter travels through your sun sign. You'll also have "up" periods every four years, when Jupiter is in the same element as your sun sign.

Jupiter in Aries

You are the soul of enthusiasm and optimism. Your luckiest times are when you are getting started on an exciting project or selling an idea that you really believe in. You may have to watch a tendency to be arrogant with those who do not share your enthusiasm. You follow your impulse, often ignoring budget or other commonsense limitations. To produce real, solid benefits, you'll need patience and follow-through wherever this Jupiter falls in your horoscope.

Jupiter in Taurus

You'll spend on beautiful material things, especially those that come from nature—items made of rare woods, natural fabrics, or precious gems, for instance. You can't have too much comfort or too many sensual pleasures. Watch a tendency to overindulge in good food, or to overpamper yourself with nothing but the best. Spartan living is not for you! You may be especially lucky in matters of real estate.

Jupiter in Gemini

You are the great talker of the zodiac, and you may be a great writer, too. But restlessness could be your weak point. You jump around, talk too much, and could be a jack-of-all-trades. Keeping a secret is especially difficult, so you'll also have to watch a tendency to spill the beans. Since you love to be at the center of a beehive of activity, you'll have a vibrant social life. Your best opportunities will come through your talent for language—speaking, writing, communicating, and selling.

Jupiter in Cancer

You are luckiest in situations where you can find emotional closeness or deal with basic security needs, such as food, nurturing, or shelter. You may be a great collector and you may simply love to accumulate things—you are the one who stashed things away for a rainy day. You probably have a very good memory and love children—in fact, you may have many children to care for. The food, hotel, child-care, or shipping businesses hold good opportunities for you.

Jupiter in Leo

You are a natural showman who loves to live in a larger-than-life way. Yours is a personality full of color that always finds its way into the limelight. You can't have too much attention or applause. Show biz is a natural place for you, and any area where you can exercise your flair for drama, your natural playfulness, and your romantic nature brings you good fortune. But watch a tendency to be overly extravagant or to monopolize center stage.

Jupiter in Virgo

You actually love those minute details others find boring. To you, they make all the difference between the perfect and the ordinary. You are the fine craftsman who spots every flaw. You expand your awareness by finding the most practical methods and by being of service to others. Many will be drawn to medical or teaching fields. You'll also have luck in publishing, crafts, nutrition, and service professions. Watch a tendency to overwork.

Jupiter in Libra

This is an other-directed Jupiter that develops best with a partner, for the stimulation of others helps you grow. You are also most comfortable in harmonious, beautiful situations, and you work well with artistic people. You have a great sense of fair play and an ability to evaluate the pros and cons of a situation. You usually prefer to play the role of diplomat rather than adversary.

Jupiter in Scorpio

You love the feeling of power and control, of taking things to their limit. You can't resist a mystery, and your shrewd, penetrating mind sees right through to the heart of most situations and people. You have luck in work that probes for solutions to matters of life and death. You may be drawn to undercover work, behind-the-scenes intrigue, psychotherapy, the occult, and sex-related ventures. Your challenge will be to develop a sense of moderation and tolerance for others' beliefs. This Jupiter can be fanatical. You may have luck in handling others' money—insurance, taxes, and inheritance can bring you a windfall.

Jupiter in Sagittarius

Independent, outgoing, and idealistic, you'll shoot for the stars. This Jupiter compels you to travel far and wide, both physically and mentally, via higher education.

You may have luck while traveling in an exotic place. You also have luck with outdoor ventures, exercise, and animals, particularly horses. Since you tend to be very open about your opinions, watch a tendency to be tactless and to exaggerate. Instead, use your wonderful sense of humor to make your point.

Jupiter in Capricorn

Jupiter is much more restrained in Capricorn. Here, Jupiter can make you overwork, and heighten any ambition or sense of duty you may have. You'll expand in areas that advance your position, putting you farther up the social or corporate ladder. You are lucky working within the establishment in a very structured situation, where you can show off your ability to organize and reap rewards for your hard work.

Jupiter in Aquarius

This is another freedom-loving Jupiter, with great tolerance and originality. You are at your best when you are working for a humanitarian cause and in the company of many supporters. This is a good Jupiter for a political career. You'll relate to all kinds of people on all social levels. You have an abundance of original ideas, but you are best off away from routine and any situation that imposes rigid rules. You need mental stimulation!

Jupiter in Pisces

You are a giver whose feeling and pocketbook are easily touched by others, so choose your companions with care. You could be the original sucker for a hard-luck story. Better find a worthy hospital or charity to appreciate your selfless support. You have a great creative imagination and may attract good fortune in fields related to oil, perfume, pharmaceuticals, petroleum, dance, footwear, and alcohol. But beware of overindulgence in alcohol—focus on a creative outlet instead.

Saturn—The Taskmaster

Saturn has suffered from a bad reputation, always cast as the heavy in the chart. However, the flip side of Saturn is that teacher whose class is the toughest in school, but whose lessons you never forget. And the tests of Saturn, which come at regular seven-year exam periods, are the ones you need to pass to survive as a conscious, independent adult. Saturn gives us the grade we've earned, so if we have studied and prepared for our tests we needn't be afraid of the big, bad wolf. Saturn in Capricorn, its ruler, is comfortable with this sign's emphasis on structure and respect for authority. Cancer, Saturn's detriment, suggests both that feeling must become responsible and that authority cannot operate effectively without concern for the chart.

Your Saturn position can illuminate your fears, your hangups, and your important lessons in life. Remember that Saturn is concerned with your maturity, and with what you need to know to survive in the world.

When Saturn returns to its location at the time of your birth, at approximately age 28, you'll have your first Saturn return. At this time, a person usually takes stock or settles down to find a mission in life and assume full adult duties and responsibilities.

Another way Saturn helps us is to reveal the karmic lessons from previous lives and give us the chance to overcome them. So look at Saturn's challenges as much-needed opportunities for self-improvement. Under a Jupiter influence, you'll have more fun, but Saturn gives you solid, long-lasting results.

Look up your natal Saturn in the tables in this book for clues on where you need work.

Saturn in Aries

Saturn here gives you great ambition and independence—you don't let anyone push you around and you know what's best for you. Following orders is not your strong point, and neither is diplomacy. Because no one quite lives up to your standards, you often wind up doing everything yourself. You are best off running your own business, though you may be quite lonely at times.

Saturn in Taurus

A big issue is getting control of the cash flow. There will be lean periods that can be frightening, but you have the patience and endurance to stick them out and the methodical drive to prosper in the end. Learn to take a philosophical attitude like Ben Franklin, who also had this placement and who said, "A penny saved is a penny earned."

Saturn in Gemini

You are a rather cold, detached, serious student, uninclined to communicate or share your knowledge. You dwell in the realms of science, theory, or abstract analysis, even when you are dealing with the emotions, like Sigmund Freud, who had this placement.

Saturn in Cancer

Your tests come with establishing a secure emotional base. In doing so, you may have to deal with some very basic fears centering on your early home environment. Most of your Saturn tests will have emotional roots in those early childhood experiences. You may have difficulty remaining objective in terms of what you try to achieve, so it will be especially important for you to deal with negative feelings such as guilt, paranoia, jealousy, resentment, and suspicion. Galileo and Michelangelo also navigated these murky waters.

Saturn in Leo

This is an authoritarian Saturn, a strict, demanding parent who may deny the pleasure principle in your zeal to see that rules are followed. Though you may feel guilty about taking the spotlight, you are very ambitious and loyal. You have to watch a tendency toward rigidity, also toward overwork and holding back affection. Joseph Kennedy and Billy Graham share this placement.

Saturn in Virgo

This is a cautious, exacting Saturn, intensely hard on yourself, most of all. You give yourself the roughest time with your constant worries about every little detail, often making yourself sick. Your tests will come in learning tolerance and understanding of others. Charles de Gaulle and Nathaniel Hawthorne had this meticulous Saturn.

Saturn in Libra

Saturn is exalted here, which makes this planet an ally. You may choose very serious, older partners in life, perhaps stemming from a fear of dependency. You need to learn to stand solidly on your own before you commit to another. You are extremely cautious as you deliberate every involvement—with good reason. It is best that you find an occupation that makes good use of your sense of duty and honor. Steer clear of fly-by-night situations. Khrushchev and Mao Tse-tung had this placement, too.

Saturn in Scorpio

You have great staying power. This Saturn tests you in matters of control and transformation. You may feel drawn to some kind of intrigue or undercover work, like J. Edgar Hoover. Or there may be an air of mystery surrounding your life and death, like Marilyn Monroe and Robert Kennedy, who had this placement. There are lessons to be learned from your sexual involvements—often sex is used for manipulation or is somehow out of the ordinary. The Roman emperor Caligula and the transvestite Christine Jorgensen are extreme cases.

Saturn in Sagittarius

Your challenges and lessons will come from tests of your spiritual and philosophical values, as happened to Martin Luther King and Gandhi. You are high minded and sincere with this reflective, moral placement. Uncompromising in your ethical standards, you could be a benevolent despot.

Saturn in Capricorn

With the help of Saturn at maximum strength, your judgment will improve with age. And, like Spencer Tracy's screen image, you'll be the gray-haired hero with a strong sense of responsibility. You advance in life slowly but steadily, always with a strong hand at the helm and an eye for the advantageous situation. Negatively, you may be a loner, prone to periods of melancholy.

Saturn in Aquarius

Your tests come from your relationships with groups. Do you care too much about what others think? You may fear being different from others and therefore slight your own unique, forward-looking gifts or, like Lord Byron and Howard Hughes, take the opposite tack and rebel in the extreme. You can apply discipline to accomplish great humanitarian goals, as Albert Schweitzer did.

Saturn in Pisces

Your fear of the unknown and the irrational may lead you to a secluded, solitary lifestyle. You may go on the run like Jesse James, who had this placement, to avoid looking too deeply inside. Or you might go in the opposite, more positive direction and develop a disciplined psychoanalytic approach, which puts you more in control of your feelings. Some of you will take refuge in work with hospitals, charities, or religious institutions. Queen Victoria, who had this placement, symbolized an era when institutions of all kinds were sustained. Discipline applied to artistic work, especially poetry and dance, or spiritual work, such as yoga or meditation, might be helpful.

Uranus, Neptune, and Pluto Affect Your Whole Generation

These three planets remain in signs such a long time that a whole generation bears the imprint of the sign. Mass movements, great sweeping changes, fads that characterize a generation, even the issues of the conflicts and wars of the time are influenced by the "outer three." When one of these distant planets changes signs, there is a definite shift in the atmosphere, the feeling of the end of an era.

Since these planets are so far away from the sun—too distant to be seen by the naked eye—they pick up signals from the universe at large. These planetary receivers literally link the sun with distant energies, and then perform a similar function in your horoscope by linking your central character with intuitive, spiritual, transformative forces from the cosmos. Each planet has a special domain and will reflect this in the area of your life where it falls.

Uranus—The Planet of Surprises

There is nothing ordinary about this quirky green planet that seems to be traveling on its side, surrounded by a swarm of at least fifteen moons. Is it any wonder that astrologers assigned it to Aquarius, the most eccentric and gregarious sign? Uranus seems to wend its way around the sun, marching to its own tune.

Uranus energy is electrical, happening in sudden flashes. It is not influenced by karma or past events, nor does it regard tradition, sex, or sentiment. The Uranian key words are surprise and awakening. Uranus wakes you up, jolting you out of your comfortable rut. Suddenly, there's that flash of inspiration, that bright idea or totally new approach to revolutionize whatever scheme you were undertaking. The Uranus place in your life is where you awaken and become your own person. And it is probably the most unconventional place in your chart.

Look up the sign of Uranus at the time of your birth and see where you follow your own tune.

Uranus in Aries—A Fiery Shocker

Birth dates: March 31–November 4, 1927; January 13, 1928–June 6, 1934; October 10, 1934–March 28, 1935. Your generation is original, creative, pioneering; it developed the computer, the airplane, and the cyclotron. You let nothing hold you back from exploring the unknown and have a powerful mixture of fire and electricity behind you. Women of your generation were among the first to be liberated. You were the unforgettable style setters. You have a surprise in store for everyone. Like Yoko Ono, Grace Kelly, and Jacqueline Onassis, your life may be jolted by sudden and violent changes.

Uranus in Taurus—Sudden Shakeups

Birth dates: June 6, 1934–October 10, 1934; March 28, 1935–August 7, 1941; October 5, 1941–May 15, 1942. You are probably self-employed or would like to be. You have original ideas about making money, and you brace yourself for sudden changes of fortune. This Uranus can cause shakeups, particularly in finances, but it can also make you a born entrepreneur.

Uranus in Gemini—The Walking Talk Show

Birth date: August 7–October 5, 1941; May 15, 1942–August 30, 1948; November 12, 1948–June 10, 1949. You were the first children to be influenced by television, and in your adult years, your generation stocks up on answering machines, cordless phones, car phones, computers, and fax machines—any new way you can communicate. You have an inquiring mind, but your interests are rather short lived. This Uranus can be easily fragmented if there is no structure and focus.

Uranus in Cancer—Domestic Disturbances

Birth date: August 30–November 12, 1948; June 10, 1949–August 24, 1955; January 28–June 10, 1956. This generation came at a time when divorce was becoming commonplace, so your home image is unconventional. You may have an unusual relationship with your parents; you may have come from a broken home or an unconventional one. You'll have unorthodox ideas about parenting, intimacy, food, and shelter. You may also be interested in dreams, psychic phenomena, and memory work.

Uranus in Leo—A Flashy Performer

Birth date: August 24, 1955–January 28, 1956; June 10, 1956–November 1, 1961; January 10–August 10, 1962. This generation understood how to use electronic media. Many of your group are now leaders in the high-tech industries, and you also understand how to use the new media to promote yourself. Like Isadora Duncan, you may have a very eccentric kind of charisma and a life that is sparked by unusual love affairs. Your children, too, may have traits that are out of the ordinary. Where this planet falls in your chart, you'll have a love of freedom, be a bit of an egomaniac, and show the full force of your personality in a unique way, like tennis great Martina Navratilova.

Uranus in Virgo—Eccentric Genius

Birth date: November 1, 1961–January 10, 1962; August 10, 1962–September 28, 1968; May 20, 1969–June 24, 1969.

You'll have highly individual work methods, and many will be finding newer, more practical ways to use computers. Like Einstein, who had this placement, you'll break the rules brilliantly. Your generation came at a time of student rebellions, the civil rights movement, and the general acceptance of health foods. Chances are, you are concerned abut pollution and cleaning up the environment. You may also be involved with nontraditional healing methods. Heavyweight champ Mike Tyson has this placement.

Uranus in Libra—On Again, Off Again Partners

Birth date: September 28, 1968–May 20, 1969; June 24, 1969–November 21, 1974; May 1–September 8, 1975. Your generation will be always changing partners. Born during the time of women's liberation, you may have come from a broken home and have no clear image of what a marriage entails. There will be many sudden splits and experiments before you settle down. Your generation will be much involved in legal and political reforms and in changing artistic and fashion looks.

Uranus in Scorpio—The New Age

Birth date: November 21, 1974–May 1, 1975; September 8, 1975–February 17, 1981; March 20–November 16, 1981. Interest in transformation, meditation, and life after death signaled the beginning of New-Age consciousness. Your generation recognizes no boundaries, no limits, and no external controls. You'll have new attitudes toward death and dying, psychic phenomena, and the occult. Like Mae West and Casanova, you'll shock 'em sexually, too.

Uranus in Sagittarius—Space Trippers

Birth date: February 17–March 20, 1981; November 16, 1981–February 15, 1988; May 27, 1988–December 2, 1988. Could this generation be the first to travel in outer space? The last generation with this placement included

Charles Lindbergh—at that time, the first Zeppelins and the Wright Brothers were conquering the skies. Uranus here forecasts great discoveries, mind expansion, and long-distance travel. Like Galileo and Martin Luther, those born in these years will generate new theories about the cosmos and man's relation to it.

Uranus in Capricorn—Movers and Shakers

Birth date: December 20, 1904–January 30, 1912; September 4–November 12, 1912; February 15–May 27, 1988; December 2, 1988–April 1, 1995; June 9, 1995–January 12, 1996. This generation will challenge traditions with the help of electronic gadgets. In these years, we got organized with the help of technology put to practical use. Great leaders, who were movers and shakers of history, like Julius Caesar and Henry VIII, were born under this placement.

Uranus in Aquarius—The Innovators

Birth date: January 30–September 4, 1912; November 12, 1912–April 1, 1919; August 16, 1919–January 22, 1920; April 1,–June 9, 1995; January 12, 1996 through the end of this century. The last generation with this placement produced great innovative minds such as Leonard Bernstein and Orson Welles. The next will become another radical breakthrough generation, much concerned with global issues that involve all humanity. Intuition, innovation, and sudden changes will surprise everyone when Uranus is in its home sign. This will be a time of experimentation on every level.

Uranus in Pisces—That's Entertainment

Birth date: April 1–August 16, 1919; January 22, 1920–March 31, 1927; November 4, 1927–January 12, 1928. In this century, Uranus in Pisces focused attention on the rise of electrical entertainment—radio and the cinema, and the secretiveness of Prohibition. This produced a generation of idealists exemplified by Judy Garland's theme, "Somewhere Over the Rainbow."

What You See Is Not What You Get With Neptune, Planet of Dreams, Imagination, Illusions

Under Neptune's influence, you see what you want to see. But Neptune also encourages you to create, letting your fantasies and daydreams run free. Neptune is often maligned as the planet of illusions, drugs, and alcohol, where you can't bear to face reality. But it also embodies the energy of glamour, subtlety, mystery, and mysticism, and governs anything that takes you out of the mundane world, including out-of-body experiences.

Neptune acts to break through your ordinary perceptions and take you to another level of reality, where you can experience either confusion or ecstasy. Neptune's force can pull you off course in the way this planet affects its neighbor, Uranus, but only if you allow this to happen. Those who use Neptune wisely can translate their daydreams into poetry, theater, design, or inspired moves in the business world, avoiding the tricky con-artist side of this planet.

Find your Neptune listed below:

Neptune in Cancer

Birth Date: July 19–December 25, 1901; May 21, 1902–September 23, 1914; December 14, 1914–July 19, 1915; March 19–May 2, 1916. Dreams of the homeland, idealistic patriotism, and glamorization of the nurturing assets of women are characterized this time. You who were born here have unusual psychic ability and deep insights into basic needs of others.

Neptune in Leo

Birth Date: September 23–December 14, 1914; July 19, 1915–March 19, 1916; May 2, 1916–September 21, 1928; February 19, 1929–July 24, 1929. This sign brought us the glamour of the 1920s and the big spenders, where gambling, seduction, theater, and lavish entertaining distracted from the realities of the age. Those born now have been part of a generation that made great advances in the arts.

Neptune in Virgo

Birth Date: September 21, 1928–February 19, 1929; July 24, 1929–October 3, 1942; April 17–August 2, 1943. Neptune in Virgo encompassed the Great Depression and World War II, while those born at this time later spread the gospel of health and fitness. This generation's devotion to spending hours at the office inspired the term "workaholic."

Neptune in Libra

Birth Date: October 3, 1942–April 17, 1943; August 2, 1943–December 24, 1955; March 12–October 19, 1956; June 15–August 6, 1957. Neptune in Libra was the romantic generation who would later be concerned with relating. As this generation matured, there was a new trend toward marriage and commitment. Racial and sexual equality became important issues, as they redesigned traditional roles to suit modern times.

Neptune in Scorpio

Birth Date: December 24, 1955–March 12, 1956; October 19, 1956–June 15, 1957; August 6, 1957–January 4, 1970; May 3–November 6, 1970. Neptune in Scorpio brought in a generation that would become interested in transformative power. Born in an era that glamorized sex, drugs, rock and roll, and Eastern religion, they matured in a more sobering time of AIDS, cocaine abuse, and New-Age spirituality. As they mature, they will become active in healing the planet from the results of the abuse of power.

Neptune in Sagittarius

Birth Date: January 4–May 3, 1970; November 6, 1970–January 19, 1984; June 23–November 21, 1984. Neptune in Sagittarius was the time when space and astronaut travel became a reality. The Neptune influence glamorized new approaches to mysticism, religion, and mind expansion. This generation will take a new approach to spiritual life, with emphasis on visions, mysticism, and clairvoyance.

Neptune in Capricorn

Birth Date: January 19, 1984–June 23, 1984; November 21, 1984–January 29, 1998. Neptune in Capricorn, which began in 1984 and will stay until 1998, brought a time when delusions about material power were first glamorized, then dashed on the rocks of reality. It was also a time when the psychic and occult worlds spawned a new category of business enterprise, and sold services on television.

Neptune in Aquarius

Birth Date: starting January 29, 1998 through the end of this century.

This should be a time of breakthroughs, when the creative influence of Neptune reaches a universal audience. This is a time of dissolving barriers, when we truly become one world.

Your Pluto Place Is the Power Spot!

To find out how someone handles power, look for the sign and house of Pluto. Because Pluto moves so slowly—only seven signs in this century—it reveals general trends for your whole generation. But if you know which house Pluto inhabits in a chart, you'll then know which area of life this little planet will pack a wallop in an individual's chart. Pluto tells you what makes your gang seem "cool" to each other, but uncool to the next generation. For example, the hedonistic rock-and-roll generation of Pluto in Leo *vs.* the workaholic Pluto in Virgo yuppies who came next.

Pluto brings our deep subconscious feelings to life

through painful probing. Nothing escapes—or is sacred—with Pluto. Because Pluto was discovered only recently, the signs of its exaltation and fall are debated. But in Scorpio, which Pluto rules, we have been able to witness this planet's fullest effect as it traveled through this sign from 1984 to 1995. Pluto symbolizes death and rebirth, the process of elimination, violence, and renewal.

Much of the strength of Pluto will depend on its position in your chart and the aspects it makes to other planets. The Pluto place in your horoscope is where you have invisible power (Mars governs the visible power), where you can transform, heal, and affect the unconscious needs of the masses. Though it is a tiny planet, its influence is great. When Pluto zaps a strategic point in your horoscope, you'll know it—your life is sure to change dramatically.

Pluto in Gemini (Late 1800s–May 28, 1914)

This is a time of mass suggestion and breakthroughs in communications, when many brilliant writers, such as Ernest Hemingway and F. Scott Fitzgerald, were born. Henry Miller, D. H. Lawrence, and James Joyce scandalized society by using explicit sexual images in their literature. "Muckraking" journalists exposed corruption. Pluto-ruled Scorpio President Theodore Roosevelt said, "Speak softly, but carry a big stick." This generation had an intense need to communicate and made major breakthroughs in knowledge. A compulsive restlessness and a thirst for a variety of experiences characterizes many of this generation.

Pluto in Cancer (May 28, 1914–June 14, 1939)

Dictators and mass media arose to wield emotional power over the masses. Women's rights was a popular issue. Deep sentimental feelings, acquisitiveness, and possessiveness characterized these times and people.

Pluto in Leo (June 14, 1939–
August 19, 1957)

The performing arts played on the emotions of the masses. Mick Jagger, John Lennon, and rock and roll were born at this time. Those born here tend to be self-centered, powerful, and boisterous. This generation does its own thing, for better or for worse.

Pluto in Virgo (August 19, 1957–October 5, 1971; April 17, 1972–July 30, 1972)

This is the "yuppie" generation that sparked a mass movement toward fitness, health, and career. During this time, machines were invented to process detail work perfectly. Inventions took on a practical turn, as answering machines, fax machines, car phones, and home office equipment all contributed to transform the workplace.

Pluto in Libra (October 5, 1971–April 17, 1972; July 30, 1972–August 28, 1984)

People born at this time will be concerned with partnerships, working together, and finding diplomatic solutions to problems. Marriage is becoming redefined for these couples along more traditional, but equal-partnership lines. This was a time of women's liberation, gay rights, ERA, and legal battles over abortion, all of which transformed our ideas about relationships.

Pluto in Scorpio (August 28, 1984–
January 17, 1995)

Pluto was in its ruling sign for a comparatively short period of time. In 1989, it was at its perihelion, or closest point to the sun and Earth. We have all felt the transforming power somewhere in our lives. This was a time of record achievements, destructive sexually transmitted diseases, nuclear power controversies, and explosive political issues. Pluto destroys in order to create new understanding—the phoenix rising from the ashes, which should be some consolation for those of you who have felt Pluto's force before 1995. Sexual shockers were par for the course during these intense years, when black clothing, transvestites, body piercing, tattoos, and sexually explicit advertising pushed the boundaries of good taste.

Pluto in Sagittarius (January 17, 1995 through the end of the century)

During our current Pluto transit, we'll be pushed to expand our horizons. For many of us, this will mean rolling down the information superhighway into the future. It signals a time of spiritual emphasis, when religion will exert much power in our political life as well. Since this is the sign that rules travel, there's a good possibility that Pluto, the planet of extremes, will make space travel a reality for some of us. Discovery of life on Mars, traveling here in meteors, could transform our ideas about where we came from. New dimensions in electronic publishing, concern with animal rights and the environment, and an increasing emphasis on extreme forms of religion could signal this period. We'll be developing far-reaching philosophies designed to elevate our lives with a new sense of purpose.

Look Up Your Planets

The following tables are provided so that you can look up the signs of seven major planets—Venus, Mars, Saturn, Jupiter, Uranus, Neptune, and Pluto. We do not have room for tables for the moon and Mercury, which change signs often.

How to Use the Venus Table

Find the year of your birth in the vertical column on the left, then follow across the page until you find the correct date. Your Venus sign is at the top of that column.

VENUS SIGNS 1901–2000

	Aries	Taurus	Gemini	Cancer	Leo	Virgo
1901	3/29–4/22	4/22–5/17	5/17–6/10	6/10–7/5	7/5–7/29	7/29–8/23
1902	5/7–6/3	6/3–6/30	6/30–7/25	7/25–8/19	8/19–9/13	9/13–10/7
1903	2/28–3/24	3/24–4/18	4/18–5/13	5/13–6/9	6/9–7/7	7/7–8/17
						9/6–11/8
1904	3/13–5/7	5/7–6/1	6/1–6/25	6/25–7/19	7/19–8/13	8/13–9/6
1905	2/3–3/6	3/6–4/9	7/8–8/6	8/6–9/1	9/1–9/27	9/27–10/21
	4/9–5/28	5/28–7/8				
1906	3/1–4/7	4/7–5/2	5/2–5/26	5/26–6/20	6/20–7/16	7/16–8/11
1907	4/27–5/22	5/22–6/16	6/16–7/11	7/11–8/4	8/4–8/29	8/29–9/22
1908	2/14–3/10	3/10–4/5	4/5–5/5	5/5–9/8	9/8–10/8	10/8–11/3
1909	3/29–4/22	4/22–5/16	5/16–6/10	6/10–7/4	7/4–7/29	7/29–8/23
1910	5/7–6/3	6/4–6/29	6/30–7/24	7/25–8/18	8/19–9/12	9/13–10/6
1911	2/28–3/23	3/24–4/17	4/18–5/12	5/13–6/8	6/9–7/7	7/8–11/8
1912	4/13–5/6	5/7–5/31	6/1–6/24	6/24–7/18	7/19–8/12	8/13–9/5
1913	2/3–3/6	3/7–5/1	7/8–8/5	8/6–8/31	9/1–9/26	9/27–10/20
	5/2–5/30	5/31–7/7				
1914	3/14–4/6	4/7–5/1	5/2–5/25	5/26–6/19	6/20–7/15	7/16–8/10
1915	4/27–5/21	5/22–6/15	6/16–7/10	7/11–8/3	8/4–8/28	8/29–9/21
1916	2/14–3/9	3/10–4/5	4/6–5/5	5/6–9/8	9/9–10/7	10/8–11/2
1917	3/29–4/21	4/22–5/15	5/16–6/9	6/10–7/3	7/4–7/28	7/29–8/21
1918	5/7–6/2	6/3–6/28	6/29–7/24	7/25–8/18	8/19–9/11	9/12–10/5
1919	2/27–3/22	3/23–4/16	4/17–5/12	5/13–6/7	6/8–7/7	7/8–11/8
1920	4/12–5/6	5/7–5/30	5/31–6/23	6/24–7/18	7/19–8/11	8/12–9/4
1921	2/3–3/6	3/7–4/25	7/8–8/5	8/6–8/31	9/1–9/25	9/26–10/20
	4/26–6/1	6/2–7/7				
1922	3/13–4/6	4/7–4/30	5/1–5/25	5/26–6/19	6/20–7/14	7/15–8/9
1923	4/27–5/21	5/22–6/14	6/15–7/9	7/10–8/3	8/4–8/27	8/28–9/20
1924	2/13–3/8	3/9–4/4	4/5–5/5	5/6–9/8	9/9–10/7	10/8–11/12
1925	3/28–4/20	4/21–5/15	5/16–6/8	6/9–7/3	7/4–7/27	7/28–8/21

Libra	Scorpio	Sagittarius	Capricorn	Aquarius	Pisces
8/23–9/17	9/17–10/12	10/12–1/16	1/16–2/9 11/7–12/5	2/9 12/5–1/11	3/5–3/29
10/7–10/31	10/31–11/24	11/24–12/18	12/18–1/11	2/6–4/4	1/11–2/6 4/4–5/7
8/17–9/6 11/8–12/9	12/9–1/5			1/11–2/4	2/4–2/28
9/6–9/30	9/30–10/25	1/5–1/30 10/25–11/18	1/30–2/24 11/18–12/13	2/24–3/19 12/13–1/7	3/19–4/13
10/21–11/14	11/14–12/8	12/8–1/1/06			1/7–2/3
8/11–9/7	9/7–10/9 12/15–12/25	10/9–12/15 12/25–2/6	1/1–1/25	1/25–2/18	2/18–3/14
9/22–10/16	10/16–11/9	11/9–12/3	2/6–3/6 12/3–12/27	3/6–4/2 12/27–1/20	4/2–4/27
11/3–11/28	11/28–12/22	12/22–1/15			1/20–2/4
8/23–9/17	9/17–10/12	10/12–11/17	1/15–2/9 11/17–12/5	2/9–3/5 12/5–1/15	3/5–3/29
10/7–10/30	10/31–11/23	11/24–12/17	12/18–12/31	1/1–1/15 1/29–4/4	1/16–1/28 4/5–5/6
11/19–12/8	12/9–12/31		1/1–1/10	1/11–2/2	2/3–2/27
9/6–9/30	1/1–1/4 10/1–10/24	1/5–1/29 10/25–11/17	1/30–2/23 11/18–12/12	2/24–3/18 12/13–12/31	3/19–4/12
10/21–11/13	11/14–12/7	12/8–12/31		1/1–1/6	1/7–2/2
8/11–9/6	9/7–10/9 12/6–12/30	10/10–12/5 12/31	1/1–1/24	1/25–2/17	2/18–3/13
9/22–10/15	10/16–11/8	1/1–1/6 11/9–12/2	2/7–3/6 12/3–12/26	3/7–4/1 12/27–12/31	4/2–4/26
11/3–11/27	11/28–12/21	12/22–12/31		1/1–1/19	1/20–2/13
8/22–9/16	9/17–10/11	1/1–1/14 10/12–11/6	1/15–2/7 11/7–12/5	2/8–3/4 12/6–12/31	3/5–3/28
10/6–10/29	10/30–11/22	11/23–12/16	12/17–12/31	1/1–4/5	4/6–5/2
11/9–12/8	12/9–12/31		1/1–1/9	1/10–2/2	2/3–2/26
9/5–9/30	1/1–1/3 9/31–10/23	1/4–1/28 10/24–11/17	1/29–2/22 11/18–12/11	2/23–3/18 12/12–12/31	3/19–4/11
10/21–11/13	11/14–12/7	12/8–12/31		1/1–1/6	1/7–2/2
8/10–9/6	9/7–10/10 11/29–12/31	10/11–11/28	1/1–1/24	1/25–2/16	2/17–3/12
9/21–10/14	1/1 10/15–11/7	1/2–2/6 11/8–12/1	2/7–3/5 12/2–12/25	3/6–3/31 12/26–12/31	4/1–4/26
11/13–11/26	11/27–12/21	12/22–12/31		1/1–1/19	1/20–2/12
8/22–9/15	9/16–10/11	1/1–1/14 10/12–11/6	1/15–2/7 11/7–12/5	2/8–3/3 12/6–12/31	3/4–3/27

VENUS SIGNS 1901–2000

	Aries	Taurus	Gemini	Cancer	Leo	Virgo
1926	5/7–6/2	6/3–6/28	6/29–7/23	7/24–8/17	8/18–9/11	9/12–10/5
1927	2/27–3/22	3/23–4/16	4/17–5/11	5/12–6/7	6/8–7/7	7/8–11/9
1928	4/12–5/5	5/6–5/29	5/30–6/23	6/24–7/17	7/18–8/11	8/12–9/4
1929	2/3–3/7	3/8–4/19	7/8–8/4	8/5–8/30	8/31–9/25	9/26–10/19
	4/20–6/2	6/3–7/7				
1930	3/13–4/5	4/6–4/30	5/1–5/24	5/25–6/18	6/19–7/14	7/15–8/9
1931	4/26–5/20	5/21–6/13	6/14–7/8	7/9–8/2	8/3–8/26	8/27–9/19
1932	2/12–3/8	3/9–4/3	4/4–5/5	5/6–7/12	9/9–10/6	10/7–11/1
			7/13–7/27	7/28–9/8		
1933	3/27–4/19	4/20–5/28	5/29–6/8	6/9–7/2	7/3–7/26	7/27–8/20
1934	5/6–6/1	6/2–6/27	6/28–7/22	7/23–8/16	8/17–9/10	9/11–10/4
1935	2/26–3/21	3/22–4/15	4/16–5/10	5/11–6/6	6/7–7/6	7/7–11/8
1936	4/11–5/4	5/5–5/28	5/29–6/22	6/23–7/16	7/17–8/10	8/11–9/4
1937	2/2–3/8	3/9–4/17	7/7–8/3	8/4–8/29	8/30–9/24	9/25–10/18
	4/14–6/3	6/4–7/6				
1938	3/12–4/4	4/5–4/28	4/29–5/23	5/24–6/18	6/19–7/13	7/14–8/8
1939	4/25–5/19	5/20–6/13	6/14–7/8	7/9–8/1	8/2–8/25	8/26–9/19
1940	2/12–3/7	3/8–4/3	4/4–5/5	5/6–7/4	9/9–10/5	10/6–10/31
			7/5–7/31	8/1–9/8		
1941	3/27–4/19	4/20–5/13	5/14–6/6	6/7–7/1	7/2–7/26	7/27–8/20
1942	5/6–6/1	6/2–6/26	6/27–7/22	7/23–8/16	8/17–9/9	9/10–10/3
1943	2/25–3/20	3/21–4/14	4/15–5/10	5/11–6/6	6/7–7/6	7/7–11/8
1944	4/10–5/3	5/4–5/28	5/29–6/21	6/22–7/16	7/17–8/9	8/10–9/2
1945	2/2–3/10	3/11–4/6	7/7–8/3	8/4–8/29	8/30–9/23	9/24–10/18
	4/7–6/3	6/4–7/6				
1946	3/11–4/4	4/5–4/28	4/29–5/23	5/24–6/17	6/18–7/12	7/13–8/8
1947	4/25–5/19	5/20–6/12	6/13–7/7	7/8–8/1	8/2–8/25	8/26–9/18
1948	2/11–3/7	3/8–4/3	4/4–5/6	5/7–6/28	9/8–10/5	10/6–10/31
			6/29–8/2	8/3–9/7		
1949	3/26–4/19	4/20–5/13	5/14–6/6	6/7–6/30	7/1–7/25	7/26–8/19
1950	5/5–5/31	6/1–6/26	6/27–7/21	7/22–8/15	8/16–9/9	9/10–10/3
1951	2/25–3/21	3/22–4/15	4/16–5/10	5/11–6/6	6/7–7/7	7/8–11/9

Libra	Scorpio	Sagittarius	Capricorn	Aquarius	Pisces
10/6–10/29	10/30–11/22	11/23–12/16	12/17–12/31	1/1–4/5	4/6–5/6
11/10–12/8	12/9–12/31	1/1–1/7	1/8	1/9–2/1	2/2–2/26
9/5–9/28	1/1–1/3	1/4–1/28	1/29–2/22	2/23–3/17	3/18–4/11
	9/29–10/23	10/24–11/16	11/17–12/11	12/12–12/31	
10/20–11/12	11/13–12/6	12/7–12/30	12/31	1/1–1/5	1/6–2/2
8/10–9/6	9/7–10/11	10/12–11/21	1/1–1/23	1/24–2/16	2/17–3/12
	11/22–12/31				
9/20–10/13	1/1–1/3	1/4–2/6	2/7–3/4	3/5–3/31	4/1–4/25
	10/14–11/6	11/7–11/30	12/1–12/24	12/25–12/31	
11/2–11/25	11/26–12/20	12/21–12/31		1/1–1/18	1/19–2/11
8/21–9/14	9/15–10/10	1/1–1/13	1/14–2/6	2/7–3/2	3/3–3/26
		10/11–11/5	11/6–12/4	12/5–12/31	
10/5–10/28	10/29–11/21	11/22–12/15	12/16–12/31	1/1–4/5	4/6–5/5
11/9–12/7	12/8–12/31		1/1–1/7	1/8–1/31	2/1–2/25
9/5–9/27	1/1–1/2	1/3–1/27	1/28–2/21	2/22–3/16	3/17–4/10
	9/28–10/22	10/23–11/15	11/16–12/10	12/11–12/31	
10/19–11/11	11/12–12/5	12/6–12/29	12/30–12/31	1/1–1/5	1/6–2/1
8/9–9/6	9/7–10/13	10/14–11/14	1/1–1/22	1/23–2/15	2/16–3/11
	11/15–12/31				
9/20–10/13	1/1–1/3	1/4–2/5	2/6–3/4	3/5–3/30	3/31–4/24
	10/14–11/6	11/7–11/30	12/1–12/24	12/25–12/31	
11/1–11/25	11/26–12/19	12/20–12/31		1/1–1/18	1/19–2/11
8/21–9/14	9/15–10/9	1/1–1/12	1/13–2/5	2/6–3/1	3/2–3/26
		10/10–11/5	11/6–12/4	12/5–12/31	
10/4–10/27	10/28–11/20	11/21–12/14	12/15–12/31	1/1–4/4	4/6–5/5
11/9–12/7	12/8–12/31		1/1–1/7	1/8–1/31	2/1–2/24
9/3–9/27	1/1–1/2	1/3–1/27	1/28–2/20	2/21–3/16	3/17–4/9
	9/28–10/21	10/22–11/15	11/16–12/10	12/11–12/31	
10/19–11/11	11/12–12/5	12/6–12/29	12/30–12/31	1/1–1/4	1/5–2/1
8/9–9/6	9/7–10/15	10/16–11/7	1/1–1/21	1/22–2/14	2/15–3/10
	11/8–12/31				
9/19–10/12	1/1–1/4	1/5–2/5	2/6–3/4	3/5–3/29	3/30–4/24
	10/13–11/5	11/6–11/29	11/30–12/23	12/24–12/31	
11/1–1/25	11/26–12/19	12/20–12/31		1/1–1/17	1/18–2/10
8/20–9/14	9/15–10/9	1/1–1/12	1/13–2/5	2/6–3/1	3/2–3/25
		10/10–11/5	11/6–12/5	12/6–12/31	
10/4–10/27	10/28–11/20	11/21–12/13	12/14–12/31	1/1–4/5	4/6–5/4
11/10–12/7	12/8–12/31		1/1–1/7	1/8–1/31	2/1–2/24

VENUS SIGNS 1901–2000

	Aries	Taurus	Gemini	Cancer	Leo	Virgo
1952	4/10–5/4	5/5–5/28	5/29–6/21	6/22–7/16	7/17–8/9	8/10–9/3
1953	2/2–3/13 4/1–6/5	3/4–3/31 6/6–7/7	7/8–8/3	8/4–8/29	8/30–9/24	9/25–10/18
1954	3/12–4/4	4/5–4/28	4/29–5/23	5/24–6/17	6/18–7/13	7/14–8/8
1955	4/25–5/19	5/20–6/13	6/14–7/7	7/8–8/1	8/2–8/25	8/26–9/18
1956	2/12–3/7	3/8–4/4	4/5–5/7 6/24–8/4	5/8–6/23 8/5–9/8	9/9–10/5	10/6–10/31
1957	3/26–4/19	4/20–5/13	5/14–6/6	6/7–7/1	7/2–7/26	7/7–8/19
1958	5/6–5/31	6/1–6/26	6/27–7/22	7/23–8/15	8/16–9/9	9/10–10/3
1959	2/25–3/20	3/21–4/14	4/15–5/10	5/11–6/6	6/7–7/8 9/21–9/24	7/9–9/20 9/25–11/9
1960	4/10–5/3	5/4–5/28	5/29–6/21	6/22–7/15	7/16–8/9	8/10–9/2
1961	2/3–6/5	6/6–7/7	7/8–8/3	8/4–8/29	8/30–9/23	9/24–10/17
1962	3/11–4/3	4/4–4/28	4/29–5/22	5/23–6/17	6/18–7/12	7/13–8/8
1963	4/24–5/18	5/19–6/12	6/13–7/7	7/8–7/31	8/1–8/25	8/26–9/18
1964	2/11–3/7	3/8–4/4	4/5–5/9 6/18–8/5	5/10–6/17 8/6–9/8	9/9–10/5	10/6–10/31
1965	3/26–4/18	4/19–5/12	5/13–6/6	6/7–6/30	7/1–7/25	7/26–8/19
1966	5/6–6/31	6/1–6/26	6/27–7/21	7/22–8/15	8/16–9/8	9/9–10/2
1967	2/24–3/20	3/21–4/14	4/15–5/10	5/11–6/6	6/7–7/8 9/10–10/1	7/9–9/9 10/2–11/9
1968	4/9–5/3	5/4–5/27	5/28–6/20	6/21–7/15	7/16–8/8	8/9–9/2
1969	2/3–6/6	6/7–7/6	7/7–8/3	8/4–8/28	8/29–9/22	9/23–10/17
1970	3/11–4/3	4/4–4/27	4/28–5/22	5/23–6/16	6/17–7/12	7/13–8/8
1971	4/24–5/18	5/19–6/12	6/13–7/6	7/7–7/31	8/1–8/24	8/25–9/17
1972	2/11–3/7	3/8–4/3	4/4–5/10 6/12–8/6	5/11–6/11 8/7–9/8	9/9–10/5	10/6–10/30
1973	3/25–4/18	4/18–5/12	5/13–6/5	6/6–6/29	7/1–7/25	7/26–8/19
1974	5/5–5/31	6/1–6/25	6/26–7/21	7/22–8/14	8/15–9/8	9/9–10/2
1975	2/24–3/20	3/21–4/13	4/14–5/9	5/10–6/6	6/7–7/9 9/3–10/4	7/10–9/2 10/5–11/9

Libra	Scorpio	Sagittarius	Capricorn	Aquarius	Pisces
9/4–9/27	1/1–1/2	1/3–1/27	1/28–2/20	2/21–3/16	3/17–4/9
	9/28–10/21	10/22–11/15	11/16–12/10	12/11–12/31	
10/19–11/11	11/12–12/5	12/6–12/29	12/30–12/31	1/1–1/5	1/6–2/1
8/9–9/6	9/7–10/22	10/23–10/27	1/1–1/22	1/23–2/15	2/16–3/11
	10/28–12/31				
9/19–10/13	1/1–1/6	1/7–2/5	2/6–3/4	3/5–3/30	3/31–4/24
	10/14–11/5	11/6–11/30	12/1–12/24	12/25–12/31	
11/1–11/25	11/26–12/19	12/20–12/31		1/1–1/17	1/18–2/11
8/20–9/14	9/15–10/9	1/1–1/12	1/13–2/5	2/6–3/1	3/2–3/25
		10/10–11/5	11/6–12/16	12/7–12/31	
10/4–10/27	10/28–11/20	11/21–12/14	12/15–12/31	1/1–4/6	4/7–5/5
11/10–12/7	12/8–12/31		1/1–1/7	1/8–1/31	2/1–2/24
9/3–9/26	1/1–1/2	1/3–1/27	1/28–2/20	2/21–3/15	3/16–4/9
	9/27–10/21	10/22–11/15	11/16–12/10	12/11–12/31	
10/18–11/11	11/12–12/4	12/5–12/28	12/29–12/31	1/1–1/5	1/6–2/2
8/9–9/6	9/7–12/31		1/1–1/21	1/22–2/14	2/15–3/10
9/19–10/12	1/1–1/6	1/7–2/5	2/6–3/4	3/5–3/29	3/30–4/23
	10/13–11/5	11/6–11/29	11/30–12/23	12/24–12/31	
11/1–11/24	11/25–12/19	12/20–12/31		1/1–1/16	1/17–2/10
8/20–9/13	9/14–10/9	1/1–1/12	1/13–2/5	2/6–3/1	3/2–3/25
		10/10–11/5	11/6–12/7	12/8–12/31	
10/3–10/26	10/27–11/19	11/20–12/13	2/7–2/25	1/1–2/6	4/7–5/5
			12/14–12/31	2/26–4/6	
11/10–12/7	12/8–12/23		1/1–1/6	1/7–1/30	1/31–2/23
9/3–9/26	1/1	1/2–1/26	1/27–2/20	2/21–3/15	3/16–4/8
	9/27–10/21	10/22–11/14	11/15–12/9	12/10–12/31	
10/18–11/10	11/11–12/4	12/5–12/28	12/29–12/31	1/1–1/4	1/5–2/2
8/9–9/7	9/8–12/31		1/1–1/21	1/22–2/14	2/15–3/10
9/18–10/11	1/1–1/7	1/8–2/5	2/6–3/4	3/5–3/29	3/30–4/23
	10/12–11/5	11/6–11/29	11/30–12/23	12/24–12/31	
	11/25–12/18	12/19–12/31		1/1–1/16	1/17–2/10
10/31–11/24					
8/20–9/13		1/1–1/12	1/13–2/4	2/5–2/28	3/1–3/24
		10/9–11/5	11/6–12/7	12/8–12/31	
			1/30–2/28	1/1–1/29	
10/3–10/26	10/27–11/19	11/20–12/13	12/14–12/31	3/1–4/6	4/7–5/4
			1/1–1/6	1/7–1/30	1/31–2/23
11/10–12/7	12/8–12/31				

VENUS SIGNS 1901–2000

	Aries	Taurus	Gemini	Cancer	Leo	Virgo
1976	4/8–5/2	5/2–5/27	5/27–6/20	6/20–7/14	7/14–8/8	8/8–9/1
1977	2/2–6/6	6/6–7/6	7/6–8/2	8/2–8/28	8/28–9/22	9/22–10/17
1978	3/9–4/2	4/2–4/27	4/27–5/22	5/22–6/16	6/16–7/12	7/12–8/6
1979	4/23–5/18	5/18–6/11	6/11–7/6	7/6–7/30	7/30–8/24	8/24–9/17
1980	2/9–3/6	3/6–4/3	4/3–5/12 8/5–8/6	5/12–6/5 8/6–9/7	9/7–10/4	10/4–10/30
1981	3/24–4/17	4/17–5/11	5/11–6/5	6/5–6/29	6/29–7/24	7/24–8/18
1982	5/4–5/30	5/30–6/25	6/25–7/20	7/20–8/14	8/14–9/7	9/7–10/2
1983	2/22–3/19	3/19–4/13	4/13–5/9	5/9–6/6	6/6–7/10 8/27–10/5	7/10–8/27 10/5–11/9
1984	4/7–5/2	5/2–5/26	5/26–6/20	6/20–7/14	7/14–8/7	8/7–9/1
1985	2/2–6/6	6/8–7/6	7/6–8/2	8/2–8/28	8/28–9/22	9/22–10/16
1986	3/9–4/2	4/2–4/26	4/26–5/21	5/21–6/15	6/15–7/11	7/11–8/7
1987	4/22–5/17	5/17–6/11	6/11–7/5	7/5–7/30	7/30–8/23	8/23–9/16
1988	2/9–3/6	3/6–4/3	4/3–5/17 5/27–8/6	5/17–5/27 8/28–9/22	9/7–10/4 9/22–10/16	10/4–10/29
1989	3/23–4/16	4/16–5/11	5/11–6/4	6/4–6/29	6/29–7/24	7/24–8/18
1990	5/4–5/30	5/30–6/25	6/25–7/20	7/20–8/13	8/13–9/7	9/7–10/1
1991	2/22–3/18	3/18–4/13	4/13–5/9	5/9–6/6	6/6–7/11 8/21–10/6	7/11–8/21 10/6–11/9
1992	4/7–5/1	5/1–5/26	5/26–6/19	6/19–7/13	7/13–8/7	8/7–8/31
1993	2/2–6/6	6/6–7/6	7/6–8/1	8/1–8/27	8/27–9/21	9/21–10/16
1994	3/8–4/1	4/1–4/26	4/26–5/21	5/21–6/15	6/15–7/11	7/11–8/7
1995	4/22–5/16	5/16–6/10	6/10–7/5	7/5–7/29	7/29–8/23	8/23–9/16
1996	2/9–3/6	3/6–4/3	4/3–8/7	8/7–9/7	9/7–10/4	10/4–10/29
1997	3/23–4/16	4/16–5/10	5/10–6/4	6/4–6/28	6/28–7/23	7/23–8/17
1998	5/3–5/29	5/29–6/24	6/24–7/19	7/19–8/13	8/13–9/6	9/6–9/30
1999	2/21–3/18	3/18–4/12	4/12–5/8	5/8–6/5	6/5–7/12 8/15–10/7	7/12–8/15 10/7–11/9
2000	4/6–5/1	5/1–5/25	5/25–6/13	6/13–7/13	7/13–8/6	8/6–8/31

Libra	Scorpio	Sagittarius	Capricorn	Aquarius	Pisces
9/1–9/26	9/26–10/20	1/1–1/26	1/26–2/19	2/19–3/15	3/15–4/8
		10/20–11/14	11/14–12/6	12/9–1/4	
10/17–11/10	11/10–12/4	12/4–12/27	12/27–1/20		
8/6–9/7	9/7–1/7				1/4–2/2
9/17–10/11	10/11–11/4			1/20–2/13	2/13–3/9
		1/7–2/5	2/5–3/3	3/3–3/29	3/29–4/23
		11/4–11/28	11/28–12/22	12/22–1/16	
10/30–11/24	11/24–12/18	12/18–1/11			
					1/16–2/9
8/18–9/12	9/12–10/9	10/9–11/5	1/11–2/4	2/4–2/28	2/28–3/24
			11/5–12/8	12/8–1/23	
10/2–10/26	10/26–11/18	11/18–12/12	1/23–3/2	3/2–4/6	4/6–5/4
			12/12–1/5		
11/9–12/6	12/6–1/1			1/5–1/29	1/29–2/22
9/1–9/25	9/25–10/20	1/1–1/25	1/25–2/19	2/19–3/14	3/14–4/7
		10/20–11/13	11/13–12/9		
10/16–11/9	11/9–12/3	12/3–12/27			1/4–2/2
8/7–9/7	9/7–1/7			1/20–3/13	2/13–3/9
9/16–10/10	10/10–11/3	1/7–2/5	2/5–3/3	3/3–3/28	3/28–4/22
		11/3–11/28	11/28–12/22	12/22–1/15	
10/29–11/23	11/23–12/17	12/17–1/10			1/15–2/9
8/18–9/12	9/12–10/8	10/8–11/5	1/10–2/3	2/3–2/27	2/27–3/23
			11/5–12/10	12/10–1/16	
10/1–10/25	10/25–11/18	11/18–12/12	1/16–3/3	3/3–4/6	4/6–5/4
			12/12–1/5		
8/21–12/6	12/6–12/31	12/21–1/25/92		1/5–1/29	1/29–2/22
8/31–9/25	9/25–10/19	10/19–11/13	1/25–2/18	2/18–3/13	3/13–4/7
			11/13–12/8	12/8–1/3	
10/16–11/9	11/9–12/2	12/2–12/26	12/26–1/19		1/3–2/2
8/7–9/7	9/7–1/7			1/19–2/12	2/12–3/8
9/16–10/10	10/10–11/13	1/7–2/4	2/4–3/2	3/2–3/28	3/28–4/22
		11/3–11/27	11/27–12/21	12/21–1/15	
10/29–11/23	11/23–12/17	12/17–1/10/97			1/15–2/9
8/17–9/12	9/12–10/8	10/8–11/5	1/10–2/3	2/3–2/27	2/27–3/23
			11/5–12/12	12/12–1/9	
9/30–10/24	10/24–11/17	11/17–12/11	1/9–3/4	3/4–4/6	4/6–5/3
11/9–12/5	12/5–12/31	12/31–1/24		1/4–1/28	1/28–2/21
8/31–9/24	9/24–10/19	10/19–11/13	1/24–2/18	2/18–3/12	3/13–4/6
			11/13–12/8	12/8	

How to Use the Mars, Jupiter, and Saturn Tables

Find the year of your birth on the left side of each column. The dates when the planet entered each sign are listed on the right side of each column. (Signs are abbreviated to the first three letters.) Your birthday should fall on or between each date listed, and your planetary placement should correspond to the earlier sign of that period.

MARS SIGN 1901–2000

1901	MAR	1	Leo	1905	JAN	13	Scp
	MAY	11	Vir		AUG	21	Sag
	JUL	13	Lib		OCT	8	Cap
	AUG	31	Scp		NOV	18	Aqu
	OCT	14	Sag		DEC	27	Pic
	NOV	24	Cap	1906	FEB	4	Ari
1902	JAN	1	Aqu		MAR	17	Tau
	FEB	8	Pic		APR	28	Gem
	MAR	19	Ari		JUN	11	Can
	APR	27	Tau		JUL	27	Leo
	JUN	7	Gem		SEP	12	Vir
	JUL	20	Can		OCT	30	Lib
	SEP	4	Leo		DEC	17	Scp
	OCT	23	Vir	1907	FEB	5	Sag
	DEC	20	Lib		APR	1	Cap
1903	APR	19	Vir		OCT	13	Aqu
	MAY	30	Lib		NOV	29	Pic
	AUG	6	Scp	1908	JAN	11	Ari
	SEP	22	Sag		FEB	23	Tau
	NOV	3	Cap		APR	7	Gem
	DEC	12	Aqu		MAY	22	Can
1904	JAN	19	Pic		JUL	8	Leo
	FEB	27	Ari		AUG	24	Vir
	APR	6	Tau		OCT	10	Lib
	MAY	18	Gem		NOV	25	Scp
	JUN	30	Can	1909	JAN	10	Sag
	AUG	15	Leo		FEB	24	Cap
	OCT	1	Vir		APR	9	Aqu
	NOV	20	Lib		MAY	25	Pic

	JUL	21	Ari		AUG	19	Can
	SEP	26	Pic		OCT	7	Leo
	NOV	20	Ari	1916	MAY	28	Vir
1910	JAN	23	Tau		JUL	23	Lib
	MAR	14	Gem		SEP	8	Scp
	MAY	1	Can		OCT	22	Sag
	JUN	19	Leo		DEC	1	Cap
	AUG	6	Vir	1917	JAN	9	Aqu
	SEP	22	Lib		FEB	16	Pic
	NOV	6	Scp		MAR	26	Ari
	DEC	20	Sag		MAY	4	Tau
1911	JAN	31	Cap		JUN	14	Gem
	MAR	14	Aqu		JUL	28	Can
	APR	23	Pic		SEP	12	Leo
	JUN	2	Ari		NOV	2	Vir
	JUL	15	Tau	1918	JAN	11	Lib
	SEP	5	Gem		FEB	25	Vir
	NOV	30	Tau		JUN	23	Lib
1912	JAN	30	Gem		AUG	17	Scp
	APR	5	Can		OCT	1	Sag
	MAY	28	Leo		NOV	11	Cap
	JUL	17	Vir		DEC	20	Aqu
	SEP	2	Lib	1919	JAN	27	Pic
	OCT	18	Scp		MAR	6	Ari
	NOV	30	Sag		APR	15	Tau
1913	JAN	10	Cap		MAY	26	Gem
	FEB	19	Aqu		JUL	8	Can
	MAR	30	Pic		AUG	23	Leo
	MAY	8	Ari		OCT	10	Vir
	JUN	17	Tau		NOV	30	Lib
	JUL	29	Gem	1920	JAN	31	Scp
	SEP	15	Can		APR	23	Lib
1914	MAY	1	Leo		JUL	10	Scp
	JUN	26	Vir		SEP	4	Sag
	AUG	14	Lib		OCT	18	Cap
	SEP	29	Scp		NOV	27	Aqu
	NOV	11	Sag	1921	JAN	5	Pic
	DEC	22	Cap		FEB	13	Ari
1915	JAN	30	Aqu		MAR	25	Tau
	MAR	9	Pic		MAY	6	Gem
	APR	16	Ari		JUN	18	Can
	MAY	26	Tau		AUG	3	Leo
	JUL	6	Gem		SEP	19	Vir

	NOV	6	Lib		APR	7	Pic
	DEC	26	Scp		MAY	16	Ari
1922	FEB	18	Sag		JUN	26	Tau
	SEP	13	Cap		AUG	9	Gem
	OCT	30	Aqu		OCT	3	Can
	DEC	11	Pic		DEC	20	Gem
1923	JAN	21	Ari	1929	MAR	10	Can
	MAR	4	Tau		MAY	13	Leo
	APR	16	Gem		JUL	4	Vir
	MAY	30	Can		AUG	21	Lib
	JUL	16	Leo		OCT	6	Scp
	SEP	1	Vir		NOV	18	Sag
	OCT	18	Lib		DEC	29	Cap
	DEC	4	Scp	1930	FEB	6	Aqu
1924	JAN	19	Sag		MAR	17	Pic
	MAR	6	Cap		APR	24	Ari
	APR	24	Aqu		JUN	3	Tau
	JUN	24	Pic		JUL	14	Gem
	AUG	24	Aqu		AUG	28	Can
	OCT	19	Pic		OCT	20	Leo
	DEC	19	Ari	1931	FEB	16	Can
1925	FEB	5	Tau		MAR	30	Leo
	MAR	24	Gem		JUN	10	Vir
	MAY	9	Can		AUG	1	Lib
	JUN	26	Leo		SEP	17	Scp
	AUG	12	Vir		OCT	30	Sag
	SEP	28	Lib		DEC	10	Cap
	NOV	13	Scp	1932	JAN	18	Aqu
	DEC	28	Sag		FEB	25	Pic
1926	FEB	9	Cap		APR	3	Ari
	MAR	23	Aqu		MAY	12	Tau
	MAY	3	Pic		JUN	22	Gem
	JUN	15	Ari		AUG	4	Can
	AUG	1	Tau		SEP	20	Leo
1927	FEB	22	Gem		NOV	13	Vir
	APR	17	Can	1933	JUL	6	Lib
	JUN	6	Leo		AUG	26	Scp
	JUL	25	Vir		OCT	9	Sag
	SEP	10	Lib		NOV	19	Cap
	OCT	26	Scp		DEC	28	Aqu
	DEC	8	Sag	1934	FEB	4	Pic
1928	JAN	19	Cap		MAR	14	Ari
	FEB	28	Aqu		APR	22	Tau

	JUN	2	Gem		AUG	19	Vir
	JUL	15	Can		OCT	5	Lib
	AUG	30	Leo		NOV	20	Scp
	OCT	18	Vir	1941	JAN	4	Sag
	DEC	11	Lib		FEB	17	Cap
1935	JUL	29	Scp		APR	2	Aqu
	SEP	16	Sag		MAY	16	Pic
	OCT	28	Cap		JUL	2	Ari
	DEC	7	Aqu	1942	JAN	11	Tau
1936	JAN	14	Pic		MAR	7	Gem
	FEB	22	Ari		APR	26	Can
	APR	1	Tau		JUN	14	Leo
	MAY	13	Gem		AUG	1	Vir
	JUN	25	Can		SEP	17	Lib
	AUG	10	Leo		NOV	1	Scp
	SEP	26	Vir		DEC	15	Sag
	NOV	14	Lib	1943	JAN	26	Cap
1937	JAN	5	Scp		MAR	8	Aqu
	MAR	13	Sag		APR	17	Pic
	MAY	14	Scp		MAY	27	Ari
	AUG	8	Sag		JUL	7	Tau
	SEP	30	Cap		AUG	23	Gem
	NOV	11	Aqu	1944	MAR	28	Can
	DEC	21	Pic		MAY	22	Leo
1938	JAN	30	Ari		JUL	12	Vir
	MAR	12	Tau		AUG	29	Lib
	APR	23	Gem		OCT	13	Scp
	JUN	7	Can		NOV	25	Sag
	JUL	22	Leo	1945	JAN	5	Cap
	SEP	7	Vir		FEB	14	Aqu
	OCT	25	Lib		MAR	25	Pic
	DEC	11	Scp		MAY	2	Ari
1939	JAN	29	Sag		JUN	11	Tau
	MAR	21	Cap		JUL	23	Gem
	MAY	25	Aqu		SEP	7	Can
	JUL	21	Cap		NOV	11	Leo
	SEP	24	Aqu		DEC	26	Can
	NOV	19	Pic	1946	APR	22	Leo
1940	JAN	4	Ari		JUN	20	Vir
	FEB	17	Tau		AUG	9	Lib
	APR	1	Gem		SEP	24	Scp
	MAY	17	Can		NOV	6	Sag
	JUL	3	Leo		DEC	17	Cap

1947	JAN	25	Aqu		MAR	20	Tau
	MAR	4	Pic		MAY	1	Gem
	APR	11	Ari		JUN	14	Can
	MAY	21	Tau		JUL	29	Leo
	JUL	1	Gem		SEP	14	Vir
	AUG	13	Can		NOV	1	Lib
	OCT	1	Leo		DEC	20	Scp
	DEC	1	Vir	1954	FEB	9	Sag
1948	FEB	12	Leo		APR	12	Cap
	MAY	18	Vir		JUL	3	Sag
	JUL	17	Lib		AUG	24	Cap
	SEP	3	Scp		OCT	21	Aqu
	OCT	17	Sag		DEC	4	Pic
	NOV	26	Cap	1955	JAN	15	Ari
1949	JAN	4	Aqu		FEB	26	Tau
	FEB	11	Pic		APR	10	Gem
	MAR	21	Ari		MAY	26	Can
	APR	30	Tau		JUL	11	Leo
	JUN	10	Gem		AUG	27	Vir
	JUL	23	Can		OCT	13	Lib
	SEP	7	Leo		NOV	29	Scp
	OCT	27	Vir	1956	JAN	14	Sag
	DEC	26	Lib		FEB	28	Cap
1950	MAR	28	Vir		APR	14	Aqu
	JUN	11	Lib		JUN	3	Pic
	AUG	10	Scp		DEC	6	Ari
	SEP	25	Sag	1957	JAN	28	Tau
	NOV	6	Cap		MAR	17	Gem
	DEC	15	Aqu		MAY	4	Can
1951	JAN	22	Pic		JUN	21	Leo
	MAR	1	Ari		AUG	8	Vir
	APR	10	Tau		SEP	24	Lib
	MAY	21	Gem		NOV	8	Scp
	JUL	3	Can		DEC	23	Sag
	AUG	18	Leo	1958	FEB	3	Cap
	OCT	5	Vir		MAR	17	Aqu
	NOV	24	Lib		APR	27	Pic
1952	JAN	20	Scp		JUN	7	Ari
	AUG	27	Sag		JUL	21	Tau
	OCT	12	Cap		SEP	21	Gem
	NOV	21	Aqu		OCT	29	Tau
	DEC	30	Pic	1959	FEB	10	Gem
1953	FEB	8	Ari		APR	10	Can

97

	JUN	1	Leo		NOV	14	Cap
	JUL	20	Vir		DEC	23	Aqu
	SEP	5	Lib	1966	JAN	30	Pic
	OCT	21	Scp		MAR	9	Ari
	DEC	3	Sag		APR	17	Tau
1960	JAN	14	Cap		MAY	28	Gem
	FEB	23	Aqu		JUL	11	Can
	APR	2	Pic		AUG	25	Leo
	MAY	11	Ari		OCT	12	Vir
	JUN	20	Tau		DEC	4	Lib
	AUG	2	Gem	1967	FEB	12	Scp
	SEP	21	Can		MAR	31	Lib
1961	FEB	5	Gem		JUL	19	Scp
	FEB	7	Can		SEP	10	Sag
	MAY	6	Leo		OCT	23	Cap
	JUN	28	Vir		DEC	1	Aqu
	AUG	17	Lib	1968	JAN	9	Pic
	OCT	1	Scp		FEB	17	Ari
	NOV	13	Sag		MAR	27	Tau
	DEC	24	Cap		MAY	8	Gem
1962	FEB	1	Aqu		JUN	21	Can
	MAR	12	Pic		AUG	5	Leo
	APR	19	Ari		SEP	21	Vir
	MAY	28	Tau		NOV	9	Lib
	JUL	9	Gem		DEC	29	Scp
	AUG	22	Can	1969	FEB	25	Sag
	OCT	11	Leo		SEP	21	Cap
1963	JUN	3	Vir		NOV	4	Aqu
	JUL	27	Lib		DEC	15	Pic
	SEP	12	Scp	1970	JAN	24	Ari
	OCT	25	Sag		MAR	7	Tau
	DEC	5	Cap		APR	18	Gem
1964	JAN	13	Aqu		JUN	2	Can
	FEB	20	Pic		JUL	18	Leo
	MAR	29	Ari		SEP	3	Vir
	MAY	7	Tau		OCT	20	Lib
	JUN	17	Gem		DEC	6	Scp
	JUL	30	Can	1971	JAN	23	Sag
	SEP	15	Leo		MAR	12	Cap
	NOV	6	Vir		MAY	3	Aqu
1965	JUN	29	Lib		NOV	6	Pic
	AUG	20	Scp		DEC	26	Ari
	OCT	4	Sag	1972	FEB	10	Tau

	MAR	27	Gem	1978	JAN	26	Can
	MAY	12	Can		APR	10	Leo
	JUN	28	Leo		JUN	14	Vir
	AUG	15	Vir		AUG	4	Lib
	SEP	30	Lib		SEP	19	Scp
	NOV	15	Scp		NOV	2	Sag
	DEC	30	Sag		DEC	12	Cap
1973	FEB	12	Cap	1979	JAN	20	Aqu
	MAR	26	Aqu		FEB	27	Pic
	MAY	8	Pic		APR	7	Ari
	JUN	20	Ari		MAY	16	Tau
	AUG	12	Tau		JUN	26	Gem
	OCT	29	Ari		AUG	8	Can
	DEC	24	Tau		SEP	24	Leo
1974	FEB	27	Gem		NOV	19	Vir
	APR	20	Can	1980	MAR	11	Leo
	JUN	9	Leo		MAY	4	Vir
	JUL	27	Vir		JUL	10	Lib
	SEP	12	Lib		AUG	29	Scp
	OCT	28	Scp		OCT	12	Sag
	DEC	10	Sag		NOV	22	Cap
1975	JAN	21	Cap		DEC	30	Aqu
	MAR	3	Aqu	1981	FEB	6	Pic
	APR	11	Pic		MAR	17	Ari
	MAY	21	Ari		APR	25	Tau
	JUL	1	Tau		JUN	5	Gem
	AUG	14	Gem		JUL	18	Can
	OCT	17	Can		SEP	2	Leo
	NOV	25	Gem		OCT	21	Vir
1976	MAR	18	Can		DEC	16	Lib
	MAY	16	Leo	1982	AUG	3	Scp
	JUL	6	Vir		SEP	20	Sag
	AUG	24	Lib		OCT	31	Cap
	OCT	8	Scp		DEC	10	Aqu
	NOV	20	Sag	1983	JAN	17	Pic
1977	JAN	1	Cap		FEB	25	Ari
	FEB	9	Aqu		APR	5	Tau
	MAR	20	Pic		MAY	16	Gem
	APR	27	Ari		JUN	29	Can
	JUN	6	Tau		AUG	13	Leo
	JUL	17	Gem		SEP	30	Vir
	SEP	1	Can		NOV	18	Lib
	OCT	26	Leo	1984	JAN	11	Scp

	AUG	17	Sag		JUL	12	Tau
	OCT	5	Cap		AUG	31	Gem
	NOV	15	Aqu		DEC	14	Tau
	DEC	25	Pic	1991	JAN	21	Gem
1985	FEB	2	Ari		APR	3	Can
	MAR	15	Tau		MAY	26	Leo
	APR	26	Gem		JUL	15	Vir
	JUN	9	Can		SEP	1	Lib
	JUL	25	Leo		OCT	16	Scp
	SEP	10	Vir		NOV	29	Sag
	OCT	27	Lib	1992	JAN	9	Cap
	DEC	14	Scp		FEB	18	Aqu
1986	FEB	2	Sag		MAR	28	Pic
	MAR	28	Cap		MAY	5	Ari
	OCT	9	Aqu		JUN	14	Tau
	NOV	26	Pic		JUL	26	Gem
1987	JAN	8	Ari		SEP	12	Can
	FEB	20	Tau	1993	APR	27	Leo
	APR	5	Gem		JUN	23	Vir
	MAY	21	Can		AUG	12	Lib
	JUL	6	Leo		SEP	27	Scp
	AUG	22	Vir		NOV	9	Sag
	OCT	8	Lib		DEC	20	Cap
	NOV	24	Scp	1994	JAN	28	Aqu
1988	JAN	8	Sag		MAR	7	Pic
	FEB	22	Cap		APR	14	Ari
	APR	6	Aqu		MAY	23	Tau
	MAY	22	Pic		JUL	3	Gem
	JUL	13	Ari		AUG	16	Can
	OCT	23	Pic		OCT	4	Leo
	NOV	1	Ari		DEC	12	Vir
1989	JAN	19	Tau	1995	JAN	22	Leo
	MAR	11	Gem		MAY	25	Vir
	APR	29	Can		JUL	21	Lib
	JUN	16	Leo		SEP	7	Scp
	AUG	3	Vir		OCT	20	Sag
	SEP	19	Lib		NOV	30	Cap
	NOV	4	Scp	1996	JAN	8	Aqu
	DEC	18	Sag		FEB	15	Pic
1990	JAN	29	Cap		MAR	24	Ari
	MAR	11	Aqu		MAY	2	Tau
	APR	20	Pic		JUN	12	Gem
	MAY	31	Ari		JUL	25	Can

	SEP	9	Leo		NOV	27	Lib
	OCT	30	Vir	1999	JAN	26	Scp
1997	JAN	3	Lib		MAY	5	Lib
	MAR	8	Vir		JUL	5	Scp
	JUN	19	Lib		SEP	2	Sag
	AUG	14	Scp		OCT	17	Cap
	SEP	28	Sag		NOV	26	Aqu
	NOV	9	Cap	2000	JAN	4	Pic
	DEC	18	Aqu		FEB	12	Ari
1998	JAN	25	Pic		MAR	23	Tau
	MAR	4	Ari		MAY	3	Gem
	APR	13	Tau		JUN	16	Can
	MAY	24	Gem		AUG	1	Leo
	JUL	6	Can		SEP	17	Vir
	AUG	20	Leo		NOV	4	Lib
	OCT	7	Vir		DEC	23	Scp

JUPITER SIGN 1901–2000

1901	JAN	19	Cap		OCT	26	Ari
1902	FEB	6	Aqu	1917	FEB	12	Tau
1903	FEB	20	Pic		JUN	29	Gem
1904	MAR	1	Ari	1918	JUL	13	Can
	AUG	8	Tau	1919	AUG	2	Leo
	AUG	31	Ari	1920	AUG	27	Vir
1905	MAR	7	Tau	1921	SEP	25	Lib
	JUL	21	Gem	1922	OCT	26	Scp
	DEC	4	Tau	1923	NOV	24	Sag
1906	MAR	9	Gem	1924	DEC	18	Cap
	JUL	30	Can	1926	JAN	6	Aqu
1907	AUG	18	Leo	1927	JAN	18	Pic
1908	SEP	12	Vir		JUN	6	Ari
1909	OCT	11	Lib		SEP	11	Pic
1910	NOV	11	Scp	1928	JAN	23	Ari
1911	DEC	10	Sag		JUN	4	Tau
1913	JAN	2	Cap	1929	JUN	12	Gem
1914	JAN	21	Aqu	1930	JUN	26	Can
1915	FEB	4	Pic	1931	JUL	17	Leo
1916	FEB	12	Ari	1932	AUG	11	Vir
	JUN	26	Tau	1933	SEP	10	Lib

1934	OCT	11	Scp	1960	MAR	1	Cap
1935	NOV	9	Sag		JUN	10	Sag
1936	DEC	2	Cap		OCT	26	Cap
1937	DEC	20	Aqu	1961	MAR	15	Aqu
1938	MAY	14	Pic		AUG	12	Cap
	JUL	30	Aqu		NOV	4	Aqu
	DEC	29	Pic	1962	MAR	25	Pic
1939	MAY	11	Ari	1963	APR	4	Ari
	OCT	30	Pic	1964	APR	12	Tau
	DEC	20	Ari	1965	APR	22	Gem
1940	MAY	16	Tau		SEP	21	Can
1941	MAY	26	Gem		NOV	17	Gem
1942	JUN	10	Can	1966	MAY	5	Can
1943	JUN	30	Leo		SEP	27	Leo
1944	JUL	26	Vir	1967	JAN	16	Can
1945	AUG	25	Lib		MAY	23	Leo
1946	SEP	25	Scp		OCT	19	Vir
1947	OCT	24	Sag	1968	FEB	27	Leo
1948	NOV	15	Cap		JUN	15	Vir
1949	APR	12	Aqu		NOV	15	Lib
	JUN	27	Cap	1969	MAR	30	Vir
	NOV	30	Aqu		JUL	15	Lib
1950	APR	15	Pic		DEC	16	Scp
	SEP	15	Aqu	1970	APR	30	Lib
	DEC	1	Pic		AUG	15	Scp
1951	APR	21	Ari	1971	JAN	14	Sag
1952	APR	28	Tau		JUN	5	Sc
1953	MAY	9	Gem		SEP	11	Sag
1954	MAY	24	Can	1972	FEB	6	Cap
1955	JUN	13	Leo		JUL	24	Sag
	NOV	17	Vir		SEP	25	Cap
1956	JAN	18	Leo	1973	FEB	23	Aqu
	JUL	7	Vir	1974	MAR	8	Pic
	DEC	13	Lib	1975	MAR	18	Ari
1957	FEB	19	Vir	1976	MAR	26	Tau
	AUG	7	Lib		AUG	23	Gem
1958	JAN	13	Scp		OCT	16	Tau
	MAR	20	Lib	1977	APR	3	Gem
	SEP	7	Scp		AUG	20	Can
1959	FEB	10	Sag		DEC	30	Gem
	APR	24	Scp	1978	APR	12	Can
	OCT	5	Sag		SEP	5	Leo

1979	FEB	28	Can		JUL	30	Can
	APR	20	Leo	1990	AUG	18	Leo
	SEP	29	Vir	1991	SEP	12	Vir
1980	OCT	27	Lib	1992	OCT	10	Lib
1981	NOV	27	Scp	1993	NOV	10	Scp
1982	DEC	26	Sag	1994	DEC	9	Sag
1984	JAN	19	Cap	1996	JAN	3	Cap
1985	FEB	6	Aqu	1997	JAN	21	Aqu
1986	FEB	20	Pic	1998	FEB	4	Pic
1987	MAR	2	Ari	1999	FEB	13	Ari
1988	MAR	8	Tau		JUN	28	Tau
	JUL	22	Gem		OCT	23	Ari
	NOV	30	Tau	2000	FEB	14	Tau
1989	MAR	11	Gem		JUN	30	Gem

SATURN SIGN 1903–2000

1903	JAN	19	Aqu	1929	MAR	15	Cap
1905	APR	13	Pic		MAY	5	Sag
	AUG	17	Aqu		NOV	30	Cap
1906	JAN	8	Pic	1932	FEB	24	Aqu
1908	MAR	19	Ari		AUG	13	Cap
1910	MAY	17	Tau		NOV	20	Aqu
	DEC	14	Ari	1935	FEB	14	Pic
1911	JAN	20	Tau	1937	APR	25	Ari
1912	JUL	7	Gem		OCT	18	Pic
	NOV	30	Tau	1938	JAN	14	Ari
1913	MAR	26	Gem	1939	JUL	6	Tau
1914	AUG	24	Can		SEP	22	Ari
	DEC	7	Gem	1940	MAR	20	Tau
1915	MAY	11	Can	1942	MAY	8	Gem
1916	OCT	17	Leo	1944	JUN	20	Can
	DEC	7	Can	1946	AUG	2	Leo
1917	JUN	24	Leo	1948	SEP	19	Vir
1919	AUG	12	Vir	1949	APR	3	Leo
1921	OCT	7	Lib		MAY	29	Vir
1923	DEC	20	Scp	1950	NOV	20	Lib
1924	APR	6	Lib	1951	MAR	7	Vir
	SEP	13	Scp		AUG	13	Lib
1926	DEC	2	Sag	1953	OCT	22	Scp

Year	Month	Day	Sign
1956	JAN	12	Sag
	MAY	14	Scp
	OCT	10	Sag
1959	JAN	5	Cap
1962	JAN	3	Aqu
1964	MAR	24	Pic
	SEP	16	Aqu
	DEC	16	Pic
1967	MAR	3	Ari
1969	APR	29	Tau
1971	JUN	18	Gem
1972	JAN	10	Tau
	FEB	21	Gem
1973	AUG	1	Can
1974	JAN	7	Gem
	APR	18	Can
1975	SEP	17	Leo
1976	JAN	14	Can
	JUN	5	Leo
1977	NOV	17	Vir
1978	JAN	5	Leo
	JUL	26	Vir
1980	SEP	21	Lib
1982	NOV	29	Scp
1983	MAY	6	Lib
	AUG	24	Scp
1985	NOV	17	Sag
1988	FEB	13	Cap
	JUN	10	Sag
	NOV	12	Cap
1991	FEB	6	Aqu
1993	MAY	21	Pic
	JUN	30	Aqu
1994	JAN	28	Pic
1996	APR	7	Ari
1998	JUN	9	Tau
	OCT	25	Ari
1999	MAR	1	Tau
2000	AUG	10	Gem
	OCT	16	Tau

How to Use the Uranus, Neptune, and Pluto Tables

Find your birthday in the list following each sign.

Look up your Uranus placement by finding your birthday on the following lists.

URANUS IN ARIES BIRTH DATES

March 31–November 4, 1927
January 13, 1928–June 6, 1934
October 10, 1934–March 28, 1935

URANUS IN TAURUS BIRTH DATES

June 6, 1934–October 10, 1934
March 28, 1935–August 7, 1941
October 5, 1941–May 15, 1942

URANUS IN GEMINI BIRTH DATES

August 7–October 5, 1941
May 15, 1942–August 30, 1948
November 12, 1948–June 10, 1949

URANUS IN CANCER BIRTH DATES

August 30–November 12, 1948
June 10, 1949–August 24, 1955
January 28–June 10, 1956

URANUS IN LEO BIRTH DATES

August 24, 1955–January 28, 1956
June 10, 1956–November 1, 1961
January 10–August 10, 1962

URANUS IN VIRGO BIRTH DATES

November 1, 1961–January 10, 1962
August 10, 1962–September 28, 1968
May 20, 1969–June 24, 1969

URANUS IN LIBRA BIRTH DATES

September 28, 1968–May 20, 1969
June 24, 1969–November 21, 1974
May 1–September 8, 1975

URANUS IN SCORPIO BIRTH DATES

November 21, 1974–May 1, 1975
September 8, 1975–February 17, 1981
March 20–November 16, 1981

URANUS IN SAGITTARIUS BIRTH DATES

February 17–March 20, 1981
November 16, 1981–February 15, 1988
May 27, 1988–December 2, 1988

URANUS IN CAPRICORN BIRTH DATES

December 20, 1904–January 30, 1912
September 4–November 12, 1912
February 15–May 27, 1988
December 2, 1988–April 1, 1995
June 9, 1995–January 12, 1996

URANUS IN AQUARIUS BIRTH DATES

January 30–September 4, 1912
November 12, 1912–April 1, 1919
August 16, 1919–January 22, 1920
April 1–June 9, 1995
January 12, 1996 through end of the century

URANUS IN PISCES BIRTH DATES

April 1–August 16, 1919
January 22, 1920–March 31, 1927
November 4, 1927–January 13, 1928

Look up your Neptune placement by finding your birthday on the following lists.

NEPTUNE IN CANCER BIRTH DATES

July 19–December 25, 1901
May 21, 1902–September 23, 1914
December 14, 1914–July 19, 1915
March 19–May 2, 1916

NEPTUNE IN LEO BIRTH DATES

September 23–December 14, 1914
July 19, 1915–March 19, 1916
May 2, 1916–September 21, 1928
February 19, 1929–July 24, 1929

NEPTUNE IN VIRGO BIRTH DATES

September 21, 1928–February 19, 1929
July 24, 1929–October 3, 1942
April 17–August 2, 1943

NEPTUNE IN LIBRA BIRTH DATES

October 3, 1942–April 17, 1943
August 2, 1943–December 24, 1955
March 12–October 19, 1956
June 15–August 6, 1957

NEPTUNE IN SCORPIO BIRTH DATES

December 24, 1955–March 12, 1956
October 19, 1956–June 15, 1957
August 6, 1957–January 4, 1970
May 3–November 6, 1970

NEPTUNE IN SAGITTARIUS BIRTH DATES

January 4–May 3, 1970
November 6, 1970–January 19, 1984
June 23–November 21, 1984

NEPTUNE IN CAPRICORN BIRTH DATES

January 19, 1984–June 23, 1984
November 21, 1984–January 29, 1998

Find your Pluto placement in the following list:
Pluto in Gemini—Late 1800s until May 28, 1914
Pluto in Cancer—May 26, 1914–June 14, 1939
Pluto in Leo—June 14, 1939–August 19, 1957
Pluto in Virgo—August 19, 1957–October 5, 1971
                April 17, 1972–July 30, 1972
Pluto in Libra—October 5, 1971—April 17, 1972
                July 30, 1972–August 28, 1984
Pluto in Scorpio—August 28, 1984–January 17, 1995
Pluto in Sagittarius—starting January 17, 1995

CHAPTER 7

The Sign Language of Astrology
Your Glyph Guide and How to Use It

The first time you see an astrology chart, you might as well be looking at a Chinese manuscript for all the sense it makes! What do those odd-looking symbols mean? Are they a code? You're right to ask. Astrology has a symbolic language, a kind of universal shorthand, which is used by astrologers all over the world, so any astrology-savvy reader, regardless of nationality, could read your chart. These symbols or *glyphs* are also used in all the new astrology programs available for your computer, so, if you want to progress in astrology enough to read a printout of a horoscope, you've got to know the meaning of the glyphs.

Learning to decipher the glyphs can not only help you read a computer chart, but can help you understand the meaning of the signs and planets, because each symbol contains clues to what it represents. And, since there are only 12 signs and 10 planets (not counting a few asteroids and other space creatures some astrologers use), it's a lot easier than learning to read than, say, Chinese!

Here's a code-cracker for the glyphs, beginning with the glyphs for the planets. If you already know their glyphs, don't just skim over the chapter! There are hidden meanings to discover, so test your glyph-ese.

The Glyphs for the Planets

The glyphs for the planets are simply combinations of the circle, the semicircle or arc, and the cross. Each component of a glyph has a special meaning in relation to the others, which combines to create the total meaning of the symbol.

The circle, which has no beginning or end, is one of the oldest symbols of spirit or spiritual forces. All of the early diagrams of the heavens—spiritual territory—are shown in circular form. The semicircle or arc symbolizes the receptive, finite soul, which contains spiritual potential in the curving line. The vertical line of the cross symbolizes movement from heaven to earth. The horizontal line describes temporal movement, here and now, in time and space. Superimposed together, the vertical and horizontal planes symbolize manifestation in the material world.

The Sun Glyph ☉

The sun is always shown by this powerful solar symbol, a circle with a point in the center. The point is you, your spiritual center, and the symbol represents your infinite personality incarnating (the point) into the finite cycles of birth and death.

This symbol was brought into common use in the sixteenth century, after a German occultist and scholar, Cornelius Agrippa (1486–1535), wrote a book called *Die Occulta Philosophia,* which became accepted as the standard work in its field. Agrippa collected many medieval astrological and magical symbols in this book, which were copied by astrologers thereafter.

The Moon Glyph ☽

This is surely the easiest symbol to spot on a chart. The Moon glyph is a left-facing arc stylized into the crescent moon, which perfectly captures the reactive, receptive, emotional nature of the moon.

As part of a circle, the arc symbolizes the potential fulfillment of the entire circle. It is the life force that is still incomplete.

The Mercury Glyph ☿

Mercury contains all three elements—the crescent, the circle, and the cross, in vertical order. This is the "Venus with a hat" glyph (compare it with the symbol of Venus). With another stretch of the imagination, can't you see the winged cap of Mercury the messenger? Think of the upturned crescent as antennae that tune in and transmit messages from the sun, reminding you that Mercury is the way you communicate and the way your mind works. The upturned arc is receiving energy into the spirit or solar circle, which will later be translated into action on the material plane, symbolized by the cross. All the elements are equally sized because Mercury is neutral—it doesn't play favorites! This planet symbolizes objective, detached, unemotional thinking.

The Venus Glyph ♀

Here the relationship is between two elements, the circle or spirit above the cross of matter. Spirit is elevated over matter, pulling it upward. Venus asks, "What is beautiful? What do you like best? What do you love to have done to you?" Venus determines both your ideal of beauty and what feels good sensually. It governs your own allure and power to attract, as well as what attracts and pleases you.

The Mars Glyph ♂

In this glyph, the cross of matter is stylized into an arrowhead pointed up and outward, propelled by the circle of spirit. You can deduce that Mars embodies your spiritual energy projected into the outer world. It's your assertiveness, your initiative, your aggressive drive, what you like to do to others, your temper. If you know someone's Mars, you know whether they'll blow up when angry or do a slow burn. Your task is to use your outgoing Mars energy wisely and well.

The Jupiter Glyph ♃

Jupiter is the basic cross of matter, with a large stylized crescent perched on the left side of the horizontal, temporal plane. You might think of the crescent as an open hand—one meaning of Jupiter is "luck," what's handed to you. You don't work for what you get from Jupiter—it comes to you if you're open to it.

The Jupiter glyph might also remind you of a jumbo jet plane with a huge tail fin, about to take off. Jupiter is the planet of travel, both mental and spiritual, and the planet of expanding your horizons via new ideas, new spiritual dimensions, and new places. Jupiter embodies the optimism and enthusiasm of the traveler about to embark on an exciting adventure.

The Saturn Glyph ♄

Flip Jupiter over and you've got Saturn. (This might not be immediately apparent, because Saturn is usually stylized into an "h" form like the one shown here.) But the principle it expresses is the opposite of Jupiter's expansive tendencies. Saturn pulls you back to earth—the receptive arc is pushed down underneath the cross of matter. Before there are any rewards or expansion, the duties and obligations of the material world must be considered. Saturn says, "Stop, wait, finish your chores before you take off!"

Saturn's glyph also resembles the sickle of old Father Time. Saturn was first known as Chronos, the Greek god of time, for time brings all matter to an end. When it was thought to be the most distant planet, before the discovery of Uranus, Saturn was believed to be the place where time stopped. After the soul, having departed from earth, journeyed back to the outer reaches of the universe, it finally stopped at Saturn, the end of time.

The Uranus Glyph ♅

The glyph for Uranus is often stylized to form a capital "H" after Sir William Herschel, the name of the planet's discoverer. But the more esoteric version curves the two pillars of the H into crescent antennae, or ears, or satellite discs receiving signals from space. These are perched on the horizontal material line of the cross (matter) and pushed from below by the circle of the spirit. To many sci-fi fans, Uranus looks like an orbiting satellite.

Uranus channels the highest energy of all, the white electrical light of the universal spiritual sun, the force that holds the cosmos together. This pure electrical energy is gathered from all over the universe. Because Uranian energy doesn't follow an ordinary celestial drumbeat, it can't be controlled or predicted—which is also true of those who are strongly influenced by this eccentric planet. In the symbol, this energy is manifested through the balance of polarities (the two opposite arms of the glyph) like the two polarized wires of a light bulb.

The Neptune Glyph ♆

Neptune's glyph is usually stylized to look like a trident, the weapon of the Roman god Neptune. However, on a more esoteric level, it shows the large, upturned crescent of the soul pierced through by the cross of matter. Neptune nails down, or materializes, soul energy, bringing impulses from the soul level into manifestation. That is why Neptune is associated with imagination or "imagining in," making an image of the soul. Neptune works through feeling, sensitivity, and mystical capacity to bring the divine into the earthly realm.

The Pluto Glyph ♇

Pluto is written two ways. One is a composite of the letters "PL," the first two letters of the wold Pluto and coincidentally in the initial of Percival Lowell, one of the planet's discoverers. The other, more esoteric, symbol is a small circle above a large open crescent which surmounts the cross of matter. This depicts Pluto's power to regenerate—imagine a new little spirit emerging from the sheltering cup of the soul. Pluto rules the forces of life and death—after this planet has passed a sensitive point in your chart, you are transformed or reborn in some way.

Sci-fi fans might visualize this glyph as a small satellite (the circle) being launched. It was shortly after Pluto's discovery that we learned how to harness the nuclear forces that made space exploration possible. Pluto rules the transformative power of atomic energy, which totally changed our lives and from which there was no turning back.

The Glyphs for the Signs

On an astrological chart, the glyph for the sign will appear after that of the planet. For example, when you see the moon glyph followed by first a number and then another glyph representing the sign, this means that the moon was passing over a certain degree of that astrological sign when the chart was cast. On the dividing lines between the segments or houses on your chart, you'll find the symbol for the sign that was passing over the house cusp (or spoke of the wheel) at the time.

Because sun-sign symbols do not contain the same geometric components as the glyphs for the planets, we must look elsewhere for clues to their meanings. Many have been passed down from ancient Egyptian and Chaldean civilizations with few modifications. Others have been adapted over the centuries. In deciphering many of the glyphs, you'll often find that the symbols reveal a dual nature of the sign, which is not always apparent in the usual sun-sign descriptions. For instance, the Gemini glyph is similar to the Roman numeral for two, and reveals this sign's longing to discover a twin soul. The Cancer glyph may be interpreted as either resembling the nurturing breasts, or the self-protective claws of the crab, both symbols associated with the contrasting qualities of this sign. Libra's glyph embodies the duality of the spirit balanced with material reality. The Sagittarius glyph shows that the aspirant must also carry along the earthly animal nature in his quest. The Capricorn sea goat is another symbol with dual emphasis. The goat climbs high, yet is always pulled back by the deep waters of the unconscious. Aquarius embodies the double waves of mental detachment, balanced by the desire for connection with others in a friendly way. And finally, the two fishes of Pisces, which are forever tied together, show the duality of the soul and the spirit that must be reconciled.

The Aries Glyph ♈

Since the symbol for Aries is the ram, this glyph's most obvious association is with a ram's horns, which characterizes one aspect of the Aries personality—an aggressive, me-first, leaping-head-first attitude. But the symbol may have other meanings for you, too. Some astrologers liken it to a fountain of energy, which Aries people also embody. The first sign of the zodiac bursts on the scene eagerly and ready to go. Another analogy is to the eyebrows and nose of the human head, which Aries rules, and to the thinking power that is initiated in the brain.

One theory of the origin of this symbol links it to the Egyptian god Amun, represented by a ram. As Amon-Ra, this god was believed to embody the creator of the universe, the leader of all the other gods. This relates easily to the position of Aries as the leader, or first sign, of the zodiac, which begins at the spring equinox, a time of the year when nature is renewed.

The Taurus Glyph ♉

This is another easy glyph to draw and identify. It takes little imagination to decipher the bull's head with long, curving horns. Like the bull, the archetypal Taurus is slow to anger but ferocious when provoked, as well as stubborn, steady, and sensual. Another association is the larynx and thyroid of the throat area (ruled by Taurus) and the Eustachian tubes running up to the ears, which coincides with the relationship of Taurus to the voice, song, and music. Many famous singers, musicians, and composers have prominent Taurus influences.

Many ancient religions involved a bull as the central figure in fertility rites or initiations, usually symbolizing the victory of man over his animal nature. Another possible origin is in the sacred bull of Egypt, who embodied the incarnate form of Osiris, god of death and resurrection. In early Christian imagery, the Taurean bull represented St. Luke.

The Gemini Glyph Ⅱ

The standard glyph immediately calls to mind the Roman numeral for two and the symbol for Gemini, the twins. In almost all images for this sign, the relationship between two persons is emphasized. This is the sign of communication and human contact; it manifests the desire to share.

Many of the figurative images for Gemini show twins with their arms around each other, emphasizing that they are sharing the same ideas and the same ground. In the glyph, the top line indicates mental communication, while the bottom line indicates shared physical space.

The most famous Gemini legend is that of the twin sons, Castor and Pollux, one of whom had a mortal father, while the other was the son of Zeus, king of the gods. When it came time for the mortal twin to die, his grief-stricken brother pleaded with Zeus, who finally agreed to let them spend half the year on earth, in mortal form, and half in immortal life, with the gods on Mt. Olympus. This reflects the basic nature of humankind, which possesses an immortal soul yet is also subject to the limits of mortality.

The Cancer Glyph ♋

Two convenient images relate to the Cancer glyph. The easiest to picture is the curving claws of the Cancer symbol, the crab. Like the crab, Cancer's element is water. This sensitive sign also has a hard protective shell to protect its tender interior. It must be wily to escape predators, scampering sideways and hiding shyly under rocks. The crab also responds to the cycles of the moon, as do all shellfish. The other image is that of two female breasts, which Cancer rules, showing that this is a sign that nurtures and protects others as well as itself.

In ancient Egypt, Cancer was also represented by the scarab beetle, a symbol of regeneration and eternal life.

The Leo Glyph ♌

Notice that the Leo glyph seems to be an extension of Cancer's glyph, with a significant difference. In the Cancer glyph, the lines curve inward protectively, while the Leo glyph expresses energy outwardly and there is no duality in the symbol (or in Leo).

Lions have belonged to the sign of Leo since earliest times and it is not difficult to imagine the king of beasts with his sweeping mane and curling tail from this glyph. The upward sweep of the glyph easily describes the positive energy of Leos; the flourishing tail, their flamboyant qualities. Another analogy, which is a stretch of the imagination, is that of a heart leaping up with joy and enthusiasm, also very typical of Leo, which also rules the heart. In early Christian imagery, the Leo lion represented St. mark.

The Virgo Glyph ♍

You can read much into this mysterious glyph. For instance, it could represent the initials of "Mary Virgin," or a young woman holding a staff of wheat, or stylized female genitalia, all common interpretations. The "M" shape might also remind you that Virgo is ruled by Mercury. The cross beneath the symbol could indicate the grounded, practical nature of this earth sign.

The earliest zodiacs link Virgo with the Egyptian goddess Isis, who gave birth to the god Horus after her husband Osiris had been killed, in the archetype of a miraculous conception. There are many statues of Isis nursing her baby son, which are reminiscent of medieval Virgin and Child motifs. This sign has also been associated with the image of the Holy Grail, when the Virgo symbol was substituted with a chalice.

117

The Libra Glyph ♎

It is not difficult to read the standard image for Libra, the scales, into this glyph. There is another meaning, however, that is equally relevant—the setting sun as it descends over the horizon. Libra's natural position on the zodiac wheel in the descendant or sunset position (as the Aries natural position is the ascendant, or rising sign). Both images relate to Libra's personality. Libra is always weighing pros and cons for a balanced decision. In the sunset image, the sun (male) hovers over the horizontal Earth (female) before setting. Libra is the space between these lines, harmonizing yin and yang, spiritual and material, male and female, ideal and real worlds. The glyph has also been linked to the kidneys, which are ruled by Libra.

The Scorpio Glyph ♏

With its barbed tail, this glyph is easy to identify with the sign of the Scorpion. It also represents the male sexual parts, over which the sign rules. However, some earlier symbols for Scorpio, such as the Egyptian, represent it as an erect serpent. You can also draw the conclusion that Mars is its ruler by the arrowhead.

Another image for Scorpio, which is not identifiable in this glyph, is the eagle. Scorpios can go to extremes, soaring like the eagle or self-destructing like the scorpion. In early Christian imagery, which often used zodiacal symbols, the Scorpio eagle was chosen to symbolize the intense apostle, St. John the Evangelist.

The Sagittarius Glyph ♐

This glyph is one of the easiest to spot and draw—an upward-pointing arrow lifting up a cross. The arrow is pointing skyward, while the cross represents the four elements of the material world, which the arrow must convey. Elevating materiality into spirituality is an important Sagittarius quality, which explains why this sign is associated with higher learning, religion, philosophy, and travel—the aspiring professions. Sagittarius can also send barbed arrows of frankness in their pursuit of truth. This is also the sign of the super salesman, who can persuade you that an ordinary item is truly extraordinary.

Sagittarius is symbolically represented by the centaur, a mythological creature who is half-man, half-horse, aiming his arrow toward the skies. Though Sagittarius is motivated by spiritual aspiration, it also must balance this with powerful earthbound appetites of the animal nature. The centaur Chiron, a figure in Greek mythology, became a wise teacher after many adventures and world travels.

The Capricorn Glyph ♑

One of the most difficult symbols to draw, this glyph may take some practice. It is a representation of the sea goat—a mythical goat with a curving fish's tail. The goat part of Capricorn wants to leave the waters of the emotions and climb to the elevated areas of life. But the fish part represents the unconscious, chaotic psychic forces that keep drawing the goat back. Capricorns often try to escape the deep, feeling part of life by submerging themselves in work, steadily rising to the top of their professions or social ladders. Another interpretation of this glyph is a seated figure with a bent knee, a reminder that Capricorn governs the knee area of the body.

An interesting aspect of this glyph is how the sharp, pointed horns of the symbol, which represent the penetrating, shrewd, conscious side of Capricorn, contrast with the swishing tail that represents its serpentine, unconscious, emotional force. One Capricorn legend, which dates from Roman times, tells of the earthy fertility god, Pan, who tried to save himself from uncontrollable sexual desires by jumping into the Nile. His upper body then turned into a goat, while the lower part became a fish. Later, Jupiter gave him a safe haven in the skies, as a constellation.

The Aquarius Glyph ♒

This ancient water symbol can be traced back to an Egyptian hieroglyph representing streams of life force.

Symbolized by the water bearer, Aquarius is distributor of the waters of life—the magic liquid of regeneration. The two waves can also be linked to the positive and negative charges of the electrical energy that Aquarius rules, a sort of universal wavelength. Aquarius is tuned in intuitively to higher forces via this electrical force. The duality of the glyph could also refer to the dual nature of Aquarius, a sign that runs hot and cold, is friendly but also detached in the mental world of air signs.

In Greek legends, Aquarius is represented by Ganymede, who was carried to heaven by an eagle in order to become the cup bearer of Zeus, and to supervise the annual flooding of the Nile. the sign became associated with aviation and notions of flight.

The Pisces Glyph)(

Here is an abstraction of the familiar image of Pisces, two fishes swimming in opposite directions, yet bound together by a cord. The fishes represent spirit, which yearns for the freedom of heaven, while the soul remains attached to the desires of the temporal world. During life on earth, the spirit and the soul are bound together and when they complement each other, instead of pulling in opposite directions, this facilitates the creative expression for which Pisceans are known. The ancient version of this glyph, taken from the Egyptians, had no connecting line; this was added in the fourteenth century.

Another interpretation is that the left fish symbolizes involution or the beginning of the cycle, the right-hand fish the direction of evolution, the completion of a cycle. It's an appropriate meaning for Pisces, the last sign of the zodiac.

CHAPTER 8

Your Astrological Love-Links
Rating Relationships Sign by Sign

"I've got your number!" is the old saying when you've finally figured out what makes someone tick. But, in astrology, this cliché takes on new meaning—getting someone's astrological number in relation to your sign can give you terrific clues, not only to how you relate to each other, but why.

Use the chart in this chapter to get the "number" of those close to you and then read the following explanation. It's called the "ultimate compatibility chart," because you can use it not only to compare sun signs, but to relate any two planets within your own horoscope chart or to compare your planets with those of another chart.

Use it to help you understand the dynamics between you and the people you interact with. You might find it the key to getting along better with your boss and coworkers. Or discover what the real dynamics are with your difficult relatives and your best friends.

What this chart won't do is tell you that there are signs you *can't* get along with. There are no totally incompatible signs—there are many happy marriages between signs that succeed because of the stimulation and chemistry their differences provide. To understand your astrological connection with another person, you need to identify the spatial relationship between signs. The sign "next door" is something like your next-door neighbor who loans you his lawn-mower or feeds your cats—or disputes your property boundaries. Signs distant from yours also have attitudes based on their "neighborhoods."

Some Sign Basics

A sign by definition is a specific territory, a division of an energy belt called the zodiac, which circles the Earth. Each division is distinguished by an element (earth, air, fire, water), a quality or modality (cardinal, fixed, mutable), and a polarity or charge (positive/negative). No two signs have the same combination. These variables alternate around the zodiac belt in an established order: first fire, followed by earth, air, and water. The qualities alternate first with cardinal (active), then fixed (growth), and last mutable (change) signs. It follows that the positive and negative signs also alternate, like the charge of a battery. As the energy flow progresses around the zodiac, starting with Aries, the signs become more complex and less self-oriented. So the place in line around the belt becomes a factor, too.

Play the Numbers Game

Since the zodiac is a circle, the signs also relate to each other according to the angle of the distance between them. Between signs of the same polarity (masculine/feminine, positive/negative, yin/yang), which are numbers 0, 2, and 4, energy flows most easily (with one exception: the sign opposite yours, number 6). Between signs of different polarity, which are numbered 1, 3, and 5, you'll experience tension or challenge (and possibly a very sexy "charge"!) Here's how it works out:

THE ULTIMATE COMPATIBILITY CHART

	AR	TA	GEM	CAN	LEO	VIR	LIB	SCO	SAG	CAP	AQ	PI
Aries	0	1	2	3	4	5	6	5	4	3	2	1
Taurus	1	0	1	2	3	4	5	6	5	4	3	2
Gemini	2	1	0	1	2	3	4	5	6	5	4	3
Cancer	3	2	1	0	1	2	3	4	5	6	5	4
Leo	4	3	2	1	0	1	2	3	4	5	6	5
Virgo	5	4	3	2	1	0	1	2	3	4	5	6
Libra	6	5	4	3	2	1	0	1	2	3	4	5
Scorpio	5	6	5	4	3	2	1	0	1	2	3	4
Sagittarius	4	5	6	5	4	3	2	1	0	1	2	3
Capricorn	3	4	5	6	5	4	3	2	1	0	1	2
Aquarius	2	3	4	5	6	5	4	3	2	1	0	1
Pisces	1	2	3	4	5	6	5	4	3	2	1	0

Find your sign in the vertical list. Then read across the row until you come to the column under the sign of your parner, mate, lover, boss and so on. Then read the descripton of the number in this chapter.

Your "0" Relationships—Signmates

"0" relationships are with those of your own sign, so naturally you'll have much in common. This could be the soulmate you've been looking for—one who understands and sympathizes with you like no other sign can! Your signmate understands your need for space, yet knows how and when to be there for you. There are many examples of long-term partnerships between sun-sign twins—Roy Rogers and Dale Evans (both Scorpio), Abigail and John Adams (Scorpio), George and Barbara Bush (Gemini), Bob and Dolores Hope (Gemini), Frank and Kathie Lee Gifford (Leo). Working relationships fare especially well with sun signs in common, though you may have to delegate unwanted tasks to others. In a public lifestyle or one where there is much separation or stimulation, your similarities can hold you together—there is the feeling of "you and me against the world."

The problem is when there is too much of a good thing with no stimulation or challenge—or when there is no "chemistry," which can often happen between signs that share so much, including the same element, quality, and polarity. The solution is to bring plenty of outside excitement into your lives.

Your "1" Relationships—Next-Door Neighbors

These signs are your next-door neighbors on the zodiac wheel. Your relationship is based on evolution—you've evolved out of the previous sign carrying energies that have been accumulating and developing through the zodiac cycle. The sign following yours is where your energy is headed, the next step. In a way, it's like sitting at a dinner table and passing the plate from left to right. You receive certain qualities from the previous sign and pass on those, plus your own, to the next.

This is also a sibling relationship where the sign before yours is like a protective older brother or sister, who's been there, and the next sign is your eager younger sibling. Every sign also has a compensating factor for its predecessor—this sign embodies lessons you should have learned (and which could trip you up if you've forgotten them).

But although both are in the same family, sibling signs actually have little in common, because you have different basic values (elements), ways of operating (qualities), and types of energy (polarity). You probably won't feel sparks of chemistry or the deep rapport of a solute unless other planets in your horoscopes provide this bond. Instead, the emphasis is on pals, best friends, working partners, who are enhanced by the sibling sign position.

The sign ahead can inspire you—they're where you are heading, but you may be afraid to take the first brave step. For example, to Pisces, Aries embodies dynamic, forceful, self-oriented will—whereas Pisces is the formless, selfless, imaginative state where Aries originated. So Aries energizes Pisces and gets Pisces moving. This sign behind backs you up and supports you. This relationship often makes one of the most lasting and contented unions—several famous examples are the Duke and Duchess of Windsor (Cancer/Gemini), Paul Newman and Joanne Woodward (Aquarius/Pisces), and Jerry Hall/Mick Jagger (Cancer/Leo).

To reveal how you'll relate to your zodiac sibling, here's how energy evolves through the twelve signs.

Aries, the first sign of the zodiac, is "born" from Pisces, the last. In Pisces, individual energy dissolved into universal energy—to be asserted again in Aries. Aries is the new "baby," while Pisces is the prebirth generation, living in the otherworldly realm of spirit. Pisces reminds self-oriented Aries that there is more to life than "me." Pisces teaches Aries compassion and a consciousness of others, while Aries infuses Pisces with new energy and gets Pisces to assert itself.

Taurus is the baby taking the first steps into the material world, feeling its way with the senses., Taurus stabilizes Aries, giving this sign direction and purpose and directing all that energy and drive. Taurus also imposes boundaries and limits to Aries, pulling it down to earth and stubbornly insisting, "You can't have it your way all the time" or "What are you really getting done?" or "What will it cost?"

Gemini teaches Taurus, who is often stuck on its own turf, to communicate, to socialize, to reach out to others, paving the way for the first emotional water sign, Cancer, where feelings are top priority and the energy becomes nurturing and self-protective. Cancer adds the dimension of caring to Gemini, who would rather not deal with emotions at all.

The nurturing qualities of Cancer burst forth in Leo. Leo's confidence and self-expression come out of the security Cancer provides. Leo, who needs this kind of caring to shine, can be quite insecure and demanding if good mothering has not been received. And that becomes a hallmark of the Cancer–Leo relationship: Ideally, Cancer nurtures Leo (in a not so ideal relationship, Cancer's fearfulness holds Leo back) and Leo in turn brings this vulnerable sign out into public life. Virgo is concerned with making things work, with helping, and says, "Leo, this is all very impressive, but is it useful? Will it work? Here's how to improve it." Virgo edits Leo creativity, which Leo might resent, but which makes for a better end result. Leo's confidence rubs off on shyer Virgo.

Like Virgo, Libra is also concerned with measuring up. While Virgo is interested in whatever is most practical, Libra is in love with beauty. When Virgo asks, "What good is something beautiful if it doesn't if it doesn't work?" Libra answers, "Beauty is its own justification." Virgo stimulates and grounds Libra; Libra takes Virgo further into aesthetics.

Scorpio plunges into deep emotional territory that Libra might prefer not to enter. However, the balance of Libra is required for Scorpio to reach its most positive, decisive expression. In return, Scorpio's intensity challenges Libra to look deeper, not to be content with superficial beauty.

Sagittarius takes Scorpio's deep understanding and then projects this to higher levels. Sagittarius adds optimism, uplifting ideals, and humor, which counteract Scorpio's pessimism. Jupiter-ruled, expansive Sagittarius then gains direction from the following sign, Saturn-ruled Capricorn, who brings the structure, discipline, and order that can help Sagittarius achieve its goals.

Though Capricorn can be inspired by Sagittarius, this bottom-line earth sign is interested in getting concrete results. Aquarius, its neighbor, then brings in higher principles, plus the elements of surprise, inventiveness, and unpredictability. There is always a higher purpose with Aquarius that lifts Capricorn out of the ordinary.

Pisces, the final sign in the cycle, is most sensitive to outside input, and as a result can be self-sacrificing or self-pitying. It shares a universal outlook with Aquarius, who reminds Pisces of detachment, social life, and the need to maintain perspective. The following sign, Aries, which has no patience for self-pity, will dry out this watery sign with its optimism and drive. In return, Pisces, which represents the amorphous prenatal world, often brings the spiritual dimension to the Aries life, which becomes an important part of their relationship.

Your "2" Relationships

With your "2" signs, you share the same electrical charge, so energy flows freely between you, and you also have compatible elements. For example, air signs and fire signs work well together—air makes fire burn brighter. But too much of either element can suffocate or blow out the flame. Earth and water signs can either make flowers, or mud flats, or wastelands.

The "2's" line up as follows:

Combination A. The earth signs (Taurus, Virgo, Capricorn) with water signs (Cancer, Scorpio, Pisces). These are usually very fertile nurturing combinations, each providing the emotional and material security the other sign needs to reach full potential. Problems arise when the earth sign's material orientation and "here-and-nowness" stifles the more cosmic water sign's creativity.

Combination B. The air signs (Gemini, Libra, Aquarius) with fire signs (Aries, Leo, Sagittarius). These are very stimulating, energetic combinations. Both kinds of signs are positive, outgoing, and active, and this usually describes their relationship as well. The problem is that the more objective, detached air sign's preference for reason over enthusiasm could cool the fire sign's ardor. And the fire sign's enthusiastic, but often egocentric and unreasonable, approach could exasperate reasoning, relationship-oriented air signs.

Your "3" Relationships

If you recognize that stress in a relationship often stimulates growth, and sexual tension can be heightened by a challenge, you can succeed with a "3" relationship. Relationships between signs of a similar quality are charged with erotic energy and sparks of passion. Some of these can thrive on difficulty. But, even though you can declare a truce with this sign, the person probably won't be easy to live with. However, these will also be your least boring partners.

"3s" share the same modality; you're both either cardinal, fixed, or mutable signs. So you'll understand how the other operates, though you won't necessarily share the same basic values or type of energy. It often happens with this relationship that you continually confront each other—here is a sign that is just as restless, stubborn, or driven as you are! This person isn't one to provide security, settle down, or back you up. So will you choose to compete or join forces, forging an equal partnership?

Mutable signs (Gemini, Virgo, Sagittarius, Pisces), which are the most changeable, understand each other's restlessness and low tolerance for boredom. This is a couple that can easily fragment, however, going off in different directions. This union often falls apart under stress, but challenges mutables to make order out of chaos. In other words, get your act together.

Cardinal couples (Aries, Cancer, Libra, Capricorn) with equal drive and energy often are characterized by goal-driven intensity—they never sit still. Fixed signs (Taurus, Leo, Scorpio, Aquarius) can be the most stable partners or, negatively, they can wrestle for control, war over territory, or have a stubborn standoff.

Positively, this is one of the sexiest aspects—these two signs challenge each other and bring about growth. Here are some of the issues likely to arise between each "3" pair-up:

Aries–Cancer Aries is forced by Cancer to consider the consequences of actions, particularly those that threaten security and hurt feelings. However, introspection cramps Aries style—this sign wants perfect freedom to act as they please and has no patience for Cancer's self-pity or self-protectiveness. Although Cancer admires Aries courage, the interaction will have to confront the conflict between the Aries outdirected desire to have their own way and Cancer's inward-turning drive to create safety and security.

Cancer–Libra Cancer is most satisfied by symbiotic, intimate, emotionally dependent relationships. So when you meet someone who is very independent, you feel hurt, rejected, and throw up a defensive shell, or you get moody and depressed. Unfortunately, you risk this happening with Libra, a romantic but rather emotionally cool sign. Libras want an equal partner and they tend to judge their partner on a detached, idealistic level, by their looks, style, ideas, and conversation. Libra recognizes that the best partnerships are between equals, but the issue here is what do you have to share? Libra won't be able to escape emotions through social activities or intellectual analysis here.

Libra–Capricorn Both of you love the good life, but you may have conflicting ideas about how to get it. Capricorn is a very disciplined, goal-directed, ordered worker, who requires concrete results. Libra is more about style and abstract principles, and can be quite self-indulgent. Libran indulgence *vs.* Capricorn discipline could be the cruncher here. Another bone to pick would be differing ideas about what's fair and just. Capricorn often believes that the end justifies the means, while Libra upholds fairness over bottom-line concerns.

Capricorn–Aries Earth signs want solidity, fire signs want freedom. Both are survivors who love to win, but Capricorn works for status and material rewards while Aries works for glory, heroism, and the joy of being first. Capricorn wants to stay in control; Aries wants freedom. In a positive way, Aries must grow up with Capricorn, but in return it can give this tradition-oriented sign a new and younger lease on life.

Taurus–Leo Leo has an insatiable appetite for admiration, Taurus for pleasure. Taurus sensuality can make Leo feel like a star, while Leo's romantic gestures appeal to Taurus on a grand scale. Taurus will have to learn courtship and flattery to keep Leo happy, bringing on the champagne and caviar! Leo will have to learn not to tease the bull, especially by withholding affection, and to enjoy simple meat-and-potatoes kinds of pleasures as well. Money can be so important here—Leo likes to spend royally, Taurus to accumulate and hoard.

Scorpio–Leo Scorpio wants adventure in the psychic underworld; Leo wants to stay in the throne room. Scorpio challenges Leo to experience life intensely, which can bring out the best in Leo. Leo burns away Scorpio negativity, with a low tolerance for dark moods. Scorpio is content to work behind the scenes, giving Leo center stage. But Leo must never mistake a quiet Scorpio for a gentle pussycat. There will be plenty of action behind the scenes. Settle issues of control without playing power games.

Scorpio–Aquarius Aquarian love of freedom and Scorpio possessiveness could clash here. Scorpio wants to own you; Aquarius wants to remain friends. This is one unpredictable sign that Scorpio can't figure out, but has fun trying. The Aquarian flair for group dynamics could bring Scorpio out, but too many outside interests could put a damper on this combination.

Taurus–Aquarius Taurus lives in the touchable realm of the earth. Aquarius is in the electric, invisible realm of air, which can't be fenced in. It's anyone's guess if Taurus can ground Aquarius or if Aquarius can uplift Taurus. The Taurean talent as a realist could be the anchor this free sprit needs, while Aquarian originality opens new territory to Taurus.

Gemini–Virgo Nerves can be stimulated or frayed when these Mercury-ruled signs sound off. Both have much to say to each other, from different points of view. Gemini deals in abstractions, Virgo in down-to-earth facts. Common interests could keep this pair focused on each other.

Virgo–Sagittarius Safety versus risk could be the hallmark of this relationship. Virgo plays it safe and cautious, while Sagittarius operates on faith and enthusiasm. You're two natural teachers who have different philosophies and have much to learn from each other. When Virgo picks things apart or gets bogged down in details, Sag urges them to look for the truth—the big picture. Sag's lack of organization or follow-though will either drive Virgo crazy or provide a job. Virgo puts Sagittarius down with facts, deflating overblown promises and sales pitches.

Sagittarius–Pisces There should be many philosophical and spiritual discussions and debates here. When Sagittarius says, "I'm right," Pisces says, "Everything's relative. We're all right and wrong. So what?" Sagittarius is about elevating the self and Pisces is about merging the self, losing the self. On a less cosmic level, these two high-flying signs may never get down to earth. Pisces' super-sensitive feelings are easily wounded by Sagittarius' moments of truth telling. But Sag can help sell those creative Piscean ideas; that is, if you don't wander off in different directions.

Pisces–Gemini Gemini is always trying to understand, abstract, and rationalize. Pisces wants to merge and flow, find a soulmate, go beyond the mind. Piscean moods get on Gemini's nerves. Gemini runs away from emotional mergers, which really matter to Pisces. Yet Piscean glamour can intrigue Gemini and Gemini lightness and wit help Pisces laugh away the blues.

Your "4" Relationships

These are considered the easiest relationship possible, the most compatible partnerships. You share the same element and the same polarity, but sometimes there is too much of a good thing. These tend to lack the dynamism and sexy sparks of the "3" and "5" relationships. They can be too comfortable as you adjust very easily to each other. But what can you teach each other? If it's too easy, you might look for excitement elsewhere.

Relationships between the three earth signs (Taurus, Virgo, Capricorn) are mutually profitable, both professionally and personally. You won't find the other sign tampering with your financial security, frittering away hard-earned funds, or flirting with danger. You could fulfill your dreams of a comfortable life together. Too much comfort could leave you yawning, however—you need someone to shake you up once in a while.

Fire signs (Aries, Leo, Sagittarius) can ignite each other, but watch out for temper and jealousy. You both demand exclusive attention and are happiest when your ego is stroked and you feel like number one, so you may have to curb any tendency to flirt. Because you tend to be big risk takers and free spenders, you may have to delegate the financial caretaking carefully or find an expert adviser.

Water signs (Cancer, Scorpio, Pisces) have found partners who aren't afraid of emotional depths or heights. These are the ones who can understand and sympathize with your moods. This could be your solute who gives you the emotional security you need. When moods collide, however, you could find it difficult to get each other out of deep water.

Air signs (Gemini, Libra, Aquarius) communicate well together. There is no heavy emotionalism or messy ego or possessiveness to deal with. You both respect the need for freedom and personal space and can make your own rules for an open, equal partnership. Staying in touch is the problem here. You could become so involved in your own pursuits that you let romance fly by or are never there for each other. Be sure to cultivate things in common because, unless there are many shared interests, it is easy to float away.

Your "5" Relationships

This is the relationship that challenges your sign the most. You have to stretch yourself to make this work. You are totally different in basic values (element), way of acting (quality), and kind of energy (polarity). And, unlike your next-door signs that also have those differences, you don't have the proximity of being next in line. Instead of being beside you, the other sign is off on the other side of the zodiac. On the other hand, this very separateness can have an exotic quality, the attraction of the unknown and the unattainable. This is someone you'll never quite figure out. And this sign also has many threatening traits—if you get into this relationship, there will be risks and you won't quite know what to expect.

The "5" relationship is the proverbial square peg and round hole. Even though the stress of making this relationship work can be great, so can the stimulation and creativity that result from trying to find out what makes each other tick.

When positive and negative signs come together, lights go on, as you discover methods in dealing with situations and different ways of viewing the world, which can move you out of the doldrums. Here is how your sign relates to the "5" partners.

Aries: Scorpio/Virgo Scorpio, who tends to be secretive and manipulative, embodies everything that is foreign to Aries. Aries is clear cut and openly demanding. If an Aries attacks, it will be swift and open. Scorpio will wait for the time when an opponent is most vulnerable— years, if necessary—to deal the lethal blow. Aries burns out much sooner. Yet your very strong differences only make the conquest more exciting.

Virgo thinks the way to solve problems is to get organized and think things through, while steamrollering Aries wants fast action and quick results. Both Scorpio and Virgo will challenge Aries to go against the grain, being careful, organized, and persevering, and delving deeply while looking at the long haul. Aries will have to tone down impulsiveness with these signs.

Taurus: Libra/Sagittarius Libra, also Venus ruled, is involved with the abstract, idealistic side of the planet, whereas Taurus is involved with the sensual, materialistic, self-indulgent side. Libra challenges Taurus to abstract, to get into the mind as well as the body. Taurus will bring Libra down to earth and provide stability for this sign.

Sagittarius challenges Taurus to expend its territory. Taurus is the most rooted of signs, and can be immobile. Sagittarius is the happy wanderer. Taurus moves outside its turf with Sagittarius, who challenges it intellectually, spiritually, and physically.

Gemini: Scorpio/Capricorn Here, playful, verbal, mental Gemini is confronted by the failure to probe, the failure to deal with passion. Gemini gets into deep, real, emotional stuff with Scorpio. Contact with Scorpio often precipitates a crisis in Gemini's life, as this sign realizes there is something powerful that it's been missing. Scorpio challenges Gemini to delve deeply and make commitments rather than deals.

Capricorn makes Gemini develop discipline, set goals, and do practical bottom-line things the signs is not prepared to do. Capricorn has no tolerance for fragmented efforts and forces Gemini to focus and produce.

Cancer: Sagittarius/Aquarius Fearful, frugal Cancer must take risks to make a relationship work with Sagittarius, who loves to gamble and has faith in the universe. Everyone's buddy, Aquarius makes Cancer give love with an open hand, placing less emphasis on personal security and property.

Cancer must give up possessiveness with both these signs, who actually enjoy the kind of freedom and insecurity that Cancer most fears. In these relationships, Cancer's expectations of what a relationship should be have to change. It gets no protection from either sign and its favorite sympathy-winning techniques (playing "poor little me," whining, clinging, or complaining) only alienate these signs further. In the process of coping with these distant signs, however, Cancer can eventually become more independent and truly secure within itself.

Leo: Capricorn/Pisces Capricorn demands that Leo deliver on promises. With this down-to-earth sign, Leo can't coast for long on looks and star power. Capricorn wants results and pushes Leo to produce, casting a cold eye on shows of ego and bluffs. Conversely, both enjoy many of the same things, such as a high-profile lifestyle, but for different reasons.

Pisces is on another planet from solar Leo—the Neptunian embodies all that is not-self. This is a sign that devalues the ego. Pisces teaches Leo to be unselfish, to exercise compassion and empathy, to walk in others' shoes. Leo has to give up arrogance and false pride for a lasting relationship with Pisces.

Virgo: Aquarius/Aries Aquarius sheds light on Virgo's problem with getting bogged down in details. Interaction with Aquarius expands Virgo, preparing this sign for the unpredictable, the sudden, and the unexpected. Aquarius gets Virgo to broaden its scope and to risk experimenting. Aries gives Virgo positive energy and draws Virgo away from self-criticism and out into the world.

Libra: Pisces/Taurus Looking for a decision maker? Libra won't find it in Pisces! Pisces and Libra both share an artistic nature, but executed in a different way. Libra can't project its need for direction onto Pisces. Libra says, "What should I do?" Pisces says, "I know how you feel. It's tough not knowing what to do." Pisces challenges Libra to go within, to understand where others are coming from, rather than expecting them to conform to an abstract ideal.

Taurus brings Libra into the practical material world and gives this sign ground, but Taurus will also insist on material value. Taurus will ask, "How much does it cost?" Libra says, "I don't care, it's so pretty." Libra would rather not worry about function and operations, which become the task of Taurus. Libra will either desperately need Taurean practicality or find it a drag.

Scorpio: Aries/Gemini Listen for the clanking of an iron shield with the Mars-ruled Aries and Scorpio combination. Both of you thrive on challenge and find it in each other. The issue here: Who's the conqueror when neither will give in or give up? You'll have to respect each other's courage and bravery, and enjoy the sparks.

Gemini is the sign you can never pin down or possess, and this is super-fascinating for Scorpio. Their quicksilver wit and ability to juggle many people and things are talents not found in the Scorpio repertoire. Scorpios never stop trying to fathom the power of Gemini—just when they've almost got them pegged, Gemini's onto something or someone else! As long as you don't expect devotion, you won't be disappointed.

Sagittarius: Taurus/Cancer This is a dialogue between the rooted and the rootless. Both Taurus and Cancer are the most home-loving signs of the zodiac, while Sagittarius is the eternal wanderer—mentally, physically, or both. Will they be content to keep the home fires burning for Sagittarius? Another sticky point: Both signs are very careful with money. However, these two financially savvy signs could help Sagittarius achieve miracles instead of talking about them. Sag will have to learn patience with Taurus, who will inevitably try to tie Sag down. Cancer could dampen Sag's spirits with self-pity if they feel neglected in any way; Sag will have to learn sensitivity to feelings. If Sag can give up the position as teacher and become a student, these relationships might last.

Capricorn: Gemini/Leo Both of these signs are social charmers who need organization, which is Capricorn's forte. They can help Capricorn get a desired position with Gemini's deft charm or Leo's warmth and poise. The trade-off is that Capricorn will have to learn to take life less seriously and be as devoted to the partnership as to work. Otherwise, these two signs will look for amusement elsewhere. Gemini should inspire Capricorn to diversify, communicate, and spread wings socially, while Leo adds confidence, authority, and status. They'll appreciate Capricorn's structure in their lives.

Aquarius: Cancer/Virgo Aquarius, the most freedom-loving sign, encounters two different dimensions here, both of which tend to bring this sign back to the realities of operating on a day-to-day level (Virgo) and honoring emotional attachments at the level of feeling (Cancer). Cancer is the home-loving sign who values security, family, and emotional connections, an area often dismissed by Aquarius. Virgo is about organization, critical judgment, and efficiency, which enhance Aquarius accomplishments.

Pisces: Leo/Libra With Leo, Pisces learns to find and project itself. Leo enjoys Pisces talent and often profits by it, and in return, Leo gives this often-insecure sign confidence. With Leo, Pisces can't hide any longer, and must come out from the depths—but Leo will not sympathize or indulge Piscean blue moods or self-pity. Pisces has to give up negativity with Leo.

Libra's instinct is to separate and analyze. Pisces instinct is to merge. The more Pisces gets emotional, the more Libra becomes cool and detached. But Pisces can gain objectivity from this relationship, which insists on seeing both sides of any matter equally. Libra can provide the balance that keeps Pisces out of the depths.

Your "6" Relationships

"6" relationships are with your opposite sign in the zodiac. This sign is your complement, your other half, who manifests qualities that you think you don't have. There are many marriages between opposite numbers, because one sign expresses what the other suppresses.

Because most lasting relationships are between equals, the attraction to your opposite number could backfire. What happens if you're an easygoing Aquarius married to a star-quality Leo and you decide it's time to show off your natural charisma on center stage? Or a disorganized Pisces with an efficient Virgo who goes on a clean-up, shape-up program and out-organizes the Virgo? No longer does the opposite partner have exclusive rights to certain talents or attitudes. If they can make adjustments to the new you, fine. Otherwise, someone could be out of a job.

It's an excellent idea to ask yourself if you are attracting your opposite number in love or other relationships, what the signs are acting out for you. It could be a clue to a side of your character you need to develop. Sometimes, after the initial chemistry dies down, and two opposite signs actually begin living together, you'll be irritated by the same qualities that at first attracted you. That's because they reveal the part you are afraid of within yourself—the part you haven't really claimed for yourself. You may resent this other person taking that part over. Here's how it works out with opposite numbers: The more you learn to express both sides of the same coin, the better chance your relationship with a "6" will have.

Aries–Libra Aries brings out Libra's placating, accommodating talents. And, at first, Libra is happy to play the charmer in exchange for Aries decisiveness. Aries revels in the chance to take charge and to be so openly needed. But in close quarters, Aries seems too pushy, too bossy. And when Libra decides to make its own decisions, Aries had better learn to charm.

Taurus–Scorpio This is one of the most powerful attractions, often found in marriages and long-term relationships. Some of these couples manage to balance out their differences nicely; others are just too stubborn to give up or give in. The uncomplicated, earthy, sensual Taurus likes safety, comfort, and pleasurable physical things. Scorpio, who enjoys the challenge and dangers of intense feelings (and could live in a monk's cell), is often attracted to danger and risk. Scorpio wants a deep powerful merger, while Taurus likes to stay above ground, enjoying innocent pleasures. both are possessive and jealous, with a need to control their own territory. Scorpio marvels at the uncomplicated basic drives of Taurus—couldn't they get into trouble together? Taurus enjoys teasing Scorpio with promises of innocent pleasure, but learns that Scorpios sting when teased. Settle issues of control early on—and never underestimate each other's strength.

Gemini–Sagittarius Gemini is the eager student of the world. Sagittarius is the perfect guide, only too happy to teach, enlighten, and expound. This is a very stimulating combination. Sagittarius enjoys telling others what to believe, however, and Gemini can't be bossed. Gemini also turns off fiery confrontations and absolute declarations of truth, and may deflate Sagittarius with barbs of wit. On a positive note, this could be a wonderful combination both socially and professionally. Romantically, the relationship works best if they can be both student and teacher to each other.

Cancer–Capricorn Both of these signs have strong defense mechanisms—Cancer's is a protective shell, while Capricorn's is a cold and stony wall. In a relationship, both of these defenses play off one another. Cancer shows weakness, complaining and whining, as a means of getting protection, which dovetails nicely with Capricorn's need to play the authoritarian father figure (even when it's a female) who takes responsibility for the vulnerable child (Cancer). But if Capricorn shows vulnerability, such as a fear of not being "right," Cancer panics, becomes insecure, and erects a self-protective shell. On the other hand, if Capricorn takes over Cancer's life, this active cardinal sign gets crabby. Learning to parent each other and reinforcing strong traditional values could be the key to happiness here.

Leo–Aquarius Here we have two stubborn fixed signs with opposite points of view. Leo is "me-oriented" and does not like to share, while Aquarius is "them-oriented" and identifies with others. The Leo charisma comes from projecting the self—others are there for applause. Aquarius shines as the symbol or spokesperson of a group, which reflects self-importance. Aquarius is the talk-show host, working from the audience. Leo is the guest star, on stage. Leo is not about to become one of the Aquarius crowd, especially if the crowd includes Aquarian ex-lovers. Aquarius will not confine interests to Leo and become an exclusive Leo fan. If Leo can learn to share and Aquarius can give one-on-one attention, these opposites could balance out.

Virgo–Pisces In Pisces, Virgo finds someone who apparently needs their services badly. Virgo in turn is attracted to Pisces because this sign can deal with the tricky side of life that can't be organized or made to run on schedule. Sensitive Pisces seems to need Virgo's clarity, orderliness, and practicality to keep together and in line. You can see how easy it is for this to become a bargain between the helper and the apparently helpless. When Pisces gets organized and Virgo gets in touch with their own irrational side, these two could form a more solid relationship.

CHAPTER 9

The Love Detector Chart

Whether you're looking for a romantic playmate, a lifetime companion, or a business partner, or whether you are searching the zodiac to find your twin soul, astrology gives you a powerful tool for discovering why you are attracted to a certain person and how the person might act or react toward you. The *five personal planets* can reveal what attracts you both, what your tastes are, your temperament and sex drive, your mutual emotional needs, and how best to communicate—all the most important clues to compatibility!

Size up the overall relationship using the elements.

Get the big picture of your relationship by comparing the elements of each partner's sun, moon, Mercury, Mars, and Venus. The interaction of elements is probably the easiest way to size up a relationship. Planets of the same element have smooth, easy chemistry; these are your *Minimum Compromise Relationships.*

For easy reference, here are the four elements and the signs of each:

EARTH ELEMENT: Taurus, Virgo, Capricorn
AIR ELEMENT: Gemini, Libra, Aquarius
FIRE ELEMENT: Aries, Leo, Sagittarius
WATER ELEMENT: Cancer, Scorpio, Pisces

When your partner has a planet in the same element as your planet in question, the energy will flow freely between these planets. Venus in Aries and Mars in Leo, for instance, should work well together. Complementary elements (fire signs with air signs and earth signs with water signs) also get along easily, though not as well as the same elements.

Some elemental combinations are more challenging. There is tension and possible combustion between fire and water signs or between earth and air signs. Taking the analogy literally, fire brings water to a boil, earth and air create dust storms. These are your *Maximum Compromise Relationships.* However, challenges can be stimulating as well, adding excitement to a relationship, especially when planets of sexual attraction—Mars and Venus—are involved.

Here's an easy chart to give you the big picture:

First find the sign of each partner's planet. Assuming you know the birthdays, you can find the Mars and Venus placements in this book. You'll have to guess the Mercury (either the same sign as the sun or in the sign before or following the sun) and moon placements, if you don't have a chart available.

Then list the planets and elements as follows, grouping earth with water and fire with air, as in the following diagram.

THE LOVE DETECTOR CHART

	EARTH	WATER	FIRE	AIR
SUN	Jack			Jill
MOON	Jack	Jill		
VENUS	Jill		Jack	
MARS		Jack & Jill		
MERCURY			Jack & Jill	

You can see from the above that Jack and Jill have Mars, Mercury, the moon, and the sun in compatible elements. Therefore, it should be a very harmonious relationship. However, Venus could present a challenge.

Now look at the following list to see what each planet stands for. Find out how each planet relates to the others.

The Lunar Link—The One You Need

The planet in your chart that governs your emotions is the moon (although the moon is not technically a planet, it is usually referred to as one by astrologers), so you would naturally take this into consideration when evaluating a potential romantic partnership. If a person's moon is in a good relationship to your sun, moon, Venus, or Mars, preferably in the *same sign or element,* you should relate well on some emotional level. Your needs will be compatible; you'll understand each other's feelings without much effort. If the moon is in a *compatible element,* such as earth with water or fire with air, you may have to make a few adjustments, but you will be able to make them easily. With a water–fire, or earth–air combination, you'll have to make a considerable effort to understand where the other is coming from emotionally.

It's worth having a computer chart done, just to find the position of your moon. Because the moon changes signs every two days, the tables are too long to include in this book.

The Mercury Message

Mercury in the same or complementary element means a meeting of minds. In a challenging element, you'll have to work harder to keep lines of communication open and guard against shutdowns.

The Venus Factor—The One You Want

The Venus position in your chart shows what you respond to, so if you and your partner have a good Venus aspect, you should have much in common. You'll enjoy doing things together; the same type of lovemaking will turn you both on. You'll have no trouble pleasing each other.

Your lover's Venus in the same sign or a sign of the same element as your own Venus, Mars, moon, or sun is best. Second-best is a sign of a compatible element (earth with water, air with fire). If Venus is in an incompatible element (water with air or earth with fire), you may have to make a special effort to understand what appeals to the other person, since your tastes are basically different.

The Mars Connection—The One Who Lights Your Fire

The Mars positions reveal your sexual energy—how often you like to make love, for instance. It also shows your temper—do you explode or do a slow burn? Here you'll find out if your partner is direct, aggressive, and hot blooded, or more likely to take the cool, mental approach. Mutually supportive partners have their Mars working together in the same or complementary elements. But any contacts between Mars and Venus in two charts can strike sexy sparks. Even the difficult aspects—your partner's Mars three or six signs away from your sun, Mars, or Venus—can offer sexual stimulation. Who doesn't get turned on by a challenge, from time to time? Sometimes the easy Mars relationships can drift into dullness.

The Solar Bond

The sun is the focus of our personality and therefore the most powerful component involved. Each pair of sun signs has special lessons to teach and learn from each other. As you'll discover, there is a negative side to the most ideal couple and a positive side to the most unlikely match—each has an up and a down side. Read the section on "Your Sign in Love" in the Sun Sign chapters for an interpretation of the upsides and downsides of each relationship.

Remember that most successful relationships have a balance of harmonious points and challenges, which stimulate you to grow and which sustain lively interest over time. So if the forecast for you and your beloved (or business associate) seems like an uphill struggle, take heart! Such legendary lovers as Juan and Eva Perón, Ronald and Nancy Reagan, Harry and Bess Truman, Julius Caesar and Cleopatra, Billy and Ruth Graham, and George and Martha Washington are among the many who have made successful partnerships between supposedly incompatible sun signs.

CHAPTER 10

Astrology Bashers
A Response to Skeptics

In 1814, the proper Bostonian descendant of two American presidents stood on trial for practicing astrology. Evangeline Adams acquitted herself with style, proving her skills with a penetrating analysis of a mystery chart, which turned out to be that of the judge's son. Reported in national media, this marked the beginning of astrology-consciousness in this country on a mass level. For the first time, astrology was recognized as much more than fortune-telling, and became a legitimate practice in its own right.

Since that time, astrology has grown in popularity, with daily horoscopes now a familiar feature in most newspapers. Where once it was difficult to find an astrologer, practitioners now advertise in newspapers and yellow pages. Some are highly qualified professionals, with years of study and proven expertise. Others simply dispense canned horoscopes from one of the many computer programs available. Still others give readings that depend more on supposed psychic talents than astrological technique.

However, astrology still comes in for its share of bashing, mainly from legal and fundamentalist religious or scientific sources. As recently as 1996, astrologers were required to be fingerprinted and subject to police inquiries in California. There has also emerged a wave of debunkers who haunt computer bulletin boards and astrology conferences looking for any opening to bait astrologers. However, most debunkers have very little knowledge of astrology. It is rare to find an attacker who has ever had his or her horoscope chart done professionally, or one who knows any astrological terminology beyond basic sun-sign information. It very often happens that once a skeptic undertakes a serious exploration of astrology, he or she becomes an ardent advocate. In fact, the profession is full of astrologers who came from scientific disciplines, studied astrology for the purpose of disproving it, and ended up with great respect for this ancient art.

One such would-be debunker was a French statistician, Michel Gauquelin, who set out back in 1953 to disprove astrology by correlating astrological data for thousands of doctors, politicians, athletes, and soldiers, and concluded that, indeed, astrology rested on verifiable premises. Among his findings, he showed that Mars and Saturn contacts held true throughout the horoscopes of military leaders, and Mars propelled the horoscopes of athletes. He also confirmed planetary links between parent and child.

Actually, astrology has never claimed to be a science, a religion, or a psychology—though it has links to all three in their mutual origin in the search for the truth and for human beings' real purpose in life. We might say that astrology is the place where science, spirit, and psyche meet. Astrology has deep roots in all religions and can be found embedded in the spiritual history of every race. However, when religion became linked to doctrine and dogma, astrology, which has been accessible to everyone who wishes to study the planets, parted company with religion. In the Christian tradition, astrology was perceived as a threat to the established church, and astrologers were driven underground or persecuted. But the study of the planets and their relationship to the affairs of humanity continued, though astrology gained an unsavory reputation as fortune-telling, a connection that still lingers in the minds of those who try to discredit it.

Astrology is actually the study of cycles, a linking of forces in our own lives with the forces of the universe at large. But most enlightened astrologers believe that you are in charge of your destiny. You can use the planetary forces at your disposal as you wish. It's not unusual to see similar charts, in which one person has used the aspects in a positive way and another, with similar aspects, has become a criminal.

In its fundamental assumption that a given moment in time embodies the forces going on at that instant in the solar system, astrology does link us to a divine plan. When man first looked toward the heavens, it was in a wish to communicate with God, whether from a Babylonian ziggurat or a Mayan pyramid. The character of each sign of the zodiac was developed in a very systematic way, linking elements, qualities, and polarities. And the influence of the planets was determined after much observation. It is interesting that Mars, in all the various systems of astrology around the world, still embodies the same aggressive force; Venus is still the same kind of benevolent energy; and, from the time of the lunar goddesses of Babylonia, Phrygia, and Greece, to modern psychological interpretations, the moon has represented our instinctive, emotional self.

Many religious people are threatened by astrologers, because they equate all astrology with what has been practiced by many charlatans of the past or because they feel that someone interested in astrology will turn away from religion. However, as anyone who has delved seriously into astrology can attest, the study of astrology tends to bring one closer to a spiritual understanding of the interchange among a universal design, the material world, and man's place in it. Astrology can, in a very practical way, help people keep in balance with the forces of the universe.

Scientists, on the other hand, attack astrology as a "pseudoscience" for its supposed lack of factual evidence. We are forever hearing comparisons between astrology and astronomy, which is really more of a parent–child relationship, since astronomy grew out of astrology. History has conveniently forgotten that five of the most famous astronomers of all time were astrologers: Copernicus, Galileo, Tycho Brahe, and Johannes Kepler.

Most scientists have not studied astrology, nor do they approach it scientifically. They do not respect astrology as a discipline in its own right, thereby missing the point of astrology. It is not concerned with linear facts, but with linking humanity to the cosmos, linking the universe without to the universe within. The rise of quantum physics could bridge the gap between science and astrology, as scientists begin to explore a different reality beyond the mechanistic, materialistic view. Scientists are realizing that their own theories of natural phenomena are creations of the mind itself, depending on the position of the observer and the observed, and by no means the last word. When science begins to look within, perhaps the parent–child respect can be renewed and, once again, science and astrology can be part of the same family.

The great psychologist Carl Jung is responsible for creating quite a different attitude—one of partnership—between astrology and psychology. Jung had great respect for astrology and used it in his practice to clarify points that he said he would otherwise have been unable to understand. "Astrology represents the summation of all the psychological knowledge of antiquity," he explained. Today, there are many psychologists who use astrology to help them penetrate in depth into the authentic personality of their clients. In turn, astrologers have benefited by psychological counseling techniques, using them to guide their clients toward personal growth and find positive ways to handle the trends evident in their birth chart.

In the Nineties, when the Aquarian Age takes root, we've all been looking for ways to expand our lives. Perhaps in this era, a new, positive relationship will be forged between astrology and science and between astrology and religion, as we find these disciplines more complementary than competitive.

Meanwhile, there are still parts of the country where, at this writing, well-organized groups work against the practice of astrology. To assist astrologers in dealing with astrology-bashers of all types, the Association for Astrological Networking (AFAN) was formed. AFAN legal committees keep constant watch over those prejudiced against astrology who try to spread misinformation and prevent astrologers from practicing. The organization also works to educate the public about astrological issues and create a network of astrology supporters who are interested in moving astrology forward and advancing the cause of professional freedom. Membership is open to the general public, as well as the professional astrological community, and it's an excellent way to participate in creating a better climate for astrology, as well as protect our individual rights. If interested, contact AFAN, 8306 Wilshire Boulevard, Suite 537, Beverly Hills, California 90211.

CHAPTER 11

Personal Readings
What They Can and Can't Do for You

Readings are everywhere—phone readings, tapes, charts, even celebrity-sponsored readings. Here's what to look for and some cautionary notes.

Though you can learn much about astrology from books such as this one, nothing compares to a personal consultation with a professional astrologer who has analyzed thousands of charts and can pinpoint the potential in yours. With your astrologer, you can address specific problems in your life that may be holding you back. For instance, if you are not getting along with your mate or coworker, you could leave the reading with some new insights and some constructive ways to handle the situation. If you are going through a crisis in your life, an astrologer who is also a trained counselor might help you examine your options; there are many astrologers who now combine their skills with training in psychology.

If you've been wondering about whether an astrological reading could give you the competitive edge in business, help you break through a personal dilemma, decide on the best day for a key event in your life, or help you make a career change, this may be the time to have a personal consultation. Before your reading, a reputable astrologer will ask for the date, time (as accurately as possible), and place of birth of the subject of the reading. (A horoscope can be cast about anything that has a specific time and place.) Most astrologers will then enter

149

this information into a computer, which will calculate your chart in seconds. From the resulting chart, the astrologer will do an interpretation.

If you don't know your exact birth time, you can usually find it filed at the Bureau of Vital Statistics at the city hall or county seat of the state where you were born. If you still have no success in getting your time of birth, some astrologers can estimate an approximate birth time by using past events in your life to determine the chart.

How to Find a Good Astrologer

Your first priority should be to choose a qualified astrologer. Rather than relying on word of mouth or grandiose advertising claims, do this with the same care you would choose any trusted adviser such as a doctor, lawyer, or banker. Unfortunately, anyone can claim to be an astrologer—to date, there is no licensing of astrologers or established professional criteria. However, there are nationwide organizations of serious, committed astrologers that can help you in your search.

Good places to start your investigation are organizations such as the American Federation of Astrologers or the National Council for Geocosmic Research (NCGR), which offers a program of study and certification. If you live near a major city, there is sure to be an active NCGR chapter or astrology club in your area—many are listed in astrology magazines available at your local newsstand. In response to many requests for referrals, the NCGR has compiled a directory of professional astrologers, which includes a glossary of terms and an explanation of specialties within the astrological field. Contact the NCGR headquarters (see the resource list in this book) for information.

As a potentially lucrative freelance business, astrology has always attracted self-styled experts who may not have the knowledge or the counseling experience to give a helpful reading. These astrologers can range from the well-meaning amateur to the charlatan or street-corner gypsy, who have for many years given astrology a bad name. Be very wary of astrologers who claim to have occult powers or who make pretentious claims of celebrated clients or miraculous achievements. You can often tell from the initial phone conversation if the astrologer is legitimate. He or she should ask for your birthday time and place and conduct the conversation in a professional way. Any astrologer who gives a reading based only on your sun sign is highly suspect.

When you arrive at the reading, the astrologer should be prepared. The consultation should be conducted in a private, quiet place. The astrologer should be interested in your problems of the moment. A good reading involves feedback on your part, so if the reading is not relating to your concerns, you should let the astrologer know. You should feel free to ask questions and get clarifications of technical terms. The reading should be an interaction between two people, rather than a solo performance. The more you actively participate, rather than expecting the astrologer to carry the reading or come forth with oracular predictions, the more meaningful your experience will be. An astrologer should help you validate your current experience and be frank about possible negative happenings, but suggest a positive course of action.

In their approach to a reading, some astrologers may be more literal, others more intuitive. Those who have had counseling training may take a more psychological approach. Though some astrologers may seem to have an almost psychic ability, extrasensory perception or any other parapsychological talent is not essential. A very accurate picture can be drawn from the data in your horoscope chart.

An astrologer may do several charts for each client, including one for the time of birth and a "progressed chart," showing the evolution from birth to the present time. According to your individual needs, there are many other possibilities, such as a chart for a different location if you are contemplating a change of place. Relationships between any two people, things, or events can be interpreted with a chart that compares one partner's horoscope with the other's. A composite chart, which uses the midpoint between planets in two individual charts to describe the relationship, is another commonly used device.

An astrologer will be particularly interested in transits—times when planets will pass over the planets or sensitive points in your chart, which signal important events in your life.

Many astrologers offer tape-recorded readings, another option to consider. In this case, you'll be mailed a tape that contains an individual reading based on your birth chart. This type of reading is more personal than a computer printout and can give you valuable insights, but it is not equivalent to a live reading, when you can have a face-to-face dialogue with the astrologer and discuss your specific interests and issues of the moment.

About Telephone Readings

Telephone readings come in two varieties. One is a dial-in taped reading, usually by a well-known astrologer. The other is a live consultation with an "astrologer" on the other end of the line. The taped readings are general daily or weekly forecasts, applied to all members of your sign and charged by the minute, and the quality depends on the astrologer. One caution: Be aware that these readings can run up quite a telephone bill, especially if you get into the habit of calling every day. Be sure that you are aware of the per-minute cost of each call beforehand. Live telephone readings also vary with the expertise of the astrologer. Ideally, the astrologer enters your birth data into a computer and refers to that chart during the consultation. The advantage of a live telephone reading is that your individual chart is used and you can ask about a specific problem. However, before you invest in any reading, be sure that your astrologer is qualified and that you fully understand in advance how much you will be charged.

About Computer Readings

Most of the companies that offer computer programs (such as ACS, Matrix, ASTROLABE) also offer a wide variety of computer-generated horoscope interpretations. These can be quite comprehensive, offering a beautiful printout of the chart plus many pages of information. A big plus is that you get a copy of your chart and a basic natal chart interpretation, which can be an ideal way to learn about your own chart, since most readings interpret all the details of the chart in a very understandable way. However, the interpretations will be general, since there is no input from you, and therefore may not cover your immediate concerns. This is still a good option for a first reading, however, especially since these printouts are much lower in cost than live consultations. You might consider them as either a supplement or preparation for a live reading—study one before you have a live reading to get familiar with your chart and plan specific questions—and they make a terrific gift for someone interested in astrology. If you are interested in this type of reading, there are several companies on our astrology resource list that offer extensive readings.

CHAPTER 12

Your Sagittarius Potential

The Sagittarius Man— A Gambler in Life and Love

Sagittarius is a man on the run, a gambler who understands that life's potential is unlimited. You'll go for broke when the occasion demands, with touching faith that luck (or the force of the universe) is on your side. More often than not, your enthusiasm for all that inspires you is contagious and your dreams catch on.

Freewheeling Sagittarius has great faith in yourself, knowing you can always sell your ideas. Though your main interest is moving ahead, sometimes you don't know quite where you're going. Or you may know your destination, but not how to get there; you'll thrust to luck (or higher forces) to put you on the fast track.

Physical and mental risks are challenges to you—most Sagittarians are superb athletes, and some are daredevils. You can also be the clown, full of practical jokes, with a boyish sense of humor and a love of games that endears you to others. You're the upbeat, fun companion, the jovial daddy, the good sportsman and great buddy, who has personal friends from all walks of life. You tend to be very male oriented, taking love lightly and making a fast getaway if someone tries to tie you down.

To reach your Sagittarius potential, you must find a

way to help others reach theirs, imparting high ideals of honesty, fairness, and love of truth. Teach others to roll with the punches (by the way, you've probably thrown a few yourself) and take a philosophical view of life's ups and downs. As Frank Sinatra, a Sagittarius, would sing, "Many a tear has to fall, but it's all in the game."

Your style is charming but confrontational, as Phil Donohue, William F. Buckley, and Rush Limbaugh have demonstrated. You thoroughly enjoy a good debate and are very articulate when challenged, though sometimes you may be overly direct when you say exactly what you think, regardless of timing. Confrontations can be fiery, especially when you don't consider the consequences of your words. However, you rarely hold a grudge.

It is difficult for Sagittarius to take direction or discipline, so you'll do best operating freelance, where you can express your visionary views and where your wise and honest words will be heard and heeded.

In a Relationship

You Sagittarians usually have some harsh lessons in store when you take on matrimonial responsibility. You tend to be very idealistic and optimistic about marriage, looking for a fun-loving, cheerful companion (with great legs), who shares your basic philosophy of life. But material realities can bog you down or cause you to bolt when you discover that marriage is more than fun and games. To keep the home fires burning, home must be more than a base of operations for outside activities, a clubhouse, or a comfortable place to relax between trips. Set common goals to hold your relationship together and include your mate in trips, work, and outside interests. Though not known for fidelity, you'll come home to someone who takes you as you are and gives you plenty of rope.

The Sagittarius Woman

The Sagittarius woman is a live wire, an enthusiastic, dynamic companion. This is a woman who tells it like it is—like it or not. But, like the "Divine Miss M," Bette Midler, you're likely to lace your truth telling with side-splitting humor and always leave 'em in an upbeat mood—if not rolling on the floor.

Sagittarius is the natural cheerleader of the zodiac, spurring others on to make the most of themselves. Like Jane Fonda, you're at your best and are most successful when you're inspiring others. You often run your own business with flair and style. You'd much rather give orders than take them and you have the ability to sell others on your schemes and dreams, whether it's an exciting promotional campaign, an all-female wrestling team, or buying up a whole town, as Kim Basinger did. Many Sagittarius women become professional athletes who enjoy the competition and the chance to stretch themselves, like Chris Evert, Suzy Chaffee, and Tracy Austin.

Once an idea appeals to you, you can elevate it to sell to a big market. With contagious optimism and enthusiasm, you get out and spread the word. You're attracted to politics, sales, public relations, or teaching, where your articulate qualities are appreciated. You'd rather delegate routine chores and you might neglect day-to-day responsibilities, often leaving others holding the bag and cleaning up after you.

Though generally blessed with good fortune (your breezy positive mental attitude attracts it!), you can get into trouble if you make promises you can't deliver, or if you run rampant over the feelings of others.

In a Relationship

The Sagittarian woman can successfully juggle a career and home life. You are usually smart enough to get a good backup staff to handle finances and routine chores, while you pursue outside interests. You are best off with a liberated man who is unthreatened by your public personality and enjoys gadding about with you (or has a demanding career of his own). He should appreciate a woman with a fine mind, well-toned body, boundless energy, and strong opinions. You'll be sure to pull your own weight in the marriage, cope with constant changes, and manage a large, active family.

The Sagittarius Family

The Sagittarius Parent

Children bring out the jovial, fun-loving child inside each Sagittarius, and you welcome the challenge of raising them. But sometimes the realities and responsibilities of parenting are more than you bargained for. Sagittarius is not a sign that welcomes dependency of any sort and may resent the obligation to be there for your child, which cuts into freewheeling career time, travel, sports, or spiritual activities. And very young children can tie you to the home, though you'll think of some ingenious ways to get out and about. Sagittarian moms usually continue to work and to be involved in community activities. A large family car or van, equipped with child seats, offers one way to take your family along with you. Sagittarians often discover that helping young minds to grow and explore life's adventures is a challenge that surpasses travels. And spending creative time with children can be more fun than gadding about—you'll discover that you're a born coach who can make learning fun. You now know when to lighten up with a joke and understand children's restlessness. Once your children have a voice of their own and get past the dependent stage, you're one of the most enthusiastic parents.

The Sagittarius Stepparent

With your breezy, casual attitude, you find it easier to adjust to being a stepparent than many other signs do. Your sense of humor will stand you in good stead when awkward situations crop up, and your honest, direct approach will help get problems out in the open. Since you allow your mate plenty of space, there will be little rivalry with the children. You'll enjoy planning outdoor activities for everyone to share. In time, you'll be a good friend to the children, one who encourages any effort to expand their horizons and supports their growth toward independence.

The Sagittarius Grandparent

Sagittarius stays young at heart right through the senior years. You'll enjoy the independence you now have, which gives you the chance to travel and pursue your interests. You may continue to work in some capacity, as a writer or teacher. You'll be well informed of global happenings, or at least what's happening outside of the home. This may be a time when you offer spiritual support and leadership in religious life. You'll enjoy the company of your grandchildren, and you'll have the energy to play right along with them. You'll encourage their educational progress, and perhaps even finance their higher studies. You'll pass on your hard-won wisdom, thrilling them with tales of youthful adventures and inspiring them to follow their dreams. Best of all, you're a grandparent who laughs with them and teaches them to look on the bright side of life.

CHAPTER 13

Your Rising Sign: Why You May Not Seem Like a Typical Sagittarius

Aries Rising—Fiery Emotions

You are the most aggressive version of your sun sign, with boundless energy that can be used productively. Watch a tendency to overreact emotionally and blow your top. You come across as openly competitive, a positive asset in business or sports. But on guard against impatience, which could lead to head injuries. Your walk and bearing could have the telltale head-forward Aries posture. You may wear more bright colors, especially red, than others of your sign, and you may also have a tendency to drive your car faster.

Taurus Rising—The Earth Mother

You'll exude a protective, nurturing quality, even if you're male, which draws those in need of TLC and support. You're slow moving, with a beautiful (or distinctive) speaking or singing voice that can be especially soothing or melodious. You probably surround yourself with comfort, good food, luxurious surroundings, sensual pleasures, and you prefer welcoming others into your home to gadding about. You may have a talent for business, especially in trading, appraising, or real estate. This ascendant gives a well-padded physique that gains weight easily.

Gemini Rising—Expressive Talents

You have an airier, lighter, more ethereal look than others of your sign, especially if you're female. You love to be with people and you express feelings easily. You may have writing or speaking talent. You need variety and a constantly changing scenario, with many different characters, though you may relate to a deeper level than others suspect and you are more sympathetic and caring than you seem. You will probably travel widely, and change partners and jobs several times—or juggle two at once. Physically, you should try to cultivate tranquillity and create a calmer atmosphere, because your nerves are quite sensitive.

Cancer Rising—Sensitive Antenna

You easily pick up others' needs and feelings, a great gift in business, the arts, and personal relationships. But guard against overreacting or taking things too personally, especially during full-moon periods. Find creative outlets for your natural nurturing gifts, such as helping the less fortunate, particularly children. Your insights would be useful in psychology; your desire to feed and care for others are appropriate in the restaurant, hotel, or child-care industries. You may be especially fond of wearing romantic old clothes, collecting antiques, and, of course, good food. Since your body will retain fluids, you should pay attention to your diet. Escape to places near water for relaxation.

Leo Rising—Scene Player

You may come across as more poised than you really feel, but you play your role to the hilt, projecting a commanding and royal presence. This ascendant gives you a natural flair for drama that masks your sensitive interior. You'll also project a much more outgoing, optimistic, sunny personality than others of your sign. You take care to please your public by always projecting your best star quality, probably tossing a luxuriant mane of hair or, if you're female, dazzling with a spectacular jewelry collection. Since you may have a strong parental nature, you could well be the regal family matriarch or patriarch.

Virgo Rising—Cool and Calculating

Virgo rising masks your inner nature with a practical, analytical outer image. You seem very neat and orderly, and more particular than others of your sign. Others in your life may feel they must live up to your high standards, for at times you may be openly critical. But this masks your well-meaning desire to have only the best for your loved ones. Your sharp eye for details could be used in the financial world, or your literary skills could draw you to teaching or publishing. The healing arts, health care, or other service-oriented professions attract many with this Virgo emphasis in their chart. Physically, you have a very sensitive digestive system.

Libra Rising—The Charmer

Libra rising makes you appear as a charmer, more of a social, public person than others of your sign. Your private life will extend beyond your home and family to include an active social life. You may tend to avoid confrontations in relationships, preferring to smooth the way or negotiate diplomatically than give in to an emotional reaction. Because you are interested in all aspects of a situation, you may be slow to reach decisions. Physically, you'll have good proportions and pleasing symmetry, along with pleasing, if not beautiful facial features. You move gracefully and have a winning smile, as well as good taste in your clothes and home decor. Legal, diplomatic, or public relations professions could draw your interest.

Scorpio Rising—Magnetic Power

You project an intriguing air of mystery when Scorpio's secretive and sense of underlying power combines with your sign. You are a master manipulator who can move in the world of power. You come across as more intense and controlled, with a direct and penetrating gaze, but you'll never reveal your private agenda. You tend toward paranoia and may even have secret love affairs. You often wear black and are happiest near water.

Sagittarius Rising—The Wanderer

You travel with this ascendant, for you are a more outdoor, sportive type, with an athletic, casual, outgoing air. Your moods are camouflaged with cheerful optimism or a philosophical attitude—you'll laugh at your troubles or crack a joke more easily than others of your sign. This ascendant can also draw you to the field of higher education or to a spiritual life. You'll seem to have less attachment to things and people and may travel widely. Your strong, fast legs are a physical bonus.

Capricorn Rising—Serious Business

This rising sign makes you come across as serious, goal oriented, disciplined, and careful with cash. You are not one of the zodiac's big spenders, though you might splurge occasionally on items with good investment value. You're the traditional, conservative type in dress and environment, and you might come across as quite formal and businesslike. You'll function well in a structured or corporate environment where you can climb to the top, always aware of who's the boss. In your personal life, you could be a loner or a single parent who is both father and mother to your children.

Aquarius Rising—One of a Kind

You come across as less concerned about what others think and could even be a bit eccentric. You're more at ease with groups of people than others of your sign, and may be attracted to public life. Your appearance may be unique, either unconventional or unimportant to you. Those with the sun in a water sign (Cancer, Scorpio, Pisces) may exercise your nurturing qualities with a large group, an extended family, or a day-care or community center.

Pisces Rising—Romantic Roles

Your creative, nurturing talents are heightened, and so is your ability to project emotional drama—your dreamy eyes and poetic air bring out the protective instinct in others. You could be attracted to the arts, especially theater, dance, film, or photography, or to careers in psychology or spiritual or charity work. Since you are vulnerable to up-and-down mood swings, it is especially important for you to find interesting, creative work where you can express your talents and boost your self esteem. Accentuate the positive and be wary of escapist tendencies, particularly involving alcohol or drugs, to which you are super-sensitive.

How to Find Your Rising Sign

At the moment you were born, your horoscope was set in movement by the sign passing over the eastern horizon: the rising sign or ascendant. Like your personal advertisement, this sign shows how you present yourself to the world.

The ascendant is one of the most important factors in your chart because it shows not only how you appear outwardly, but it sets up the path you are to follow. After the rising sign is determined, then each area of your chart is governed by the signs following in sequence.

The rising sign gives the planets a specific context, an area of life where they will operate. Without a valid rising sign, your collection of planets would have no home. Once the rising sign is known, it becomes possible to analyze a chart accurately—that is why many astrologers insist on an accurate birth time before they analyze a chart.

Rising signs change every two hours with the Earth's rotation. If you were born early in the morning, when the sun was on the horizon, you'll most likely project an accurate image of the sun sign, as the sun and ascendant reinforce each other. Look up your rising sign on the following chart. Since rising signs change rapidly, it is important to know your birth time as close to the minute as possible. Even a few minutes difference could change the rising sign and the setup of your chart. If you are unsure about the exact time, but know within a few hours, check the descriptions before and after your estimated rising sign to see which is most like the personality you project.

	1 AM	2 AM	3 AM	4 AM	5 AM	6 AM	7 AM	8 AM	9 AM	10 AM	11 AM	12 NOON
Jan 1	Lib	Sc	Sc	Sc	Sag	Sag	Cap	Cap	Aq	Aq	Pis	Ar
Jan 9	Lib	Sc	Sc	Sag	Sag	Sag	Cap	Cap	Aq	Pis	Ar	Tau
Jan 17	Sc	Sc	Sc	Sag	Sag	Cap	Cap	Aq	Aq	Pis	Ar	Tau
Jan 25	Sc	Sc	Sag	Sag	Sag	Cap	Cap	Aq	Pis	Ar	Tau	Tau
Feb 2	Sc	Sc	Sag	Sag	Cap	Cap	Aq	Pis	Pis	Ar	Tau	Gem
Feb 10	Sc	Sag	Sag	Sag	Cap	Cap	Aq	Pis	Ar	Tau	Tau	Gem
Feb 18	Sc	Sag	Sag	Cap	Cap	Aq	Pis	Pis	Ar	Tau	Gem	Gem
Feb 26	Sag	Sag	Sag	Cap	Aq	Aq	Pis	Ar	Tau	Tau	Gem	Gem
Mar 6	Sag	Sag	Cap	Cap	Aq	Pis	Pis	Ar	Tau	Gem	Gem	Cap
Mar 14	Sag	Cap	Cap	Aq	Aq	Pis	Ar	Tau	Tau	Gem	Gem	Can
Mar 22	Sag	Cap	Cap	Aq	Pis	Ar	Ar	Tau	Gem	Gem	Can	Can
Mar 30	Cap	Cap	Aq	Pis	Pis	Ar	Tau	Tau	Gem	Can	Can	Can
Apr 7	Cap	Cap	Aq	Pis	Ar	Ar	Tau	Gem	Gem	Can	Can	Leo
Apr 14	Cap	Aq	Aq	Pis	Ar	Tau	Tau	Gem	Gem	Can	Can	Leo
Apr 22	Cap	Aq	Pis	Ar	Ar	Tau	Gem	Gem	Gem	Can	Leo	Leo
Apr 30	Aq	Aq	Pis	Ar	Tau	Tau	Gem	Can	Can	Can	Leo	Leo
May 8	Aq	Pis	Ar	Ar	Tau	Gem	Gem	Can	Can	Leo	Leo	Leo
May 16	Aq	Pis	Ar	Tau	Gem	Gem	Can	Can	Can	Leo	Leo	Vir
May 24	Pis	Ar	Ar	Tau	Gem	Gem	Can	Can	Leo	Leo	Leo	Vir
June 1	Pis	Ar	Tau	Gem	Gem	Can	Can	Can	Leo	Leo	Vir	Vir
June 9	Ar	Ar	Tau	Gem	Gem	Can	Can	Leo	Leo	Leo	Vir	Vir
June 17	Ar	Tau	Gem	Gem	Can	Can	Can	Leo	Leo	Vir	Vir	Vir
June 25	Tau	Tau	Gem	Gem	Can	Can	Leo	Leo	Leo	Vir	Vir	Lib
July 3	Tau	Gem	Gem	Can	Can	Can	Leo	Leo	Vir	Vir	Vir	Lib
July 11	Tau	Gem	Gem	Can	Can	Leo	Leo	Leo	Vir	Vir	Lib	Lib
July 18	Gem	Gem	Can	Can	Can	Leo	Leo	Vir	Vir	Vir	Lib	Lib
July 26	Gem	Gem	Can	Can	Leo	Leo	Vir	Vir	Vir	Lib	Lib	Lib
Aug 3	Gem	Can	Can	Can	Leo	Leo	Vir	Vir	Vir	Lib	Lib	Sc
Aug 11	Gem	Can	Can	Leo	Leo	Leo	Vir	Vir	Lib	Lib	Lib	Sc
Aug 18	Can	Can	Can	Leo	Leo	Vir	Vir	Vir	Lib	Lib	Sc	Sc
Aug 27	Can	Can	Leo	Leo	Leo	Vir	Vir	Lib	Lib	Lib	Sc	Sc
Sept 4	Can	Can	Leo	Leo	Leo	Vir	Vir	Vir	Lib	Lib	Sc	Sc
Sept 12	Can	Leo	Leo	Leo	Vir	Vir	Lib	Lib	Lib	Sc	Sc	Sag
Sept 20	Leo	Leo	Leo	Vir	Vir	Vir	Lib	Lib	Lib	Sc	Sc	Sag
Sept 28	Leo	Leo	Leo	Vir	Vir	Lib	Lib	Lib	Sc	Sc	Sag	Sag
Oct 6	Leo	Leo	Vir	Vir	Vir	Lib	Lib	Sc	Sc	Sc	Sag	Sag
Oct 14	Leo	Vir	Vir	Vir	Lib	Lib	Lib	Sc	Sc	Sag	Sag	Cap
Oct 22	Leo	Vir	Vir	Lib	Lib	Lib	Sc	Sc	Sc	Sag	Sag	Cap
Oct 30	Vir	Vir	Vir	Lib	Lib	Sc	Sc	Sc	Sag	Sag	Cap	Cap
Nov 7	Vir	Vir	Lib	Lib	Lib	Sc	Sc	Sc	Sag	Sag	Cap	Cap
Nov 15	Vir	Vir	Lib	Lib	Sc	Sc	Sc	Sag	Sag	Cap	Cap	Aq
Nov 23	Vir	Lib	Lib	Lib	Sc	Sc	Sag	Sag	Sag	Cap	Cap	Aq
Dec 1	Vir	Lib	Lib	Sc	Sc	Sc	Sag	Sag	Cap	Cap	Aq	Aq
Dec 9	Lib	Lib	Lib	Sc	Sc	Sag	Sag	Sag	Cap	Cap	Aq	Pis
Dec 18	Lib	Lib	Sc	Sc	Sc	Sag	Sag	Cap	Cap	Aq	Aq	Pis
Dec 28	Lib	Lib	Sc	Sc	Sag	Sag	Sag	Cap	Aq	Aq	Pis	Ar

RISING SIGNS—P.M. BIRTHS

	1 PM	2 PM	3 PM	4 PM	5 PM	6 PM	7 PM	8 PM	9 PM	10 PM	11 PM	12 MIDNIGHT
Jan 1	Tau	Gem	Gem	Can	Can	Can	Leo	Leo	Vir	Vir	Vir	Lib
Jan 9	Tau	Gem	Gem	Can	Can	Leo	Leo	Leo	Vir	Vir	Vir	Lib
Jan 17	Gem	Gem	Can	Can	Can	Leo	Leo	Vir	Vir	Vir	Lib	Lib
Jan 25	Gem	Gem	Can	Can	Leo	Leo	Leo	Vir	Vir	Lib	Lib	Lib
Feb 2	Gem	Can	Can	Can	Leo	Leo	Vir	Vir	Vir	Lib	Lib	Sc
Feb 10	Gem	Can	Can	Leo	Leo	Leo	Vir	Vir	Lib	Lib	Lib	Sc
Feb 18	Can	Can	Can	Leo	Leo	Vir	Vir	Vir	Lib	Lib	Sc	Sc
Feb 26	Can	Can	Leo	Leo	Leo	Vir	Vir	Lib	Lib	Lib	Sc	Sc
Mar 6	Can	Leo	Leo	Leo	Vir	Vir	Vir	Lib	Lib	Sc	Sc	Sc
Mar 14	Can	Leo	Leo	Vir	Vir	Vir	Lib	Lib	Lib	Sc	Sc	Sag
Mar 22	Leo	Leo	Leo	Vir	Vir	Lib	Lib	Lib	Sc	Sc	Sc	Sag
Mar 30	Leo	Leo	Vir	Vir	Vir	Lib	Lib	Sc	Sc	Sc	Sag	Sag
Apr 7	Leo	Leo	Vir	Vir	Lib	Lib	Lib	Sc	Sc	Sc	Sag	Sag
Apr 14	Leo	Vir	Vir	Vir	Lib	Lib	Sc	Sc	Sc	Sag	Sag	Cap
Apr 22	Leo	Vir	Vir	Lib	Lib	Lib	Sc	Sc	Sc	Sag	Sag	Cap
Apr 30	Vir	Vir	Vir	Lib	Lib	Sc	Sc	Sc	Sag	Sag	Cap	Cap
May 8	Vir	Vir	Lib	Lib	Lib	Sc	Sc	Sag	Sag	Sag	Cap	Cap
May 16	Vir	Vir	Lib	Lib	Sc	Sc	Sc	Sag	Sag	Cap	Cap	Aq
May 24	Vir	Lib	Lib	Lib	Sc	Sc	Sag	Sag	Sag	Cap	Cap	Aq
June 1	Vir	Lib	Lib	Sc	Sc	Sc	Sag	Sag	Cap	Cap	Aq	Aq
June 9	Lib	Lib	Lib	Sc	Sc	Sag	Sag	Sag	Cap	Cap	Aq	Pis
June 17	Lib	Lib	Sc	Sc	Sc	Sag	Sag	Cap	Cap	Aq	Aq	Pis
June 25	Lib	Lib	Sc	Sc	Sag	Sag	Sag	Cap	Cap	Aq	Pis	Ar
July 3	Lib	Sc	Sc	Sc	Sag	Sag	Cap	Cap	Aq	Aq	Pis	Ar
July 11	Lib	Sc	Sc	Sag	Sag	Sag	Cap	Cap	Aq	Pis	Ar	Tau
July 18	Sc	Sc	Sc	Sag	Sag	Cap	Cap	Aq	Aq	Pis	Ar	Tau
July 26	Sc	Sc	Sag	Sag	Sag	Cap	Cap	Aq	Pis	Ar	Tau	Tau
Aug 3	Sc	Sc	Sag	Sag	Cap	Cap	Aq	Aq	Pis	Ar	Tau	Gem
Aug 11	Sc	Sag	Sag	Sag	Cap	Cap	Aq	Pis	Ar	Tau	Tau	Gem
Aug 18	Sc	Sag	Sag	Cap	Cap	Aq	Pis	Pis	Ar	Tau	Gem	Gem
Aug 27	Sag	Sag	Sag	Cap	Cap	Aq	Pis	Ar	Tau	Tau	Gem	Gem
Sept 4	Sag	Sag	Cap	Cap	Aq	Pis	Pis	Ar	Tau	Gem	Gem	Can
Sept 12	Sag	Sag	Cap	Aq	Aq	Pis	Ar	Tau	Tau	Gem	Gem	Can
Sept 20	Sag	Cap	Cap	Aq	Pis	Pis	Ar	Tau	Gem	Gem	Can	Can
Sept 28	Cap	Cap	Aq	Aq	Pis	Ar	Tau	Tau	Gem	Gem	Can	Can
Oct 6	Cap	Cap	Aq	Pis	Ar	Ar	Tau	Gem	Gem	Can	Can	Leo
Oct 14	Cap	Aq	Aq	Pis	Ar	Tau	Tau	Gem	Gem	Can	Can	Leo
Oct 22	Cap	Aq	Pis	Ar	Ar	Tau	Gem	Gem	Can	Can	Leo	Leo
Oct 30	Aq	Aq	Pis	Ar	Tau	Tau	Gem	Can	Can	Can	Leo	Leo
Nov 7	Aq	Aq	Pis	Ar	Tau	Tau	Gem	Can	Can	Can	Leo	Leo
Nov 15	Aq	Pis	Ar	Tau	Gem	Gem	Can	Can	Can	Leo	Leo	Vir
Nov 23	Pis	Ar	Ar	Tau	Gem	Gem	Can	Can	Leo	Leo	Leo	Vir
Dec 1	Pis	Ar	Tau	Gem	Gem	Can	Can	Can	Leo	Leo	Vir	Vir
Dec 9	Ar	Tau	Tau	Gem	Gem	Can	Can	Can	Leo	Leo	Vir	Vir
Dec 18	Ar	Tau	Gem	Gem	Can	Can	Can	Leo	Leo	Vir	Vir	Vir
Dec 28	Tau	Tau	Gem	Gem	Can	Can	Leo	Leo	Vir	Vir	Vir	Lib

CHAPTER 14

The Sagittarius Route to Success

Sagittarius Power

You're a breezy, informal boss who covers a wide territory. Though you may be hard to pin down, you'll keep on friendly terms with everybody and rarely hang around long enough to get into office politics. Unless of course, someone challenges your territory—then you'll send them packing fast. You tell it like it is and expect others to change their tune accordingly and quickly. Even though you may step on their toes occasionally, subordinates know where they stand with you.

Organization is not your strong point, however, so your business structure may be unconventional and sometimes nonexistent. It will take a solid, well-organized backup team to make your high-flying ideas happen, Therefore, you must learn the hard way not to trust to luck when you really need solid, practical support.

Sagittarius Teamwork

You're a born optimist whose energy and cheerful, positive attitude wins you a top place on the team. However, you'll travel ahead faster if you are allowed to run your own show. You work best when you have plenty of freedom and very loose reins. You'd rather give orders than follow them any day, and you might sound off rather than take strong direction. Diplomacy is not one of your strong points. You do respond to a challenge, however, be it intellectual or physical, and, when you're inspired, you don't need to be coddled on the job. You'll take it to the limit, making the job much more meaningful than it was originally intended. You're capable of making every job a high-flying adventure. But guard against getting carried away and losing your grounding by making promises you can't deliver or taking uncalculated risks.

Sagittarius Careers

To get on the fast track to success, you need a job with plenty of scope for your soaring ambitions. Avoid stodgy offices and tradition-bound businesses. Instead, head straight for a field where your ideas will be recognized and appreciated, where you'll have plenty of room to explore new territory and expand your mind. You are very ambitious and motivated when you find a job that inspires you. Consider anything in sales, travel, or tourism, or make your athletic skills a profession in the sports or fitness fields. Your philosophical ideals could be expressed in education, politics or publishing, or you might be drawn to New-Age spiritual work. Any profession involving animals, especially horses, or the outdoors, is very appealing. Don't even think about a desk job or any work that could get bogged down in details or requires great patience. Go for a fast-paced job with lots of challenge and a constant change of scenery. Play up your strong points:

- Sales and motivation ability
- Energy and good physical shape
- Honesty
- Enthusiasm and positive attitude
- Decisiveness

Famous Sagittarius Millionaires

Study the success stories of these colorful Sagittarians, some of them legends in their own time. Most are featured in biographies, business magazine profiles, or reference books. You might get some useful tips for moving ahead on the fast track.

Steven Spielberg (film)
Jean Paul Getty
Gordon Getty
Meshulam Riklis
William F. Buckley
Andrew Carnegie
Doris Duke
Don King (boxing promoter)
Alexis Lichine (the "Pope of Wine")
Walt Disney

CHAPTER 15

Sagittarius in Love: How You Get Along with Every Other Sun Sign

Look up your lover, your boss, your potential roommate. But bear in mind that we're all a combination of many different planets, most likely in other signs. So be tolerant of your choices—there could be another planet in the picture that will make a big difference in how well you do—or don't—get along.

Sagittarius/Aries

Turn-ons: You're good buddies who love the great outdoors, risk-taking adventures, travel, and a high-action lifestyle. You'll support each other's goals. This works especially well if you share spiritual ideals. You're both independent and understand each other's need for space.

Turn-offs: You both tend to be self-involved and may not invest enough time in maintaining the relationship. Common goals may not be enough to keep you together, especially if you lack solid financial backup. Unless you become more available to each other, you may find yourself heading off in a different direction, in search of more ego support.

Celebrity couples: Sagittarius Kim Basinger and Aries Alec Baldwin

Sagittarius Kenneth Branagh and Aries Emma Thompson (divorced)

Sagittarius/Taurus

Turn-ons: Sagittarius energizes Taurus and gets this sign to take calculated risks, daring to think big. Taurus provides the solid support and steady income to make Sagittarius ideas happen. Sagittarius will be challenged to produce, Taurus to stretch and grow.

Turn-offs: You are very different types who are not especially sympathetic to each other's needs. Taurus believes in hard work, Sagittarius in luck. Sagittarius is a rolling stone, Taurus a quiet meadow. Sagittarius appreciates freedom, Taurus substance.

Celebrity couple: Sagittarius Don Johnson and Taurus Barbra Streisand (split up)

Sagittarius/Gemini

Turn-ons: These polar opposites shake each other up—happily. Sagittarius helps Gemini see higher truths, to look beyond the life of the party and the art of the deal. Gemini adds mental challenge and flexibility to Sagittarius.

Turn-offs: Gemini pokes holes in Sagittarian theories, while Sagittarius can brand Gemini as a superficial party animal. Work toward developing nonthreatening, nonjudgmental communication. However, you can't talk away practical financial realities—you need a well-thought-out program to make things happen.

Celebrity couple: Sagittarius Bette Midler and Gemini Barry Manilow (professionally)

Sagittarius/Cancer

Turn-ons: Sagittarius gets a sensual partner who will keep the home fires burning and the coffers full, while Cancer gets a strong dose of optimism that could banish the blues. The Sagittarian carefree, outgoing outdoor lifestyle expands Cancer's sometimes narrow point of view and gets that sign physically fit.

Turn-offs: This joyride could reach a dead end when Sagittarius shows little sympathy for Cancer's need for mothering or runs roughshod over sensitive feelings. Cancer could withdraw into a protective shell or use claws when Sagittarius exercises a free hand with the budget.

Celebrity couples: Sagittarius actress Liv Ullman and Cancer director Ingmar Bergman.
Sagittarius Robin Givens and Cancer Mike Tyson (divorced)

Sagittarius/Leo

Turn-ons: Under Sagittarian optimism and good humor, Leo's luck soars. You both inspire each other and boost each other creatively. If you like the outdoor life, have a spirit of adventure, and love to travel, you're a winning combination that could feel fated to be together.

Turn-offs: Sagittarius is not one to pour on the flattery Leo loves, nor is this sign known for monogamy. When both your fiery tempers explode, Leo roars and Sagittarius heads for the door. Leo must tone down bossiness and give Sagittarius a very long leash. Sag must learn to coddle the Leo ego and keep that blazing temper on hold.

Celebrity Couple: Sagittarius Don Johnson and Leo Melanie Griffith (divorced)

Sagittarius/Virgo

Turn-ons: Sagittarius inspires Virgo to take risks and win, and brings fun, laughter and mental stimulation to Virgo's life. Virgo supplies a much-needed support system, organizing and following through on Sagittarius ideas. These two signs fulfill important needs for each other.

Turn-offs: Virgo won't relate to the Sagittarian happy-go-lucky financial philosophy and reluctance to make firm commitments. Sagittarius would rather deal with the big picture, and may resent Virgo's preoccupation with details. Sexual fidelity could be a key issue if this Sagittarian's casual approach to sex conflicts with Virgo's desire to have everything perfect.

Celebrity couple: Sagittarius Steven Spielberg and Virgo Amy Irving (divorced)

Sagittarius/Libra

Turn-ons: Libra's charm smooths over the rough spots, while Sagittarius provides lofty goals and a spirit of adventure. This can be a blazing romance, full of action and fun on the town together. Neither of you are stay-at-homes.

Turn-offs: Libra vacillations and Sagittarian wanderlust could keep you from making a firm commitment. You both need to find a solid launching pad—either mutual interest or career goals that give this relationship structure. Libra needs a partner, but Sagittarius, who travels fastest alone, resents being tied down in any way.

Celebrity couple: Sagittarius Darryl Hannah and Libra Jackson Browne

Sagittarius/Scorpio

Turn-ons: Sagittarius sees an erotic adventure in Scorpio—and doesn't mind playing with fire. Scorpio's impressed with Sagittarian high ideals, energy, and competitive spirit. Sagittarian humor diffuses Scorpio intensity, while Scorpio provides the focus for Sagittarius to reach those goals.

Turn-offs: Scorpio sees through schemes and won't fall for a sales pitch unless it has substance. Sagittarius may object to Scorpio's drive for power, rather than for higher goals and will flee from Scorpio possessiveness or heavy-handed, controlling tactics.

Celebrity couples: Sagittarius Jane Fonda and Scorpio Ted Turner
Sagittarius Phil Donohue and Scorpio Marlo Thomas

Sagittarius/Sagittarius

Turn-ons: This pair functions best on the road. You share each other's ideals and goals—and you are the greatest of traveling companions, never tying each other down.

Turn-offs: In the real world, your life together may be like a series of one-night stands—rarely are you in the same place for long, unless you arrange to travel together. You'll need to make an effort to establish a solid home base, delegating financial matters to a disciplined, responsible third party. Otherwise, you could have no one to come home to.

Celebrity couple: Darryl Hannah and John F. Kennedy, Jr. (split up)

Sagittarius/Capricorn

Turn-ons: Capricorn has a built-in job organizing Sagittarius, but the challenge of doing something for the greater good could bring Capricorn status and recognition. Sagittarius encourages Capricorn to elevate goals beyond the material and brings out both the spiritual side and the humor of this sign.

Turn-offs: Optimistic Sagittarian meets pessimistic Capricorn—and you cancel each other out! Ultimately, you can't play it for laughs—Capricorn pushes Sagittarius to produce and commit. And Sagittarius was off to do his or her own thing.

Celebrity couple: Sagittarius John F. Kennedy, Jr. and Capricorn Carolyn Bessette-Kennedy

Sagittarius/Aquarius

Turn-ons: Aquarian unpredictability and concern for humanitarian causes meshes well with the Sagittarian adventurous spirit and lofty ideals. You'll give each other plenty of freedom and probably invent a unique, unconventional lifestyle.

Turn-offs: Dealing with everyday realities could be problematic. This pair-up may not be able to get things done—there is lots of talk, a fiery debate, but little concrete action. Each may go your own way or look elsewhere for backup support.

Celebrity couple: Sagittarius Woody Allen and Aquarius Mia Farrow (split up)

Sagittarius/Pisces

Turn-ons: You spark each other creatively and romantically. Pisces imagination and Sagittarius innovation work well on all levels. Variety, mental stimulation, and spiritual understanding, plus an appreciation of exotic places, could draw and keep you together.

Turn-offs: Pisceans can turn from a gentle tropical angel fish to a vengeful shark, when Sagittarians disregard their tender feelings. Sagittarius goes for direct attacks and could feel that self-protective Pisces hides truths far beneath the surface.

Celebrity couple: Sagittarius Frank Sinatra and Pisces Barbara Sinatra

CHAPTER 16

Your Sagittarius Lifestyle and Fashion Guide

Astrology can help you with all kinds of decisions, from what kind of clothes to wear to what color to paint your room. Here are some of the ways you can use the stars to guide you to the style that suits you best.

How Should I Furnish My Home?

Many Sagittarians have great decorating flair and dress a room with drama, highlighting exotic souvenirs. Even if you are the rare Sagittarian who has never traveled, you are sure to collect some form of exotica, books, athletic trophies, or sporting pictures. Since many Sagittarians get involved with horses, you might like a western or equestrian theme, with hunter green walls, plaid upholstery, and horse prints. Or yours may be a relaxed, casual hangout to rest between trips and entertain chums. You'll be unhappy in any room with a closed-in feeling. You need plenty of space and a fireplace, and you may need dog- and cat-proof furniture to accommodate your pets!

What Music Will Put Me in a Good Mood?

Your musical tastes can be as exotic and varied as your travels! Your gypsy soul soars to flamenco beats, salsa, and tangos. Your spiritual side is uplifted by all sorts of religious music. Frank Sinatra, Noel Coward, Puccini, and George Gershwin also speak your musical language. Sagittarius singers Sinead O'Connor, Tina Turner, Bette Midler, and Dionne Warwick are on your wavelength.

Where Should I Go on Vacation?

Almost anyplace is a Sagittarius place, but not for long! Sagittarians are born globe-trotters, always on the move. You may want to settle down for a while in a place with great sports facilities, or attend a horse show in Ireland or the grand prix in Monaco. There's always the Olympics somewhere! Sagittarians like the challenge of outward-bound expeditions, or trips to remote places such as Antarctica, or Finland, Spain, Chile, Thailand, and Hungary resonate to your Sagittarius frequency.

Keep a bag packed with items you can't live without (that Swiss Army knife, copies of your favorite tapes, video workouts, portable exercise equipment, rollerblades). Choose hotels that have fitness equipment, pools, or jogging tracks, so you won't miss a workout. Keep a separate notebook for your contacts and favorite haunts in each city, so all your relevant numbers will be instantly available.

What Are My Best Sagittarius Colors?

Purple, red, and royal blue with white are special Sagittarius colors. You are usually not the pastel type, preferring exciting and dramatic combinations. Some of you love bright orange (the color Buddhist monks wear).

What Should I Wear?

You need clothes that travel well, move with your body, and yet have flair and style. You love to look dashing and you're usually up to the minute on the latest trends. Stay away from fussy ruffles or demure patterns—you're naturally better suited to well-cut sports clothes and short skirts that show off your fabulous legs. Go all out for the most sensational jogging suits and workout wear, especially if you're in great shape like Jane Fonda or *Sports Illustrated* cover girl Carol Alt. Get a stock of great stockings and beautiful shoes (from Sagittarian designer Monolo Blahnik). Versatile, packable knits in bold colors are made especially for you!

Who Are the Sagittarius Fashion Designers?

Your Sagittarian designers—Gianni Versace and Thierry Mugler—understand how to use bright colors, bold jewelry, and dramatic lines. It was Versace who designed fellow Sagittarius Don Johnson's trademark style for Miami Vice.

Where Should I Go for Dinner?

Travel via your dinner, by choosing an exotic restaurant that serves Latin American, Thai, or Middle Eastern food. You'll love the spicier forms of Chinese foods, from Szechuan or Hunan. Italian food is a perennial Sagittarian favorite. Or pick a restaurant with flair, a new hot spot with plenty of social action and lots of good-looking people. Even better, pack a tailgate picnic and head for a football or baseball game, a polo match, or a triathlon event. Combining food and sports events is a Sagittarius specialty.

CHAPTER 17

Stay Fit and Healthy the Sagittarius Way

Your Health

In maintaining health, Sagittarians would do well to remember that yours is a goal-setting sign. So aim for the best you can be, then set a plan to achieve it. Good health for you is often a matter of staying motivated. Once you've decided on a course of action, get going—being on the move and physically active keeps you in the best of health, improves your circulation, and protects your arteries. Your difficulties could come from injuries to the hip or thigh area and arterial problems, so be sure to protect yourself with the proper equipment for your activity and don't push yourself beyond your capacity.

Your Diet

Since your sign is naturally expansive, you may have difficulty staying with a diet. One that is part of a spiritually oriented lifestyle, such as vegetarianism, might have the most lasting appeal. Beware of fad diets that promise instant results and come with a high-pressure sales pitch. Avoid gimmicks, pills, or anything instant. Since patience is not a Sagittarian strong point, aim for long-range benefits and balance a sane, practical eating plan with plenty of exercise.

Exercise Tips

Your sign loves working out in classes or groups, so combine socializing with athletic activities. Touch football games, bike riding, hikes, and long walks with your dog are fun as well as healthy. Let others know that you'd like a health-promoting gift, such as sports equipment, a gym membership, or an exercise video, for Christmas. In your workouts, concentrate on Sagittarius-ruled areas—the hips, legs, and thighs. Yours is a sports-loving sign, ideal for downhill or cross-country skiing or rollerblading and basketball. Since you're likely to travel a lot, plan an exercise routine that can be done anywhere. Isometric-type exercises, which work one muscle group against another, can be done in a car or plane seat. If you travel often, investigate equipment that fits easily in your suitcase, such as water-filled weights, home gym devices, elastic bands.

Celebrity Role Models: Jane Fonda, Katarina Witt, John F. Kennedy, Jr.

CHAPTER 18

Astro-Outlook for Sagittarius in 1998

From its outset, 1998 is a momentous year. You are strongly bent on conserving good health and economic prosperity. Mighty Jupiter, your planetary ruler, is moving forward in your third house and its conjunction with the moon on New Years Day augurs well for applicable knowledge. Uranus is also in your third house, as is motivational Mars and retrograde Venus, all of which constitutes a stellium of forceful inner resources that spell gain and advancement.

Before January ends, the sun and Neptune also enter this part of your horoscope, strongly accenting the fortuitous changes, improvements, and corrections that advance your studies, hobbies, communications skills, and everyday routines and schedules.

Face up to any challenges that touch your family values, residential matters, and ownership and property interests as February moves toward a close. The presence of transiting Jupiter in Pisces during the late-February solar eclipse empowers you to handle the family's economy well.

You can count on stability in your love life over the January–June interval, with Saturn transiting your fifth house, which rules your loving, romantic overtures and interludes, courtship, spontaneous socializing, and the affairs of your children.

After June 9, Saturn will be in Taurus, where it gives stability and permits consolidation in health and work matters. May is one of your best months for happiness in loving and being loved. This period also favors real estate and ownership interests.

Ways to increase your earning power and income will be illuminated for you in early June, while late July sees the lunar spotlight on travel plans. It might be a good idea to return from any travel prior to August 22, when some pressures show up in long-range and long-distance interests.

October empowers you to straighten out any problems that may be confusing your love life. Bond more closely with your mate and offspring during October. Your social life will go well over the last ten days of the month.

Pay attention to health maintenance and working out effective preventive-medicine routines as November gets under way.

December belongs to you, especially after the 11th, when Mercury increases all your involvements in the holiday season. While others in your immediate environment may tend to panic, remember Kipling's advice, to handle imposters (be they people or situations) with courage and a little contempt. Many look to you constantly over the summer and fall for guidance, encouragement, and inspiration. You do not fail people, and your optimistic manner is once again a mark of your leadership abilities.

One of your special strengths in 1998 stems from the transit of Pluto through Sagittarius, where it confers unusual awareness that offers direction on handling uncertainties and concerns.

CHAPTER 19

Eighteen Months of Day-by-Day Predictions—July 1997 to December 1998

JULY 1997

Tuesday, July 1 (Moon in Taurus to Gemini 7:35 a.m.)
Cooperation is recommended for it is the way to success.
A Gemini can provide the flexibility and imagination
you may require to handle this day wisely. There is no
guarantee against annoyances, even a demonstration of
anger in partnership interests. Your winning color is
lemon. Hot combination numbers: 9 and 6.

Wednesday, July 2 (Moon in Gemini) A good sense
of proportion and balance can improve the potential of
this day of partnerships, marital bonding, and gains from
sharing and keeping your sense of humor. It's a busy
day with a lot of demands and complaints coming your
way. Cherry is your color. Lucky lottery: 2, 11, 20, 29,
38, 47.

***Thursday, July 3 (Moon in Gemini to Cancer 2:33
p.m.)*** You may feel somewhat trapped by the ideas
and desires of others. You could feel that the system is
pegged against you. Overcome this negativism by talking
things over with an Aquarius. The demands of children
could cut into your free time. Be patient and use your
sense of humor to diffuse tension. Your lucky number
is 4.

Friday, July 4 (Moon in Cancer)   The new moon in your eighth house illuminates security, savings, expenses, cost of living, and the changes you and others are trying to bring about. Read the financial pages of your newspaper carefully for hints about what you can expect over this month. Your lucky number is 6.

Saturday, July 5 (Moon in Cancer to Leo 11:45 p.m.)   A Cancer and a Libra can clue you on improved security matters. The changes you inaugurate now are in the nature of important improvements and corrections. Financial and business discussions could produce the information you need for a great leap forward. Orange is your color. Lucky lottery: 8, 17, 26, 35, 44, 2.

Sunday, July 6 (Moon in Leo)   Excellent trends exist in travel, getting away with youngsters to appreciate summer's potential for rest and relaxation. The kids will keep you on the go, but there's plenty of fun and good times for all. Long-range and long-distance interests capture your attention. Flame is your color; your lucky number is 1.

Monday, July 7 (Moon in Leo)   Fine rays exist for sightseeing, talking with fellow travelers, and enjoying socializing with kids on vacation. Leo and Aquarius figure prominently. Visit relatives and old friends. You enjoy being away from the grind and seeing new and exciting scenes. Your lucky number is 5.

Tuesday, July 8 (Moon in Leo to Virgo 11:22 a.m.)   There's a faster pace and lots of momentum to this day, and your sense of adventure is stronger than ever. You are fascinated by the rare sights, special animals, beautiful flowers and shrubbery, and amusement parks and off-beat restaurants. You are willing to gamble and try them all. Hot combination numbers: 7 and 3.

Wednesday, July 9 (Moon in Virgo)   Back to obligations, responsibilities, and duties, and you bring a special determination and realism with you. You will have no trouble making up for lost time, for Virgo and Taurus are in your corner. You can give your best shot to your career now by keeping your weather eye on a higher economic and social goal. All the colors of the rainbow are yours. Lucky lottery: 9, 18, 27, 36, 45, 6.

Thursday, July 10 (Moon in Virgo) You can take a great leap forward in career, professional, and authority matters. You may be able to put to use some of the studies in your distant past that you haven't been able to use until now. You have the feeling that very little time was ever wasted by you on either side of maturity. Your number is 2.

Friday, July 11 (Moon in Virgo to Libra 12:21 a.m.) It's a grand day for enjoying friendships, spending time with those special kindred spirits who really understand what you are all about. Libra and Gemini have something to say to you. Parties, group activities, and church and club membership and participation get green lights. Hot combination numbers: 4 and 3.

Saturday, July 12 (Moon in Libra) Today is perfect for entertaining in your home and bringing both old and new friends together. Patio and backyard cookouts will serve to put people in a festive mood. People who share your interests want to see more of you. Amber is your color. Lucky lottery: 6, 15, 24, 33, 42, 51.

Sunday, July 13 (Moon in Libra to Scorpio 12:20 p.m.) Invite friends and neighbors to drop in for a chat and a good pot of black Ceylon tea—every problem that ever arose during the Victorian era was solved over that pot of tea. You are reaching out for approval, appreciation, and affection and your friends are anxious to comply. Your lucky number is 8.

Monday, July 14 (Moon in Scorpio) Scorpio is available to help you complete tasks and chores. Size the job up well before actually undertaking it. Be sure you have all the facts and information about what you hope to achieve. It's a good day for dealing with the subtle, sublime, and complex matters of life. Your lucky number is 3.

Tuesday, July 15 (Moon in Scorpio to Sagittarius 9:02 p.m.)   Your awareness in submitting and presenting ideas and projects is particularly good. Use your creativity and originality to promote yourself. What is going on behind the scenes and all confidential matters are going to impact this day. Your winning colors are coral and buff. Hot combination numbers: 5 and 2.

Wednesday, July 16 (Moon in Sagittarius)   You are now in your lunar high cycle, when you can win others over to your point of view. This is the time to change course and direction, if that is what you have been contemplating. Hold the initiative and demonstrate self-reliance and self-confidence. Pastels are your colors. Lucky lottery: 7, 16, 25, 34, 43, 3.

Thursday, July 17 (Moon in Sagittarius)   Push highly personalized interests. Be self-confident, stand by basic convictions, ask questions, and air your intentions and aspirations for success. Another Sagittarius and a Gemini workaholic can be vital assistants in your drive forward. Be optimistic and enthusiastic—and smile. Your lucky number is 9.

Friday, July 18 (Moon in Sagittarius to Capricorn 1:45 a.m.)   Increase your earning power and income. Look for a new source of income. You can tutor, teach, inspire, guide, and encourage with the marvelous help of your powerful ruling orb, Jupiter. As a fervent spreader of goodwill, companies and people want you around. Your lucky number is 2.

Saturday, July 19 (Moon in Capricorn)   Big savings while shopping in two or more stores is just like money in the bank. It's a day for buying your meat in one store, your fish in another, bakery products in still a third.

Know where the prices are best. Fine trends exist for garage and other types of personal sales ventures. Violet and purple are your colors. Lucky lottery: 4, 13, 22, 31, 40, 49.

Sunday, July 20 (Moon in Capricorn to Aquarius 3:29 a.m.)   The full moon illuminates your overall wealth production and gives enlightenment in what you can do or refrain from doing in order to increase your total income for the rest of summer. Harmonize your efforts with those of your spouse or other partner. Cinnamon is your color; your number is 6.

Monday, July 21 (Moon in Aquarius)   Concentrate on the job at hand, then zero in on ways to improve the required skills. Local, immediate, and pressing matters get green lights. Studies, communications, and short-distance travel are on your agenda. Aquarius and Libra have key roles. Silver and pink are your colors; your number is 1.

Tuesday, July 22 (Moon in Aquarius to Pisces 4 a.m.)   Pisces is represented, along with your Pisces-ruled interests: domestic, property, and ownership matters. The community is making some demands upon your time. Talks with teenagers will help them and may give you a chance to contribute to the nation's future. Hot combination numbers: 3 and 6.

Wednesday, July 23 (Moon in Pisces)   Fine aspects exist for beginning your summer vacation. Travel gets bright green lights, and there is plenty of excitement and a fabulous sense of adventure represented in your horoscope. Leo and Aries figure prominently. Each member of your family will have their own ideas about a trip. Primrose is your color. Lucky lottery: 5, 14, 23, 32, 41, 50.

Thursday, July 24 (Moon in Pisces to Aries 5:03 a.m.)   Aries has interesting suggestions. You feel good about yourself and about your love life and your children. You relax and enjoy the company and the scenery. This is the kind of day when you are glad to be alive—it's pleasure all the way. Azure blue is your color; your lucky number is 7.

Friday, July 25 (Moon in Aries)   Be daring in love, romance, courtship, and your quests for adventure. At home or on the road, you want to feel part of everything that is going on. How the strangers love it when you toss them your big smile! You are exceptionally good at inspiring and encouraging children. White is your color; your lucky number is 9.

Saturday, July 26 (Moon in Aries to Taurus 7:53 a.m.)   It's a good day for health maintenance, reading about herbal medicines through the ages, activating a new exercise program or just walking about, and breathing in the fresh air. The chores you undertake today seem to be different than usual. Lucky lottery: 2, 11, 20, 29, 38, 47.

Sunday, July 27 (Moon in Taurus)   Something you see, read about, or hear today can be used in your career and professional work. You may stumble across some good financial and business advice. The day has many saving graces and gives off a vibratory power that will serve you the rest of the month. Your lucky number is 4.

Monday, July 28 (Moon in Taurus to Gemini 1:04 p.m.)   Taurus and Capricorn give a special stability to the day. You control your time and your money effectively, making healthful contributions to your longevity. You are building up pleasant memories of summer for those long cold winter evenings ahead. Turquoise is your color; your number is 8.

Tuesday, July 29 (Moon in Gemini)   There is a strongly competitive dimension to the day. Acting in concert with your mate or business partner may be required for best results. Going it alone can see you get off on tangents. Discussions prior to decisions should be

189

your rule of thumb. Fuchsia is your color. Hot combination numbers: 1 and 4.

Wednesday, July 30 (Moon in Gemini to Cancer 8:38 p.m.)   Gemini has the instructions and suggestions, but you might prefer to make up your own mind. Even so, there's a strong sense of unity every now and then and you do well to involve yourself in multiple interests. You can stretch this day to suit yourself. Your color is buff. Lucky lottery: 3, 12, 21, 30, 39, 48.

Thursday, July 31 (Moon in Cancer)   You tend to extract what you learned this past month from all other happenings. You excel in saving ideas as well as things. You can increase your sense of security today and some of your effort will rub off on others in your household. It's a good day for bargain hunting and experiencing small savings that can build up your nest egg. Your lucky number is 5.

AUGUST 1997

Friday, August 1 (Moon in Cancer)   Review anticipated expenses as this month gets under way. Changes, improvements, and corrections can be taken in stride if you consider your Sagittarius strengths. You could hear some unusual news about the future potential of your career and allied matters. Cherry is your color; your lucky number is 4.

Saturday, August 2 (Moon in Cancer to Leo 6:27 a.m.)   Let Leo lead. You'll do well today if you look ahead and work on long-range and long-distance projects. There is good illumination of travel plans and of ways to convince others to accompany you to a place where you've been happy in the past. Lucky lottery: 6, 15, 24, 33, 42, 50.

Sunday, August 3 (Moon in Leo)   Today's new moon illuminates the future, what you have perking for your-

190

self at a distance, and the rises and falls in the stock market this month. Travel plans can be honed and sculptured. What you should be buying and not buying is in strong focus. Your lucky colors are indigo and taupe; your lucky number is 8.

Monday, August 4 (Moon in Leo to Virgo 6:15 p.m.)   Travel, keep on the go, recycle in memory a trip you took several years ago. Write letters to friends you met while traveling. Relatives at a distance may be thinking about you, for there is a strong mental telepathy trend to the day. Your lucky number is 3.

Tuesday, August 5 (Moon in Virgo)   You have strong support in career, professional, and authority matters and can gain and profit from discussions with employers and supervisors. Virgo and Capricorn have key roles. You have to do some pitch-hitting on the job for a coworker who is not present. Cinnamon is your color; your lucky number is 5.

Wednesday, August 6 (Moon in Virgo)   Push career opportunities and cash in on any preference, special advantages, and longevity you may have chalked up earlier. Your diplomatic and gracious ways most likely have endeared themselves to those with whom you do business and these will run interference for you. Fuchsia is your color. Lucky lottery: 7, 16, 25, 34, 43, 3.

Thursday, August 7 (Moon in Virgo to Libra 7:17 a.m.) Libra brings balance and a good sense of proportion to the day. You allocate your leisure time well under prevailing aspects—there's work and play, business talks, and friendly exchanges. Group activities are also represented. Your winning colors are emerald and aquamarine. Hot combination numbers: 9 and 6.

Friday, August 8 (Moon in Libra)   Your social agenda is lengthy. Gemini and Aquarius will be interested in what you have to say as you elaborate on some of your social plans. Friendships, chats with kindred spirits, and applications for special financial stipends connected with charitable or humanitarian work are favored. Your lucky number is 2.

Saturday, August 9 (Moon in Libra to Scorpio 7:50 p.m.)   Kick work aside and spend the day socializing, enjoying people, moving about, and appreciating the summer scenes. Dining out is pleasurable and late afternoon get-togethers can increase the sense of approval and appreciation that comes to you from many directions. Pastels are your colors. Lucky lottery: 4, 13, 22, 31, 40, 49.

Sunday, August 10 (Moon in Scorpio)   Write reports, checks, and summaries of work recently done. You can get a good view of the way the month has been going and draw some conclusions as to what you can expect over the next several weeks. Today is fine for writing both business and friendly letters. White and off-white are your colors; your number is 6.

Monday, August 11 (Moon in Scorpio)   Today is fine for finishing work, getting presentations ready for a higher level of approval, and dealing with confidences, and for the subtle and more complex features of your responsibilities. Scorpio and Taurus have important roles. Your winning colors are magenta and ecru; your number is 1.

Tuesday, August 12 (Moon in Scorpio to Sagittarius 5:45 a.m.)   Today, tomorrow, and the next days are part of a power cycle for you. You can accept challenges; rise above obstacles; and, with a great deal of self-confidence, make strong, lasting, and immediately winning impressions. The benefits come rolling in. Indigo is your color. Hot combination numbers: 3 and 9.

Wednesday, August 13 (Moon in Sagittarius)   Air your aspirations and ambitions; let others know that you intend to capture the rainbow, the dream, the well-fortified castle. Speak up in your own behalf. Dress appropriately so that you give off the aura of success and leadership. Reddish-purple and cerulean blue are your colors. Lucky lottery: 5, 14, 23, 32, 41, 50.

Thursday, August 14 (Moon in Sagittarius to Capricorn 11:42 a.m.)   Self-confidence and self-reliance are your armor and weapons, and another Sagittarius and a Leo are in your corner. Your employer and supervisor are seeing you as a promising worker from whom much can be expected. You'll be lucky today, when your optimism and positive thinking pay off. Your number is 7.

Friday, August 15 (Moon in Capricorn)   Now you can collect money, get what is due you, and hear some good news about your salary potential. Pay attention to your hairstyle, favoring that wholesome look that your ruling orb Jupiter prefers. Be enthusiastic, loving, and quick to compliment and do favors. Coral is your color; your number is 9.

Saturday, August 16 (Moon in Capricorn to Aquarius 1:58 p.m.)   Capricorn brings approval and good news. If money is a problem, now is the time to shop around for a second job to get you over the rest of this month. With financial Jupiter in your third house, the job is not far away, and it may be connected with a travel office, school, or neighborhood park. Lucky lottery: 2, 11, 20, 29, 38, 47.

Sunday, August 17 (Moon in Aquarius)   Local, immediate, pressing, and everyday routines are favored. Neighbors, siblings, and Aquarians are in the picture. You can gain via your learning processes. Read up on the many new high-tech devices that could be mastered by people like you. Then sign up for a course at your local college. Your lucky number is 4.

Monday, August 18 (Moon in Aquarius to Pisces 2:01 p.m.)   Today's full moon illuminates your local scene. There is lunar enlightenment for you in communications, transportation, studies, hobbies, and the easier way to get information out to those who are waiting for it. You can capture the attention of someone who earlier seemed to ignore you. Your number is 8.

Tuesday, August 19 (Moon in Pisces)　Career demands are slowing down for the moment. Family requirements and property-ownership interests can fill the vacuum. Some decisions have to be made regarding the education of dependents. Also, this is the time to schedule minor surgery for kids on vacation from school. Beige is your color; your number is 1.

Wednesday, August 20 (Moon in Pisces to Aries 1:45 p.m.)　Pisces exerts a subtle and hard-to-define influence on your day. Domestic and residential interests are looking to you for solutions and explanations. You may question the advantage of summer vacations for children and parents. Don't argue with neighbors over family, pets, or fences. Carmine red is your color. Lucky lottery: 3, 12, 21, 30, 39, 48.

Thursday, August 21 (Moon in Aries)　Today is perfect for making love, enjoying the romance of the season and the August scene. Parties and entertainment are well within your scope. You can break through any shell a difficult child has placed about himself or herself. At the end of the day, you will feel in the pink. Brown and blue are your colors. Hot combination numbers: 5 and 2.

Friday, August 22 (Moon in Aries to Taurus 2:57 p.m.)　Aries can shake you out of any possible rut. You enjoy quality time with your beloved and children. Be spontaneous in your invitations for best results. You can help many people enjoy themselves. Cookouts, lounging in a torchlit patio, and dining late are represented. Your number is 7.

Saturday, August 23 (Moon in Taurus)　It's an earthy day, with Virgo and Taurus and the things they rule in sharp focus. Attending to the grounds of your home, landscaping, visiting coworkers, or inviting them over to your home are all within your scope today. You can come through to others as practical and self-disciplined. Canary and white are your colors. Lucky lottery: 9, 18, 27, 36, 45, 6.

Sunday, August 24 (Moon in Taurus to Gemini 6:56 p.m.) Relax in the sunshine with a few magazines or a good book—a veranda glider comes to mind when one considers the aspects as they pertain to Sagittarius. Simple meals are in order with a scrumptious desert this evening. Phone, keeping in touch with any coworker who is in trouble. Your number is 2.

Monday, August 25 (Moon in Gemini) Your personality will blend well with that of your beloved under these aspects. The conversation is exciting, dramatic, and at times mercurial, with Gemini very much on the scene. Marriage, other partnerships, and the fine art of sharing are all in the bigger picture. Mauve and lilac are your colors; your number is 6.

Tuesday, August 26 (Moon in Gemini) It's an airy day and the conversation can go ultra-intellectual. People want substantiating evidence of the opinions you present. Getting together with a campus roommate or long-ago fellow student could meet many of the trends of this day. You are looking back in pleasure. Hot combination numbers: 8 and 2.

Wednesday, August 27 (Moon in Gemini to Cancer 4:11 a.m.) Good trends exist in beach and water activities. A Cancer and a Pisces are on the scene. Give children a special treat as their vacations come to a close—a boat trip is an ideal way of saying adieu to the July—August cycle. Phone parents and other senior citizens who are probably thinking about you. Lucky lottery numbers: 1, 10, 19, 28, 37, 46.

Thursday, August 28 (Moon in Cancer) It's another good day for enjoying the beach, an amusement park, games of chance, and a brief relief from employment

195

situations. You are in a very giving mood, at your enthusiastic and optimistic best. All around you are people who would like to know you better. You invest your time well. Violet is your color. Hot combination numbers: 3 and 6.

Friday, August 29 (Moon in Cancer to Leo 12:19 p.m.)   Today is excellent for increasing your sense of security, and fine for inaugurating changes in your life and career. You know instinctively what you should be doing; it's all a matter of showing the clout and pluck to bring these improvements about. Increase savings and push wiser investments. Flame is your color; your number is 5.

Saturday, August 30 (Moon in Leo)   It would be a goods idea to claim these last days of August for yourself. A short trip, a grand return, capturing the sense of vacation by leaving it all behind temporarily are all part of this good picture. Leo and Aries can be in on your plans and secrets. Lucky lottery: 7, 16, 25, 34, 43, 3.

Sunday, August 31 (Moon in Leo)   Enjoy the scene and the sense of being free from all the ties that bind. Take summer's grand finale with a sense of personal freedom and the ability to, now and then, do what you want to do. Expand your thinking, invite the sunshine, enjoy beach and water activities. Tawny is your color; your number is 9.

SEPTEMBER 1997

Monday, September 1 (Moon in Leo to Virgo 12:27 a.m.)   The new moon is born in your tenth house and illuminates career, professional, and authority matters. You can make excellent decisions about employment matters now. There are ways to impress those in power which occur to you now. Your lucky number is 1.

196

Tuesday, September 2 (Moon in Virgo)   Virgo and Capricorn figure prominently in the day's events. You make marked progress in your career. All your talent will be visible to those who are interested in you and your work. A discussion with a supervisor or employer augurs well. Crimson is your color; your number is 3.

Wednesday, September 3 (Moon in Virgo to Libra 1:30 p.m.)   You may find Taurus your ideal assistant under today's aspects. The earthy qualities of coworkers can appeal strongly to you. Still, you shy away from some of the possessive tactics of these folk. Your colors are claret and orchid. Lucky lottery: 5, 14, 23, 32, 41, 50.

Thursday, September 4 (Moon in Libra)   Libra brings a sense of balance and rightness to the day. Friendships offer you peace of mind and a sense of participation in life. Group activities are more and more to your liking as the day moves along. Married people are better for socializing this evening. Hot combination numbers: 7 and 3.

Friday, September 5 (Moon in Libra)   Goods trends exist for enjoying group activities and for serving the social side of your job. Supervisors and coworkers should be encouraged to talk to one another once in a while. Your employer will appreciate your special tact and diplomacy. Azure blue is your color. Hot combination numbers: 9 and 6.

Saturday, September 6 (Moon in Libra to Scorpio 2:10 a.m.)   Scorpio and Virgo have key roles. Fine aspects exist for finishing odd jobs around your home and place of business; yard work especially is awaiting your pleasure. There is debris to be cleared away and shrubbery requiring special attention. Consider buying appliances to help with these chores. Lucky lottery: 2, 11, 20, 29, 38, 47.

Sunday, September 7 (Moon in Scorpio)   As fall approaches, you may want to move some furniture around your living room and dining rooms. If drapes and rugs have been away at the cleaners, schedule their return by phone calls. Pisces and a Cancer have good ideas for creating the impression of more space. Your lucky number is 4.

Monday, September 8 (Moon in Scorpio to Sagittarius 12:54 p.m.)   Your employer and supervisors may wish you would do more straightening up around your working place. Coworkers may wish you would help them understand orders and suggestions connected with the work. A Taurus may be overly possessive of real and imaginary rights. Your number is 8.

Tuesday, September 9 (Moon in Sagittarius)   In many ways the month is really getting started. You come into your own now that you are in your lunar-cycle high. The world is conscious of your presence; all the more so when you seize the initiative and stand out in front of others. Your increase in self-confidence makes you a force to be reckoned with. Hot combination numbers: 1 and 7.

Wednesday, September 10 (Moon in Sagittarius to Capricorn 8:23 p.m.)   Career interests gather momentum; you can make extraordinary contributions to your professional future. Another Sagittarius and Leo figure prominently. Self-confidence pays off now and others will follow your directions. The mantle of the leader rests lightly on your strong shoulders. Orchid and lilac are your colors. Lucky lottery: 3, 12, 21, 30, 39, 48.

Thursday, September 11 (Moon in Capricorn)   Capricorn and Virgo are involved in your improved lifestyle. There's money to be claimed, won, and earned. This is a good day for familiarizing yourself with the newer services being offered by your bank and brokerage firm. Ask the right questions and your fund of knowledge will be increased. Your lucky number is 5.

Friday, September 12 (Moon in Capricorn)   Venus, newly arrived in your twelfth house, brings special strengths from reminiscences and memories of lovemaking, and also from the truth that you are loved most where past, present, and future come together. Financial security and wealth production are assured. Ruby and burgundy are winning colors; your lucky number is 7.

Saturday, September 13 (Moon in Capricorn to Aquarius 12:10 a.m.)   There are good aspects for handling everyday matters, and for the insignificant, usual, and familiar routines and schedules. Studies, hobbies come in for their share of your time. Communications and transportation matters are strongly supported. Winning colors are titian gold and reddish-orange. Lucky lottery: 9, 18, 27, 36, 45, 6.

Sunday, September 14 (Moon in Aquarius)   Aquarius and Gemini have key roles. Today's accent falls on communications with members of your family, with a strong trend of honesty involved in these personal exchanges. Today is fine for your learning processes, and for helping youngsters with their school work. Your color is lapis; your lucky number is 2.

Monday, September 15 (Moon in Aquarius to Pisces 12:59 a.m.)   Give your best shot to a family situation you may have been ignoring. Real estate values are fluctuating again. The accent falls on your community and residence, and on efforts to keep your family values stabilized. Violet and aquamarine are your colors; your lucky number is 6.

Tuesday, September 16 (Moon in Pisces)   The full moon illuminates family interests as well as any possible deterioration in property you own, and it can help you make decisions about selling or buying property. The opinions of older and younger relatives make a strong impression on you. Turquoise is your color. Hot combination numbers: 8 and 1.

Wednesday, September 17 (Moon in Pisces to Aries 12:25 a.m.)   Your love department is strongly stimulated. Romantic prologues and epilogues will make your world all the lighter and brighter. Courtship takes great leaps forward toward the wedding license bureau. Aries gives your lovemaking a spirit of rare adventure—spontaneity becomes you. Lucky lottery: 1, 10, 19, 28, 37, 46.

Thursday, September 18 (Moon in Aries) This is one of those quality-time days when you should bond more closely with your beloved, for courtesy and kindness are friends to sexual ecstasy. Leo and another Sagittarius will have much to say under the right circumstances. Your colors are mauve and blue; your lucky number is 3.

Friday, September 19 (Moon in Aries to Taurus 12:21 a.m.) Let Taurus in on your plans, and on the changes, improvements, and corrections you hope to bring about in health and in work. You could encounter unhappiness in a supervisor or coworker and feel that you should be doing more to help. Rest and relaxation make their contribution to longevity. Your lucky number is 5.

Saturday, September 20 (Moon in Taurus) There's a lot of work to be done around your residence and the grounds of your home. Be sure you have the proper tools and appliances to make everything go more quickly. A Virgo can be helpful in explaining the simpler methods. Wear plaid today. Lucky lottery: 7, 16, 25, 34, 43, 3.

Sunday, September 21 (Moon in Taurus to Gemini 2:38 a.m.) Try to keep a sense of proportion and balance to make this day pay off. Equality, sharing, and cooperating are the top trends. Gemini-ruled communications can help partnerships make progress, including the partnership of marriage and/or long-term emotional relationships. Your lucky number is 9.

Monday, September 22 (Moon in Gemini) Give your partners the benefit of every doubt, even when they seem to be difficult and irritable. You may have the feeling that you are being tugged in the wrong direction, for the person in question can come up with some very convincing arguments. Libra is in the picture. Violet is your color, your number is 4.

Tuesday, September 23 (Moon in Gemini to Cancer 8:33 a.m.)   Do what you can to help a partner without delivering your head on a saucer. Give a little in order to gain much more. Aquarius is in the picture. Marriage prospers where you and your spouse are good friends. Do what you can to improve relationships with in-laws. Yellows and orangy reds are your colors. Hot combination numbers: 6 and 1.

Wednesday, September 24 (Moon in Cancer)   Good trends exist in security matters, and in making changes that improve and correct situations related to savings and investments. Review tax shelters, insurance, bequests, and inheritances. All accumulations—money, time, and energies—are part of this progressive picture. Lucky lottery: 8, 17, 26, 35, 44, 1.

Thursday, September 25 (Moon in Cancer to Leo 6:12 p.m.)   Water signs and the interests they rule are front and center. A Cancer, Scorpio, and Pisces are represented in your chart. It's a good day for security matters; for finishing projects that should not extend into October; and for handling domestic, residential, property, and ownership matters. Your lucky number is 1.

Friday, September 26 (Moon in Leo)   You're wide awake, alert, ready to spring into positive action. You want to keep on the move today and travel gets green lights. You look ahead rather than into the past. You can master some of the new appliances and systems related to the information highway. Leo and Aries get top billing. Champagne is your color; your number is 3.

Saturday, September 27 (Moon in Leo)   Keep on the go, move about, get your exercise, and don't slip into any rut. What you have going for yourself at a distance is about to pay off. It's not enough to be in the present today; you have to place your thinking and some of your doing in the future. Ecru is right for you. Lucky lottery: 5, 14, 23, 32, 41, 50.

Sunday, September 28 (Moon in Leo to Virgo 6:27 a.m.) Push your career interests, planning the work you will be responsible for during the week ahead. Virgo and Capricorn can keep you in a practical mode. Your self-discipline, patience, and perseverance will pay handsome dividends. Hard work can be mastered better when you're alone and away from distractions. Your lucky number is 7.

Monday, September 29 (Moon in Virgo) Excellent aspects exist in all career matters, and in the use of logic, self-discipline, and method. You can impress those in power by the sheer effort you put into your work. Virgo is in your corner and can help you work well beyond par. Your lucky color is amber; your lucky number is 2.

Tuesday, September 30 (Moon in Virgo to Libra 7:32 p.m.) As the month ends, you can advance in your career, professional, and authority matters. Where you apply your knowledge, you are going to stand taller than most and capture the attention of those who are in a position to promote you. Spread goodwill now. Be charming and work oriented. Your color is wheat; your number is 4.

OCTOBER 1997

Wednesday, October 1 (Moon in Libra) The new moon illuminates friendships, group activities, and the social side of your job. Libra and Aquarius have key roles. Kindred spirits can bring inspiration as well as encouragement and, as a result, you feel wonderful about the month ahead. Your lucky color is claret. Lucky lottery: 4, 13, 22, 31, 40, 49.

Thursday, October 2 (Moon in Libra)   Party, entertain, enjoy being the center of attention. Good friends show the approval, appreciation, and affection that can put you on success street. You warm up to this time of the year and enjoy October's bright blue weather. Yellow and blues are in; your lucky number is 6.

Friday, October 3 (Moon in Libra to Scorpio 7:57 a.m.)
Scorpio will help you bring projects to a successful conclusion. The secret sensations of your soul have their day, as you are interested in prophecies, mysteries, and the esoteric things of life. Read about these paranormal subjects and you will know a greater peace of mind. Dove gray is your color; your number is 8.

Saturday, October 4 (Moon in Scorpio)   Complete tasks that you want out of the way soon. Finish, file away, deal in epilogues, close out no-win involvements, and be prepared for a cycle of challenges and opportunities. A Cancer and a Pisces can be helpful if you are being pinned down to decisions. Lucky lottery: 1, 10, 19, 28, 37, 46.

Sunday, October 5 (Moon in Scorpio to Sagittarius 6:43 p.m.)   You have a power period coming up and today is ideal for preparing for it. Know which job you are going to tackle tomorrow. Gather information, records, and other assistance you may require to do a first-class job. Complete what you want to get out of the way. Pale and deep greens are your colors; your lucky number is 3.

Monday, October 6 (Moon in Sagittarius)   Pounce on the chores you want to accomplish today, seizing and holding the initiative in bigger projects. Lead, demonstrating the highest in self-confidence and self-reliance. Air your aspirations and ambitions so that others know you mean business. Be positive and optimistic. Your fortunate number is 7.

Tuesday, October 7 (Moon in Sagittarius)   Sagittarius-ruled strengths help greatly in your march to triumph and victories today. Be informed; know your facts; and be diplomatic, tactful, and enthusiastic. Picture yourself wearing the laurel wreath of victory, and the profits and gains you seek will come to you. Hot combination numbers: 9 and 6.

Wednesday, October 8 (Moon in Sagittarius to Capricorn 3:04 a.m.)   A Capricorn and another Sagittarius have key roles. You can elevate your earning power under the prevailing aspects. You gain much from sticking to the job until it is finished—perseverance will be your greatest strength under these aspects. Creamy white is your color. Lucky lottery: 2, 11, 20, 29, 38, 47.

Thursday, October 9 (Moon in Capricorn)   Another big money day is at hand. To save a little is to earn more. Though you can't attain the level of pay you want, wait until the end of the year, when you'll have more luck. It's the little ways, the little savings that count most at this time. Cherry is your color; your lucky number is 4.

Friday, October 10 (Moon in Capricorn to Aquarius 8:29 a.m.)   Today is favorable for special sales, and for ridding the premises of clutter. Advertise your wares in local newspapers, shoppers' guides, and so on. Wardrobe items you are tired of will attract the eyes of a Gemini, Libra, and Aquarius. Buy remnants for little and sell them for more. Your number is 6.

Saturday, October 11 (Moon in Aquarius)   Aquarius and Leo have key roles. You narrow your sights to solve any possible pressing problem. You zero in on situations and conditions that are pattern made for your attention. Today is excellent for finding the pertinent answers right under your nose. Emerald is your color. Lucky lottery: 8, 17, 26, 35, 44, 2.

Sunday, October 12 (Moon in Aquarius to Pisces 10:59 a.m.)   Take care of the little, insignificant, minor details on a day when you excel in seeing the trees as well

as the forest surrounding them. You know what to do
and it would be well not to let others talk you out of it.
Gemini may see only the big picture. You pinpoint now.
Your number is 1.

Monday, October 13 (Moon in Pisces)   Pisces takes
over under these trends. You may feel hemmed in by
family, residence, property, ownership, or community.
The day is full of traps if you begin anything haphaz-
ardly. There are times when you feel you have too many
irons in too many fires, but if you stop and organize
your time, things will get done well. Your number is 5.

*Tuesday, October 14 (Moon in Pisces to Aries 11:25
a.m.)*   This is an excellent day for dealing with family
situations, and it's fine for winning cooperation from
younger relatives so that a family problem might be
solved. Things aren't out in the open today—people are
secretive or unwilling to talk about personal affairs.
Your own contemporaries are the culprits. Your lucky
number is 7.

Wednesday, October 15 (Moon in Aries)   Now you
can bounce back and get all the cooperation you need.
You are approved and appreciated; you're on the receiving end of a great deal of affection. Spontaneity in social
arrangements will do well. Children are loving and con-
siderate. This is a fine day for giving a party to entertain
many. Lucky lottery: 9, 18, 27, 36, 45, 3.

*Thursday, October 16 (Moon in Aries to Taurus 11:16
a.m.)*   The full moon illuminates both your love life
and your social agenda. There is enlightenment for you
in bonding more closely with loved ones, for successfully
handling an in-law situation, or for proving to the friends
of your beloved that you are the right one. Your colors
are plum and canary. Hot combination numbers: 2 and 4.

Friday, October 17 (Moon in Taurus)   It's a day for
watching your health, staying out of drafts, and eating
properly in establishments you can trust. Sanitation and

hygiene are suffering more now than in a long time. The work you have to perform can seem particularly boring, and fatigue can overtake you. Gray is your color; your number is 4.

Saturday, October 18 (Moon in Taurus to Gemini 12:26 p.m.)   Taurus and Scorpio figure in the day's script. If you are at all under the weather—or even merely slothful—give yourself a break for best results in health and labor. You can catch up later on and the day may just not be your time to conquer. A TV movie, videotape, or a good mystery novel are better for you. Lucky lottery: 6, 15, 24, 33, 42, 51.

Sunday, October 19 (Moon in Gemini)   Gemini enters talking and delivers some pep to you. Jobs can be cut in half for this is a great day for sharing the responsibilities. Also, air signs (Gemini, Libra, and Aquarius) can make tiresome projects more interesting and somehow easier. So take advantage of all assistance. Silver is your color; your number is 8.

Monday, October 20 (Moon in Gemini to Cancer 4:45 p.m.)   You can finish projects that have been neglected, postponed, or otherwise delayed. Scorpio and Taurus have key roles. Keep on top of chores. Help youngsters organize a harvest festival. The smoky woods appeal to you strongly at this time. Your winning color is wheat; your lucky number is 3.

Tuesday, October 21 (Moon in Cancer)   Fine trends exist in savings, investments, and discussions with your broker. The gambling dimension to investments at this time appeals to you. Schools, business institutions, travel businesses, bookstores, casinos, and magazines are all good investments for you while your ruling orb is in Sagittarius. Wear plaid. Your lucky number is 5.

Wednesday, October 22 (Moon in Cancer)   Listen to what a Pisces and a Cancer are telling you. Today is fine for handling accumulations of money, energies, and leisure time, and it's an excellent day for inaugurating changes, improvements, and corrections you have been entertaining in the back of your mind. Your winning colors are magenta and indigo. Lucky lottery: 7, 16, 25, 24, 43, 3.

Thursday, October 23 (Moon in Cancer to Leo 1:10 a.m.) Scorpio- and Leo-ruled interests prevail. Travel; return to places where you have been happy in the past; and the free flow of information and long-range and long-distance matters are all featured. You feel lucky today—preferred and on top of things, with an enormous perspective and scope. Your lucky number is 9.

Friday, October 24 (Moon in Leo)   Travel, keep on the go, expand your thinking, and take in the bigger picture. No limitations, restraints, or major obstacles dog this wonderful cycle. Push highly personalized interests, wherever they take you. You cash in on your special character assets. Hot combination numbers: 2 and 6.

Saturday, October 25 (Moon in Leo to Virgo 12:59 p.m.)   This is one weekend you should spend visiting a kindred spirit a distance beyond your usual weekend trek. Get into the country, taking in the clear, blue October weather. Relax as you do so well with one of those friends beyond mere friendship. Let your hair down and confide. Bright blue is your color. Lucky lottery: 4, 13, 22, 31, 40, 49.

Sunday, October 26—Standard Time (Moon in Virgo)   There is a trend of practicality in your conversation and actions today. What pays off now is your acceptance of duties, responsibilities, and obligations, as well as your self-discipline, restraint, and persistence. Virgo and Taurus have key roles. The more you think about your career now, the better the week ahead will go for you. Your lucky number is 6.

Monday, October 27 (Moon in Virgo)   Stick to the subject being discussed, focusing your attention on the target your employer has in mind. You can handle all delegated authority wisely now and make a favorable impression on executives. Some will find it difficult to get back into the saddle after a big weekend, so be sure to make allowances for them. Your number is 1.

Tuesday, October 28 (Moon in Virgo to Libra 1:05 a.m.) Friends are in your corner and very much on your side of any altercation or misunderstanding. Group activities, the social side of your job, and church and social club membership and participation are all represented in your chart. Your winning colors are pumpkin and melon. Hot combination numbers: 3 and 9.

Wednesday, October 29 (Moon in Libra) Wonderful trends exist in friendship; spending time with kindred spirits; and enjoying a sense of approval, appreciation and affection. Gemini and Aquarius have dual roles in extracting the best in effort, creativity, and imagination from you. Your winning color is aquamarine. Lucky lottery: 5, 14, 23, 32, 41, 50.

Thursday, October 30 (Moon in Libra to Scorpio 1:15 p.m.) Positive thinking will work wonders for you today, along with enthusiasm for the ideas and projects of your friends. Be jovial in the best Jupiterian sense and ferret out those opportunities and advantages that will help you get the most out of this day. Your winning color is yellow; your number is 7.

Friday, October 31 (Moon in Scorpio) The new moon is born in your twelfth house and illuminates the darker places of the mind, leaving nothing foggy or mysterious. You understand and appreciate the invisible, the sacred, and the spiritual. You feel very much in control of your own past and able to let it serve present and future. Your number is 9.

Saturday, November 1 (Moon in Scorpio to Sagittarius 11:27 p.m.) Move everything along in an orderly way. Prepare for the approach of colder weather. Put up storm doors and windows, get shrubbery ready for frost, and clear away summer's debris to work on garage and basement. Your winning colors are blue and pumpkin. Scorpio and Taurus are helpful. Lucky lottery: 8, 17, 26, 35, 44, 1.

Sunday, November 2 (Moon in Sagittarius) Push personal strengths and personality assets to get what you want. You are in your lunar-cycle high and can hold the initiative and the lead. Excellent trends exist in studies, learning new rules and new methods, and making decisions that can improve your financial life. Your lucky number is 1.

Monday, November 3 (Moon in Sagittarius) Complete, file away, draw conclusions, and present work for approval. What is transpiring behind the scenes can impact the outcome of the day so, investigate, evaluate, and estimate for best results. Another Sagittarius and a Gemini have key roles. Prepare for important actions. Your lucky number is 5.

Tuesday, November 4 (Moon in Sagittarius to Capricorn 7:31 a.m.) Air your aspirations and ambitions so that others will take you seriously. Accent the personal and the individualistic, and make sure you are able to see yourself as others perceive you. Leo and Aries will make their contributions. The evening and its activities play into your hands. Hot combination numbers: 7 and 3.

Wednesday, November 5 (Moon in Capricorn) There's money and more money, as you warm up to the sense of gain, profit, and financial power that comes with the Venus ingress of Capricorn. There is enlightenment as to how you can keep this productive trend continuing.

Violet and beige are your colors. Lucky lottery: 9, 18, 27, 36, 45, 6.

Thursday, November 6 (Moon in Capricorn to Aquarius 1:33 p.m.)   Today is fine for locating a new source of income, as your earning power rises and the future looks pretty. Positive trends exist for funding special projects without government subsidies or interference. Taurus and Virgo are on your side. Your lucky colors are auburn and canary. Hot combination numbers: 2 and 4.

Friday, November 7 (Moon in Aquarius)   Aquarius and Leo have key roles. You make progress in the usual, familiar, everyday tasks and chores of life. Hobbies and studies are strongly supported by the dominant aspects. You communicate effectively and will enjoy short-distance travel. Siblings and neighbors have their own axes to grind. Your lucky number is 4.

Saturday, November 8 (Moon in Aquarius to Pisces 5:35 p.m.)   All personal interests are speeded up by Mercury, as usual routines and established schedules work out better. Too much time could be wasted trying to make some assignment more interesting. Extra effort can lead to overproduction. Yellow and forest green are your colors. Lucky lottery: 6, 15, 24, 33, 42, 51.

Sunday, November 9 (Moon in Pisces)   In a relaxed atmosphere, talks with loved ones can produce a strong consensus. Property and ownership interests are represented in the day's chart. Pisces and a Cancer have front seats. Nothing is wasted today, and there is a strong spiritual dimension to the evening. Purple is your color; your lucky number is 8.

Monday, November 10 (Moon in Pisces to Aries 7:44 p.m.)   In this society, where people often isolate themselves from other couch potatoes, zero in on what your loved ones are thinking. There is power for bringing children out of themselves and encouraging older people to speak up about their worries and anxieties. Your lucky number is 3.

Tuesday, November 11 (Moon in Aries)   Aries assures and reassures you, as aspects favor expressions of love and concern. Spontaneity in socializing will go well. Offspring may want a larger part of your attention. What is taking place in the schools your children attend may not be known by you. Start prying and probing. Burgundy is your color; your number is 5.

Wednesday, November 12 (Moon in Aries to Taurus 8:45 p.m.)   Parties and entertainment will do well under existing aspects. Make love and reassure older lonely relatives that you are available to them. Social involvements may be going up in cost and some economizing may be a necessary so that these aren't winnowed out completely. Lucky lottery: 7, 16, 25, 34, 43, 3.

Thursday, November 13 (Moon in Taurus)   Watch your health and remain alert to all discussions and print stories about amazing advances in medicine and nutrition matters. Any possible change in the weather now could contribute to the spread of virus-type ailments. Mother Nature is fooling people. Emerald is your color. Hot combination numbers: 9 and 6.

Friday, November 14 (Moon in Taurus to Gemini 10:05 p.m.)   Taurus accents the truth that overall physical well-being is the most valuable possession. Fine trends exist for discussions with your physician. The health of coworkers can be a topic of conversation, as tardiness and absenteeism increases. Fatigue can come early. Pumpkin is your color; your number is 2.

Saturday, November 15 (Moon in Gemini)   Gemini upholds equality between the sexes. Partnerships may be under review also. The need to share more willingly is a lesson to be taught the very young. Cooperative effort in money and other security matters can work wonders. Lucky lottery: 4, 13, 22, 31, 40, 49.

Sunday, November 16 (Moon in Gemini)   Your mar-ital state, sharing, unity, and unification of ideas are all topping your agenda. In-laws are in the shadows, as are some questionable friends of your mate. Know how to curtail unnecessary criticism when a quarrel is getting too vocal and provocative. Russet is your color; your number is 6.

Monday, November 17 (Moon in Gemini to Cancer 1:32 a.m.)   Today is excellent for improving your house-hold and auto security. Is it time to change ancient locks with more up-to-date versions? If you leave garage doors open all day, don't complain when your garden imple-ments, ladder, and wheelbarrow are stolen. More than ever, this is the time for resolving not to invite thievery. Pinecone is your color; your lucky number is 1.

Tuesday, November 18 (Moon in Cancer)   A Cancer and Scorpio are center stage. Good aspects exist for bringing about changes, improvements, and corrections in your life. Self-criticism and self-analysis are strongly supported. Also, savings may be increased under these trends and investments can be made wiser. Your number is 3.

Wednesday, November 19 (Moon in Cancer to Leo 8:38 a.m.)   Talks with your banker and broker may be in order. There can be some surprising economic instability coming into view this month and today permits you to come to a greater understanding of overall trends. Re-budget, curtail expenses, and consult a Taurus. Lucky lottery: 5, 14, 23, 32, 41, 50.

Thursday, November 20 (Moon in Leo)   The yen to get away for a while can be strong. If you can't make tracks, then recycle in your memory some of the high-points of last summer's vacation. Long-range and long-distance matters will show up better than the immediate and/or pressing. Leo and another Sagittarius are helpful. Your number is 7.

Friday, November 21 (Moon in Leo to Virgo 7:33 p.m.)   Today is excellent for pace and momentum. You cover a lot of territory and get many boring tasks out of the way. You also can give quality time to one important project that is more futuristic than immediate. Find the person who knows the most about your subject and enjoy a good idea exchange. Chestnut is your color. Hot combination numbers: 9 and 3.

Saturday, November 22 (Moon in Virgo)   Things are more settled now and you gain from conversation and preservation. Avoid extreme ideas and people—Horace's "Golden Mean of Moderation" is the best way. Virgo takes the lead in self-discipline, practicality, and realism. Determination and persistence mark the day. Lucky lottery: 2, 11, 20, 29, 38, 47.

Sunday, November 23 (Moon in Virgo)   It's a fine day for considering some career moves you want to make during the week ahead. Professional, authority, prestige, and status matters are favored. Gather all your wits and ideas together to put on the table tomorrow. Your winning colors are gold and black; your number is 4.

Monday, November 24 (Moon in Virgo to Libra 8:29 a.m.)   Excellent trends exist for raising your economic and social status at the same time. Encourage younger loved ones to avoid virulent demonstration tactics, for true gains come to people who reason, discuss peacefully, and practice respect for each other's opinions and problems. Your lucky number is 8.

Tuesday, November 25 (Moon in Libra)   Spread goodwill, be cheerful, and appreciate your friendships. Socialize and enjoy group activities. The social side of your job, hobbies, and professional membership will do well under prevailing aspects. The air signs (Gemini, Libra, and Aquarius) are center stage. Your number is 1.

Wednesday, November 26 (Moon in Libra to Scorpio 8:43 p.m.)   Approach people in good humor. Justice is a strong dimension of the day. Friendship with your mate will make your marriage all the more enduring. Goodwill on the work scene is appreciated by your employer, and working toward this will win preferential treatment. Lucky lottery: 3, 12, 21, 30, 39, 48.

Thursday, November 27 (Moon in Scorpio)   Scorpio brings strong psychic awareness to the problem and should be heeded. Minor successes can be transformed into major gains, for if you begin small you still can tackle the truly significant concerns. People whose names you've never heard can be great pillars of stability. It's a big parade, so let's join in. Your number is 5.

Friday, November 28 (Moon in Scorpio)   Today is good for completing projects that don't belong in December. Draw conclusions only when you have all the facts, making allowances for what isn't visible, for the spiritual and the mysterious—all of these are activated with the moon in your twelfth house. Violet and saffron are your colors. Hot combination numbers: 7 and 3.

Saturday, November 29 (Moon in Scorpio to Sagittarius 6:28 a.m.)   The month proceeds at your pleasure, for you are now in your lunar-cycle high and can familiarize yourself with everything that you have going for yourself in experience, educational achievements, and basic intelligence. Put them together. On a day like this, you win big. Lucky lottery: 9, 18, 27, 36, 45, 6.

Sunday, November 30 (Moon in Sagittarius)   The new moon illuminates highly personalized interests, enlightening you in ways to put your personality and character assets to most effective use. These closing days of November belong to you more than to others. Hold the initiative and lead. Your lucky color is turquoise; your lucky number is 2.

Monday, December 1 (Moon in Sagittarius to Capricorn 1:38 p.m.)   You are at an advantage as you begin this month. You are in your lunar-cycle high, when matters tend to work out in your favor. Hold the initiative, make decisions, and lead the big parade from aspiration to realization. Consolidate new gains. Your mind is agile. Wear a little gold; stick with the lucky number 4.

Tuesday, December 2 (Moon in Capricorn)   Figure out approximate costs of the month's holidays and its increased expenses. Make lists, becoming familiar with the current prices of items you want to buy. Budgeting may be more necessary that you believed. You should maintain your current level of earning power and income. Your number is 6.

Wednesday, December 3 (Moon in Capricorn to Aquarius 6:58 p.m.)   Listen to Capricorn and Taurus in financial and business interests. Government policies and new legislation should be understood before you spend money or make any new investments. Know what the current gross national product is. Your lucky colors are beige and russet. Lucky lottery: 8, 17, 26, 35, 44, 1.

Thursday, December 4 (Moon in Aquarius)   Concentrate, taking care of small but still important things. Discuss some of your plans with relatives, neighbors, and an Aquarius. Address holiday greeting cards and test lights for your outdoor decorating. You may feel that a loved one is critical of your plans. Saffron is your color; your lucky number is 1.

Friday, December 5 (Moon in Aquarius to Pisces 11:07 p.m.)   You are in a cheerful mood and can bond well with siblings and neighbors. Excellent trends exist for discussing local plans for the holidays with people you see every day. Involve kids in some of the work that will be done over the next week or so. There are no holiday decorations as memorable as those you create yourself. Reds and greens are your colors; your number is 3.

Saturday, December 6 (Moon in Pisces) House-cleaning and decorating, and decorating the grounds of your home will do well under these aspects. Strong creativity is available to you, all the more so if you invite a Gemini to help you. You'll want to move some furniture around; trust those developing their biceps. Lucky lottery: 5, 14, 23, 32, 41, 50.

Sunday, December 7 (Moon in Pisces) Pisces is of major assistance in domestic, real estate, property, and ownership matters. Today is fine for talks with children about what you expect from them during this busy month. Give some time to addressing greeting cards that must travel a long way. Shopping, with more looking than buying, will go well during late afternoon. Crimson is your color; your lucky number is 7.

Monday, December 8 (Moon in Pisces to Aries 2:24 a.m.) You are up and at responsibilities early this morning. Aries is aboard and has a way of coaxing you out of any possible rut and into vigorous actions. It's an enjoyable day, with good aspects governing your love life and your ability to bond more closely with your children. Your lucky number is 2.

Tuesday, December 9 (Moon in Aries) Make love, party, entertain, and enjoy the season and its beautiful lights. It may be difficult to keep rambunctious and overly eager children in line under these prevailing aspects. There is a lot of joy, delight, fascination, and eagerness represented in your horoscope. Hot combination numbers: 4 and 7.

Wednesday, December 10 (Moon in Aries to Taurus 5 a.m.) There is some possibility of overdoing represented; know when to rest and do a bit of postponing. Watch the health of your busy children and keep in contact with any older relative whose health has been sus-

216

pect. Taurus and Capricorn have key roles. Your winning color is gold. Lucky lottery: 6, 15, 24, 33, 42, 51.

Thursday, December 11 (Moon in Taurus)   Give due attention to all security matters. A change of pattern is indicated. You may feel bored doing things the same old way again and again. Budgeting can be annoying, but it would be wise to continue your war on waste. Look for sales in out-of-the-way places. Hot combination numbers: 8 and 1.

Friday, December 12 (Moon in Taurus to Gemini 7:35 a.m.)   You warm up to the local scene and to good bubbling conversation as Venus moves into Aquarius. Don't be too quick to kick the practical and methodical ways of doing things out of your path. Waste at this time, or ultragenerosity, will bring regrets later on. Canary is your color; your number is 1.

Saturday, December 13 (Moon in Gemini)   This is a day favoring marriage and other partnerships, sharing, cooperation, and shows of unity. Good trends exist for dividing responsibilities connected with family, neighborhood, and community up into smaller groups or individuals. There's many a slip between the cup and the lip under upcoming strictures. Lucky lottery: 3, 12, 21, 30, 39, 48.

Sunday, December 14 (Moon in Gemini to Cancer 11:25 a.m.)   The full moon forms in Gemini and illuminates ways you and others can cooperate more fully. Communicate directly under these trends. Speak up; don't take instructions for granted. Marriage and marital bonding get high grades. Be a good partner and make allowances where necessary. Your lucky number is 5.

Monday, December 15 (Moon in Cancer)   Today's excellent for a review of lighting, both outdoor and indoor, to make certain that all precautions and safety rules are being honored. A Cancer and Pisces have key roles. Good trends exist for bargain hunting, buying items in quantity at a lower price, especially toys that have been reduced in price, as gifts for children. Auburn is one of your reds; your lucky number is 9.

Tuesday, December 16 (Moon in Cancer to Leo 5:58 p.m.)   Some changes may have to be considered the closer you move to the holiday. Family scheduling and rescheduling can take place. Community involvements also are being pressured. There are some who are a little piqued about the scheduling of events. Hot combination numbers: 2 and 6.

Wednesday, December 17 (Moon in Leo)   Travel, both long-range and long-distance, are favored. What is taking place afar can impact your day and activities. It would be nice and pleasing if you could deliver some gifts before the holidays. Leo and another Sagittarius are taking steps to see that things move swiftly. Lucky lottery: 4, 13, 22, 31, 40, 49.

Thursday, December 18 (Moon in Leo)   Keep on the move, getting responsibilities well in hand. Phone, write letters, get some holiday gifts on their way. Good news arrives in the mail, leading you to feel much better about people at a distance. Your winning colors are scarlet red and kelly green. It's not a bad evening for giving a small party. Your number is 6.

Friday, December 19 (Moon in Leo to Virgo 4 a.m.)   Virgo and Taurus have front seats. Career, authority and professional matters will demand their share of your day—the holiday plans of supervisors and co-workers are laid on the table and may impact your time in the days ahead. Today's fine for some celebrations and gift exchanging if people are leaving town. Your color is strawberry. Hot combination numbers: 8 and 2.

Saturday, December 20 (Moon in Virgo)   Be prepared for many demands on your time today. The evening is favorable for entertaining coworkers in your own home. Make your plans swiftly, securing the assistance of a dependable Virgo or Capricorn. Be sure that younger members of your family understand that more is expected of them when you are this busy. Lucky lottery: 1, 10, 19, 28, 37, 46.

Sunday, December 21 (Moon in Virgo to Libra 4:35 p.m.) Put morning and early-afternoon hours to good and effective use and you will be able to get in some genuine relaxation or enjoyable shopping ventures over the late-afternoon hours. The practical and methodical are your better paths to real progress. Your winning colors are silver and white; your lucky number is 3.

Monday, December 22 (Moon in Libra) This is a friendly day and a wonderful cycle for parties and entertainment. Groups are cheerful and involved with the holiday spirit. Libra and Aquarius figure prominently. The social side of your job can be served well. Your winning colors are cherry and ivory; your lucky number is 7.

Tuesday, December 23 (Moon in Libra) Smile, be cheerful, and spread goodwill for best results. Have lunch in an intimate setting with old friends you haven't had time to see lately. It's an *auld lange syne* meeting and all the more so if one of you will be traveling far away. Former coworkers are represented in your chart. Your lucky number is 9.

Wednesday, December 24 (Moon in Libra to Scorpio 5:07 a.m.) Scorpio is the one to help you make up for lost time, to finalize plans and make whatever switches, maneuvers and changes have to be implemented. The unspoken and the invisible, the spiritual and mysterious come into fuller play as the day advances. Emerald is your color. Lucky lottery: 2, 11, 20, 29, 38, 47.

Thursday, December 25 (Moon in Scorpio) The past—old traditions, memories, nostalgia, and sentiment—are all represented in your holiday as the moon is in your twelfth house. You want to be with those who mean most to you under these aspects. Silver is among your luckiest colors. Hot combination numbers: 4 and 7.

Friday, December 26 (Moon in Scorpio to Sagittarius 3:07 p.m.)   Yesterday's moods and sensitivities are carried over into today. Events often give the impression that they are being engineered in the best Scorpio traditions. You do well to consider changes you want to inaugurate over the weekend. A Cancer and a Pisces are helpful. Your lucky number is 6.

Saturday, December 27 (Moon in Sagittarius)   Local, immediate, and pressing matters slow down. More importantly, you are now in a magnificent lunar high cycle, when you can change direction of your life and move the emphasis from one strength to another. Hold the initiative and demonstrate self-confidence. Lucky lottery: 8, 17, 26, 35, 44, 1.

Sunday, December 28 (Moon in Sagittarius to Capricorn 9:48 p.m.)   Push personal assets and tone down any possible liabilities on a day when you can win big. You can lead, winning others over to your point of view and generally making a wonderful impression on them. Obstacles are overcome—where there were objections in the past, you have green lights all the way now. Your number is 1.

Monday, December 29 (Moon in Capricorn)   Now that the month is passing, there are some special money opportunities for you, with the accent on sales, bargain hunting, and the merchants' desire to keep stock moving. Discuss your wishes with business people for best results. You can increase your earning power in unusual ways. Your lucky number is 5.

Tuesday, December 30 (Moon in Capricorn)   Discuss salary potential and requirements with somebody who is in the know and in a position to encourage your hopes. A Capricorn and a Virgo have key roles. What you don't spend in a willy-nilly fashion, you are saving and adding on to the year's financial achievement. Hot combination numbers: 7 and 3.

Wednesday, December 31 (Moon in Capricorn to Aquarius 1:58 a.m.) The old year ends on a dimension of familiarity. Today's fine for taking stock, evaluating, and deciding what the year has taught you and how you can apply this lesson to the future. Celebrate with good friends and neighbors, staying close to your own community. The group effort makes everybody feel good. Beige and taupe are your colors. Lucky lottery: 9, 18, 27, 36, 45, 6.

HAPPY NEW YEAR!

JANUARY 1998

Thursday, January 1 (Moon in Aquarius) Look around you for advantages and opportunities. Local, usual, expected, anticipated, and familiar matters are getting star billing, and everyday situations are favored. So are discussions with relatives and neighbors. Communicate and keep on the go. Cherry is your color; your number is 6.

Friday, January 2 (Moon in Aquarius to Pisces 4:56 a.m.) Domestic issues take over. Family, residential, property, ownership, and community happenings top your agenda, and maintenance and renovation matters are favored. Know what your family has in mind for the month ahead. Even though plans will change often, be prepared. Your number is 8.

Saturday, January 3 (Moon in Pisces) Pisces and Scorpio have vital roles. You could have the feeling that a loved one is playing his or her cards close to the chest and that you are being left out. Within the community, changes are threatening that are not to your liking. Your winning colors are chestnut and tan. Lucky lottery: 1, 10, 19, 28, 37, 46.

Sunday, January 4 (Moon in Pisces to Aries 7:43 a.m.)
Today is favorable for spiritual, subtle, sublime situations, and for keeping your own feelings under wraps rather than complaining or expressing surprise and dissatisfaction. What you want to know will soon be revealed and all will be well. Improvements are taking place in important relationships. Your number is 3.

Monday, January 5 (Moon in Aries)   Things are looking up. This is a grand day for joy, delight, lovemaking, keeping in close touch with loved ones, and knowing what your children are thinking. You can bond more closely with your beloved and will enjoy having many dear ones around you in a promising social setting. Your number is 7.

Tuesday, January 6 (Moon in Aries to Taurus 10:52 a.m.)   Aries is interested in what you are thinking, and in your desires and hopes for the future. Fine trends exist for giving a party, enjoying a sports event, and attending the theater. It's the right day for a winter ball, an annual seasonal event, and for improving relationships with in-laws. Hot combination numbers: 9 and 6.

Wednesday, January 7 (Moon in Taurus)   Taurus and Virgo have key roles. Take care of your health and stick to usual preventive-medicine routines. Know when to work and when to relax. If the weather is inclement, know what to expect in travel situations, and prepare for delays. Dress appropriately. Lucky lottery: 2, 11, 20, 29, 38, 47.

Thursday, January 8 (Moon in Taurus to Gemini 2:42 p.m.)   Working routines are of vital importance on a day when the effort of assistants may be lower than usual. It is important to organize your time well and to make allowances for tardiness and absenteeism. Freakish slowdowns are threatening. Snow white and cream are your colors; your number is 4.

Friday, January 9 (Moon in Gemini)   Today is excellent for teamwork, sharing, cooperation, and being able to count on help. Your marital state, business partnerships, contracts, and agreements are all favored, but do a little more than usual. Your winning colors are magenta and off-white. Hot combination numbers: 6 and 1.

Saturday, January 10 (Moon in Gemini to Cancer 7:43 p.m.) Love of luxuries is indicated along with enjoyment of what you own, thanks to Venus' entry into your second house. The moon illuminates your marital and business partnership potential. This is not the day for going it alone or going off on tangents. Irritability is present. Lucky lottery: 8, 17, 26, 35, 44, 2.

Sunday, January 11 (Moon in Cancer) Cancer and Scorpio have front seats at all happenings. Good trends exist for saving, being cautious, and working on tax, insurance, or investment matters. Be thorough. Take the economic news programs and magazine articles in fully. What you read or otherwise come to know can improve your security. Cherry red is your color; your number is 1.

Monday, January 12 (Moon in Cancer) The full moon forms in your eighth house and illuminates the changes you want to make, as well as all corrections and improvements. Shift your financial emphasis to handling upcoming tax matters. The security of your family and home gets top priority. Turquoise is your color; your number is 5.

Friday, January 13 (Moon in Cancer to Leo 2:45 a.m.) All financial trends are speeded up as Mercury enters your second house. This is the day to head where your presence might be required. A Leo and another Sagittarius have important roles. Long-range and long-distance interests need attention. Hot combination numbers: 7 and 3.

Wednesday, January 14 (Moon in Leo) Keep on the go. What you have perking for yourself at a distance can assume even greater importance. The fire signs (Aries, Leo, and Sagittarius) impact your thinking and activities.

You gain from anticipating and from looking into the future. Emerald is your color. Lucky lottery: 9, 18, 27, 36, 45, 3.

Thursday, January 15 (Moon in Leo to Virgo 12:31 p.m.)   Information is flowing freely. News that has been held up can finally arrive. What was lost or misplaced can be found. It's a good day for looking far ahead and also for dealing in long-distance matters. People at a distance are ultra-important to you. Hot combination numbers: 2 and 6.

Friday, January 16 (Moon in Virgo)   Virgo will help you finish up the week's work. You can catch up socially under the prevailing aspects. Push career interests, knowing what your boss is thinking and expecting from you. Do what you can to encourage a depressed coworker. Ruby and burgandy are your colors; your number is 4.

Saturday, January 17 (Moon in Virgo)   You won't be able to get away completely from your job today. Career ups and downs can interfere with your desire to catch up on household chores. The telephone and mail bring some surprises. Others may be expecting more from you than you care to give. Lucky lottery: 6, 15, 24, 33, 42, 15.

Sunday, January 18 (Moon in Virgo to Libra 12:44 a.m.)   Libra imparts a sense of balance and proportion. Friendships can do much for your ego and morale and the group is supportive in your plans and potential. Phone, write social notes, and keep in touch with those who care and are concerned. Your winning colors are mauve and lilac; your number is 8.

Monday, January 19 (Moon in Libra)   This can be a day for spreading happiness. People expect you to be outgoing, cheerful, lucky, and anxious to please. It's time to consider the possibility of putting your talents, tools, and available space to an activity that can bring in additional money. Gold is your color; your number is 3.

Tuesday, January 20 (Moon in Libra to Scorpio 1:34 p.m.) It's an excellent day for knowing your own mind and communicating effectively. Aquarius and Libra will work well together. It's a very airy and intellectual day, when you are easily amused, humored, and entertained by the passing panorama of life. Narrow your sights and pounce on opportunities. Hot combination numbers 5 and 2.

Wednesday, January 21 (Moon in Scorpio) Scorpio takes over. Fine trends exist for finishing up odd chores and taking advantage of what you suspect, surmise, or intuitively become aware of. What you know can be transformed into a real advantage and opportunity. Realize that much is happening behind the scenes. Lucky lottery: 7, 16, 25, 34, 43, 3.

Thursday, January 22 (Moon in Scorpio) The past may seem too much with you and others as the day gets under way. Forgiveness is a must, so don't dwell on unhappy events that should be buried once and for all. Past love affairs, romantic involvements, and in-law troubles should be relegated to oblivion. Pinecone is your color; your number is 9.

Friday, January 23 (Moon in Scorpio to Sagittarius 12:25 a.m.) Now you are in your enviable lunar-cycle high and can move into the driver's seat with a strong sense of control. Hold the initiative and keep in the lead, changing situations to your liking and advantage. Another Sagittarius and a Leo are helpful. Chartreuse is your color; your number is 2.

Saturday, January 24 (Moon in Sagittarius) Keep on the go. Know that you are a winner with lucky Jupiter your ruling star. Let the world see you at your best, strongly self-confident and self-reliant. It's a day for moving into first place, winning through the default of others. Control your time. Lucky lottery: 4, 13, 22, 31, 40, 49.

Sunday, January 25 (Moon in Sagittarius to Capricorn 7:39 a.m.) Pay attention to your career potential and to socializing with those who can who help your aspirations. Air your ambitions and be completely honest and self-respectful as you forge ahead. The spiritual element should not be overlooked in your good fortune. Silver and pink are your colors; your number is 6.

Monday, January 26 (Moon in Capricorn) Capricorn is helpful in getting your financial show on the road. Your earning power and income get top billing now that you are in the advantageous position of increasing your financial status. New sources of income are waiting for you. Your winning color is taupe; your lucky number is 1.

Tuesday, January 27 (Moon in Capricorn to Aquarius 11:27 a.m.) Keep your earning power up to par. Don't let a temporary situation discourage you. Inefficient assistance is a strong possibility and those prone to errors and accidents require careful scrutiny. Remember, it's always darkest before the dawn. Cherry is your color; your number is 3.

Wednesday, January 28 (Moon in Aquarius) The new moon is born in your third house and illuminates what is happening. Local, immediate, and pressing matters get star billing. Relatives and neighbors are in your corner and expect you to call on them. Your strength of purpose is first rate. Push hard. Lucky lottery: 5, 14, 23, 32, 41, 50.

Thursday, January 29 (Moon in Aquarius to Pisces 1:08 p.m.) Push for a higher salary or an additional one in order to permit greater investment in yourself for your future. Aquarius and Leo have front seats. An independent attitude, rather than just tagging along with the opinions of others, would be your better bet. Your colors are indigo and olive; your lucky number is 7.

Friday, January 30 (Moon in Pisces) Pisces and Cancer have important roles in the day's activities. Family values require your strong support, as the generation gap is something of a problem. Community changes are not to your liking, as property values have to be watched. Strawberry is your color. Hot combination numbers 9 and 6.

Saturday, January 31 (Moon in Pisces to Aries 2:21 p.m.)   Talks with members of your household can result in better economic collaboration. The cost of living may be inching up, so acquaint all with the need to be thrifty. It may be necessary to do your shopping a little farther from home. Lucky lottery: 2, 11, 20, 29, 38, 47.

FEBRUARY 1998

Sunday, February 1 (Moon in Aries)   Aries will help you, if that is what you want. Fine rays exist for making love and for drawing closer to children and parents. People want to celebrate, have fun, and give a party, and you can give them the help to get things started. The more spontaneous you are, the better. Your lucky number is 1.

Monday, February 2 (Moon in Aries to Taurus 4:25 p.m.)   Romantic overtures and interludes are favored. You are in a good partying and entertaining mood, when you react spontaneously to events and draw closer to your beloved, your children, and parents. It's a fine day to communicate true feelings. Ivory and gold are your colors; your lucky number is 5.

Tuesday, February 3 (Moon in Taurus)   Local interests are stimulated and start moving faster, now that Mercury is in your third house. Taurus has a role to play. Take care of your health and don't push too hard. Know when to push and when to relax and just take it easy. Titian gold is your color. Hot combination numbers: 7 and 3.

Wednesday, February 4 (Moon in Taurus to Gemini 8:09 p.m.)   The health of older loved ones can cause

227

some concern. Weather permitting, visit loved ones who most likely are expecting to hear from you. You are in a good mood to cheer others up and to give them some of your own marvelous self-confidence. Mauve and beige are your colors. Lucky lottery: 9, 18, 27, 36, 45, 6.

Thursday, February 5 (Moon in Gemini) Gemini will both assist and do battle with you. A lot of talk is taking place. Your marital state, business partnerships, and existing and future contracts may be under discussion. There is a need to share and to cooperate, but ideas and attitudes can clash. Later, you reach a compromise. Your number is 2.

Friday, February 6 (Moon in Gemini) Do what you can to keep your partners happy. You may have to give a little more than you want, but with genuine effort, you can bond more closely with your spouse and other partners. Compromise shouldn't be despised, for it often is required. Cherry red is your color. Hot combination numbers: 4 and 7.

Saturday, February 7 (Moon in Gemini to Cancer 1:57 a.m.) The day brings many saving graces, mental escape routes, and much joy from the wise use of money. Today is fine for studying both the standard and the cost of living, with an eye toward saving even more. Talks with somebody who is interested in your financial future may be a good idea. Amber is your color. Lucky lottery: 6, 15, 24, 33, 42, 51.

Sunday, February 8 (Moon in Cancer) Cancer and Pisces figure prominently. A show of wisdom may be required when discussing money with loved ones. Don't expect all generations to have similar ideas about how money should be spent or saved. Changes require some study before being implemented. Dandelion yellows and greens are right; try the number 8.

Monday, February 9 (Moon in Cancer to Leo 9:57 a.m.) Good trends exist in tax, insurance, savings, and investments. Today is fine for talks with your brokers and for some consideration of personal, family, residential, and business security. Your winning colors are sand and olive. A Scorpio and a Taurus have key roles. Protect all your financial flanks. Your lucky number is 3.

Tuesday, February 10 (Moon in Leo)   Leo makes a grand entry. Faraway people, places, and situations are in focus. You may want to travel, but still wonder about the welcome when you get there or weather troubles along the way. You could find yourself in the company of an overbearing person. Hot combination numbers: 5 and 2.

Wednesday, February 11 (Moon in Leo to Virgo 8:10 p.m.)   The full moon forms in your ninth house and illuminates what is perking at a distance. Long-range and futuristic involvements can be considered. An Aries and another Sagittarius have explanations for you. You are inclined to stop, start, and begin all over again. Lucky lottery: 7, 16, 25, 34, 43, 3.

Thursday, February 12 (Moon in Virgo)   Virgo and Capricorn are in this script. Your career is crying for attention and new ideas, but what is traditional, acceptable, and familiar tends to win out. Self-discipline is necessary if you are to make progress. Coworkers aren't always pleasant. Your lucky number is 9.

Friday, February 13 (Moon in Virgo to Libra 8:17 a.m.) Push career potential. Know what your job is all about and what supervisors expect from you, and encourage assistants to do their best. Avoid bringing outside pressures and problems into the business situation and make sure others follow suit. Cherry is your color. Hot combination numbers: 2 and 6.

Saturday, February 14 (Moon in Libra)   It's wise to keep busy today, as work, duties, responsibilities, and obligations tend to pile up. You can't do everything at once, but you can knock big jobs down to handling size and get a lot of minor details out of the way. Your winning colors are apricot and chestnut. Lucky lottery: 4, 13, 22, 31, 40, 49.

Sunday, February 15 (Moon in Libra)   Today is perfect for enjoying talks with dear friends. Group activities connected with church or hobby groups will produce for you. You want to be yourself today, to laugh with a Libra or an Aquarius, and to enjoy a sense of camaraderie. Avoid anything controversial or too serious. Whites and blacks are right; your number is 6.

Monday, February 16 (Moon in Libra to Scorpio 9:13 p.m.)   Are you neglecting to apply for a financial stipend that might be yours due to charitable and humanitarian involvements? There are other opportunities for increasing you income, if you look around for part-time jobs that would utilize talents, available tools, space, and time. Your lucky number is 1.

Tuesday, February 17 (Moon in Scorpio)   Scorpio comes aboard and will help you finish up tasks that have been neglected, postponed, or otherwise delayed. You successfully tackle and engineer projects under the prevailing aspects. Also, you are alert to ways to transform an idea into something more profitable. Hot combination numbers: 3 and 9.

Wednesday, February 18 (Moon in Scorpio)   Your sympathy and compassion can be easily stirred today. Something you hear or observe can remind you of a past event. What was important to your parents and grandparents must not be put down or laughed at under these trends. Chocolate and mocha are your colors. Lucky lottery: 5, 14, 23, 32, 41, 50.

Thursday, February 19 (Moon in Scorpio to Sagittarius 8:56 a.m.)   Family values come to the fore as the sun enters Pisces. You tend to take a more serious view of something you heretofore regarded as frivolous. You may suddenly realize that there is something you can do about a festering social matter. Cream and snow are your colors; your number is 7.

Friday, February 20 (Moon in Sagittarius) Welcome to your lunar high cycle, in which you can control situations, rise to challenges today, get your way. You demonstrate unbeatable self-confidence and self-reliance. Another Sagittarius and a Leo have key roles. Aquamarine is your color; your lucky number is 9.

Saturday, February 21 (Moon in Sagittarius to Capricorn 5:30 p.m.) You are very much in the driver's seat today. Others are offering less interference and are recognizing that you are in charge. You can maneuver and redirect your life, if that is what you want, making good and lasting impressions on former critics. Turquoise is your color. Lucky lottery: 2, 11, 20, 29, 38, 47.

Sunday, February 22 (Moon in Capricorn) You get some good financial ideas or tips today. Watch what you read and otherwise learn. Today is fine for budgeting, figuring out ways to increase your earning power and income, or running down a new source of income. Discuss family standard and cost of living with loved ones. Your number is 4.

Monday, February 23 (Moon in Capricorn to Aquarius 10:10 p.m.) Capricorn and Virgo figure prominently. It's an excellent day to pounce on earning power opportunities as soon as you arrive on the business scene. Volunteer to take on more responsibility with your weather eye on future financial gains. Make sure that the front office knows that you are working hard. Try the number 8.

Tuesday, February 24 (Moon in Aquarius) Pay due attention to local, immediate and pressing matters. Seek assistance where necessary from relatives and neighbors. Studies, hobbies, and your learning processes are all getting high marks. Move about your own community

231

rather than venturing too far from home. Hot combination numbers: 1 and 7.

Wednesday, February 25 (Moon in Aquarius to Pisces 11:42 p.m.)   Encourage a loved one to come off any financial tangent. You may feel obliged to offer a loan today. Communications and transportation matters can be somewhat pressured. You could notice that household expenses are rising. Cerulean blue is your color. Lucky lottery: 3, 12, 21, 30, 39, 48.

Thursday, February 26 (Moon in Pisces—Solar Eclipse 12:37 p.m. EST)   A total solar eclipse can bring pressures in family, residential, property, and ownership matters. Expenses connected with home maintenance are rising. You hear many complaints under these aspects and some can be coming from loved ones. Be on guard against water and plumbing disasters. Your number is 5.

Friday, February 27 (Moon in Pisces to Aries 11:42 p.m.)   Flooding, along with problems with boats, docks, and waterfront property, are strong possibilities. It's not a good day for traveling when the weather is inclement or subject to sudden changes. Know what your loved ones are doing and where. It will be easy to have your attention shifted from one problem to another. Your number is 7.

Saturday, February 28 (Moon in Aries)   You are flexible and can rise above it all. You are a born survivor and you take the challenges of these times in stride. Aries has the best way of getting around major obstacles. Make sure your time counts. The loving side of your nature works to your advantage. Lucky lottery: 9, 18, 27, 36, 45, 6.

MARCH 1998

Sunday, March 1 (Moon in Aries)   The month begins with strong shows of moral and physical courage. It's a day for loving and being loved, with Aries in the picture. The lady is ultra-feminine, a little shy, but still as self-confident. Romance, adventure, pioneering, and socializing are all strong trends. Your number is 2.

Monday, March 2 (Moon in Aries to Taurus 12 a.m.)
Taurus and Virgo have compelling ideas. You may dislike the weather and long for spring, as winds and rains try to get a strong hold. Work can keep you busier than you want to be and you may tire of all the complaints you hear. Absenteeism and tardiness are problems. Hazel is your color; your number is 6.

Tuesday, March 3 (Moon in Taurus) Employment matters are high on your agenda. There is considerable fear about downsizing making the rounds. Where confidence is strong, there is recognition that, while old jobs disappear, new ones are being born; chances are, they will be far more interesting. Emerald is your color. Hot combination numbers: 8 and 2.

Wednesday, March 4 (Moon in Taurus to Gemini 2:15 a.m.) Gemini has the right word for it. It is important that you check things out with your mate and business partners before jumping to conclusions or making hard-and-fast decisions. Approval and appreciation are there, but demand protection and wise moves on your part. Lucky lottery: 1, 10, 19, 28, 37, 46.

Thursday, March 5 (Moon in Gemini) You warm up to the local scene and to studies, hobbies, communications, and transportation matters, as Venus moves into your third house. There is a need for more sharing and cooperation permeating the day, and talks with partners can't be postponed any longer. Turquoise is your color. Hot combination numbers: 3 and 6.

Friday, March 6 (Moon in Gemini to Cancer 7:27 a.m.)
Fine trends exist for compromising, reconciling, and patching up any misunderstanding. Teamwork will be productive. Is it time to renew or rewrite an old con-

233

tract? Agreements may require more than a handshake in the days ahead. Know what a lawyer will charge before hiring one. Taupe is your color; your lucky number is 5.

Saturday, March 7 (Moon in Cancer) Fine trends exist in savings, investments, budgeting, and bargain hunting. The dollar becomes more important in your scheme of things. All around you are economic complaints, as the cost of living keeps inching up. Changes should not be made too quickly or without proper consideration. Hot combination numbers: 7 and 3.

Sunday, March 8 (Moon in Cancer to Leo 3:46 p.m.) Romance, courtship, and socializing are all stepped up by Mercury's entry into your fifth house. Cancer and Aries may be at cross-purposes, but you are able to rise above it all. Draw closer to your beloved and keep a critical eye on rebellious teenagers. Ivory is your color; your number is 9.

Monday, March 9 (Moon in Leo) Leo makes an important point. Travel, along with long-range and long-distance matters, are high on your agenda. Information is arriving that can be put to good use. Keep in close touch with your interests at a distance, because something could be changing there for the better. Watch your standard of living. Purple is your color; your number is 4.

Tuesday, March 10 (Moon in Leo) Keep on the go and much will be accomplished. Look bright and eager for best results—no sleepy or lackadaisical approach is acceptable under these keen trends. Aries and Sagittarius are feeding the flames of ambition. Don't ignore the one who makes financial contributions. Hot combination numbers: 6 and 1.

Wednesday, March 11 (Moon in Leo to Virgo 2:35 a.m.) Virgo and Taurus have key roles. Your job demands more attention and quality time. Progress can be chalked up if you give the requirements of others your best shot. Supervisors may be playing their cards closer to their chests, so it's up to you to figure out what they expect. Lucky lottery: 8, 17, 26, 35, 44, 2.

Thursday, March 12 (Moon in Virgo—Lunar Eclipse 11:34 p.m.) Don't let distractions or interruptions detract from the quality of your work. You may have to speak sharply to an agitator at work, demanding that criticism be backed up with explanations and alternatives. The practical can't be denied. Orange is your color. Hot combination numbers: 1 and 7.

Friday, March 13 (Moon in Virgo to Libra 2:58 p.m.) The demands of your career can be stepped up. There may be some additional work responsibilities put on your shoulders because of downsizing or other cutbacks. At the same time, you could hear of some marvelous job opportunities in the far Western states. Old rose is your color; your number is 3.

Saturday, March 14 (Moon in Libra) Today is excellent for taking a breather from career and professional obligations. Work on your lawn or backyard, enjoy a conversation with your helpful hardware store proprietor, and look over the ever-increasing cost of seeds. Consider overall household renovation. Lucky lottery: 5, 14, 23, 32, 41, 50.

Sunday, March 15 (Moon in Libra) Friendships, group activities, church and club-related matters, and fund raising are all favored. You enjoy visiting people today, and can get a new view of some important controversy. Emerald is your color. A Libra and a Gemini, and the matters they rule, take precedence. Your number is 7.

Monday, March 16 (Moon in Libra to Scorpio 3:51 a.m.) Scorpio and Cancer figure prominently. This is a fine cycle for finishing projects and for giving the axe to no-win situations and money-losing interests. Expectations may be higher than they should be. Behind the

235

scenes, things are taking place that are not very nice. Your number is 2.

Tuesday, March 17 (Moon in Scorpio)   Conferences, decision-making board meetings, and teaching employees how to use computers and other electronic equipment are all favored. Things have to be talked over today, before some projects can be given the green lights. Changes threaten and improvements are required. Hot combination numbers: 4 and 7.

Wednesday, March 18 (Moon in Scorpio to Sagittarius 3:56 p.m.)   The light touch at work won't help—you have to engineer your working activities and be fully conscious of what may go wrong. Systems analysis and quality control may require an overhauling. You are in a good position to contribute to the improvement of a product. Lucky lottery: 6, 15, 24, 33, 42, 51.

Thursday, March 19 (Moon in Sagittarius)   Great news! You can rearrange things to suit yourself now that you are in your lunar high cycle. It's important that you look and act the part of winner, and that you hold the initiative and keep in the lead. Others will not interfere when they see your enormous self-confidence. Gold is your color. Hot combination numbers: 8 and 2.

Friday, March 20 (Moon in Sagittarius)   Still in your lunar high cycle, keep in control, be swift to move into any deteriorating system, and let the world know that you are handling things. Your aspirations and ambitions are honored today, and opposition and competition are not able to deter you. Beige is your color; your lucky number is 1.

Saturday, March 21 (Moon in Sagittarius to Capricorn 1:44 a.m.)   Spring begins as the sun attains the first degree of Aries; as a result, you are now in the season of love. Your relationships with in-laws can be improved and you can bond more closely with your mate and children. Also, with the moon in Capricorn, you can serve your earning power needs. Lucky lottery: 3, 12, 21, 30, 39, 48.

Sunday, March 22 (Moon in Capricorn)   Stay alert to some good financial news that can develop for you today. What you hear, read, and view on television may be translated into more money in your bank. You are strongly self-disciplined in the matter of spending. Some statistics can make more sense to you than to others. Your lucky number is 5.

Monday, March 23 (Moon in Capricorn to Aquarius 8:02 a.m.)   You remain in a good financial cycle, when what you achieve on the job will bring enduring favorable results. You gain from discussions with supervisors and others in the chain of command. Fine trends exist also for reviewing more promising assignments with an eye on major progress. Deep pink is your color; your number is 9.

Tuesday, March 24 (Moon in Aquarius)   Narrow your sights and concentrate on what can be done right now. Everyday matters, as well as the usual, familiar, and expected, are all stimulated favorably. Studies, hobbies, communications, and transportation matters need special attention. A relative or a neighbor will be helpful. Hot combination numbers: 2 and 6.

Wednesday, March 25 (Moon in Aquarius to Pisces 10:43 a.m.)   Aquarius and Leo have key roles. You can gain much from taking care of small details, and from making sure that you aren't overlooking anything that should be done now. Often, what is right under your nose or at your elbow might be unnoticed. Lucky lottery: 4, 13, 22, 31, 40, 49.

Thursday, March 26 (Moon in Pisces)   Domestic, residential, property, ownership, and community matters get top billing. Pisces and Virgo are on the scene. There are things to discuss with teens and younger children now that spring is here and they will be spending more time outdoors. Auburn is your color; your lucky number is 6.

Friday, March 27 (Moon in Pisces to Aries 10:49 a.m.)
Fine trends exist for taking off with a new idea, pet project, or desire to really do something in your own interest. Your family is cheering your aspirations and will be supportive, even if you find yourself biting off more than you can chew. Ask questions rather than run the risk of wasting time looking for leads. Your winning colors are lavender and khaki; your lucky number is 8.

Saturday, March 28 (Moon in Aries)   The new moon is born in your fifth house of love, romance, courtship, affairs of children, and spontaneous socializing. It's an active, rewarding, and strongly satisfying day. You are loved, approved, appreciated, and complimented, and you want to please everybody. Your color is magenta. Lucky lottery: 1, 10, 19, 28, 37, 46.

Sunday, March 29 (Moon in Aries to Taurus 10:06 a.m.)   You may find your lover restive and in need of much encouragement. You are in good shape to build up the ego and morale of your beloved. Business partners may seem edgy and need understanding. Contracts are not enough now. Titian gold is your color; your lucky number is 3.

Monday, March 30 (Moon in Taurus)   Taurus and Virgo figure prominently. Work is not to your liking, as you could meet evasion and a dearth of cooperation from supervisors and those who pull their rank. With strength of character and self-confidence, you ultimately get around the opposition and turn the day to good account. Your lucky number is 7.

Tuesday, March 31 (Moon in Taurus to Gemini 10:37 a.m.)   Today is excellent for health corrections and improvements. Work can at times be therapeutic under the prevailing aspects. You do well when you feel good about yourself, and this can be achieved through the

238

responsibilities you assume. Capricorn can prove helpful. Hot combination numbers: 9 and 6.

APRIL 1998

Wednesday, April 1 (Moon in Gemini)   There can be minor disagreements with your beloved and with business partners. You feel very independent now and see through the pretense and guesswork of others. All the shortcomings of a contract or agreement can be evident now. Gold is your color. Lucky lottery: 8, 17, 26, 35, 44, 2.

Thursday, April 2 (Moon in Gemini to Cancer 2:10 p.m.)   Patch up arguments—everybody wants to believe that they're in the right under these trends, but compromise can keep the day from getting lost in disagreements and details. Sometimes there is too much discussion, which makes situations worse. Hot combination numbers: 1 and 7.

Friday, April 3 (Moon in Cancer)   Cancer and Pisces figure prominently, and good trends exist for completing income-tax returns, finding a tax shelter, deciding on more insurance, or getting into a promising mutual-funds agreement. You can save a little more under the prevailing aspects and you can gain from bartering. Beige and taupe are your colors; your lucky number is 3.

Saturday, April 4 (Moon in Cancer to Leo 9:36 p.m.)   Changes that have been hovering in the back of your mind can be inaugurated now. Security is topping your agenda, and it would be a good idea to check all locks on windows and doors. Don't park your car in a dark and unfamiliar area. Be cautious while walking or driving in parking lots. Lucky lottery: 5, 14, 23, 32, 41, 50.

Sunday, April 5—Daylight Saving Time (Moon in Leo)   A trip may be what you would like now, but it may be difficult to drop what you are doing. Look to the future and plan your fantasy vacation. It's never too early to gather the travel folders and brochures. Write letters to keep in touch with long-range and long-distance interests. Your lucky number is 7.

Monday, April 6 (Moon in Leo)   With Venus entering Pisces, you warm up to family values and want to know the plans of your beloved and your children. Spring housecleaning can get under way by getting estimates of costs from painters and decorators. You could become fascinated by imported works of art. Your lucky number is 2.

Tuesday, April 7 (Moon in Leo to Virgo 9:25 a.m.)   Leo and Sagittarius have key roles. Career assignments may get in the way of some activities and socializing you would rather be doing. There also can be conflicts between the various members of your family. Navy and electric blue are your colors. Hot combination numbers: 4 and 7.

Wednesday, April 8 (Moon in Virgo)   Virgo and Taurus show up. The day demands more attention to duty, to what your employer expects of you, and to the possibility of career advancement. Look very serious and dress rather formally, with nothing outlandish or too chic. You could be evaluated now. Lucky lottery: 6, 15, 24, 33, 42, 51.

Thursday, April 9 (Moon in Virgo to Libra 10:04 p.m.)   Give career, professional, and authority matters your best shot and endear yourself to those responsible for the production line. Keep everything moving today and your efforts will pay off. Conferences and important discussions are indicated. Pearl gray is your color; your lucky number is 8.

Friday, April 10 (Moon in Libra)   It's a friendly and cheerful day, when you are popular and stand out in any group. The positive side of your personality is strongly activated: your quiet intelligence, universal mind, and flexibility. Another Sagittarius and a Libra have fascinating suggestions. Flame red is your color. Hot combination numbers: 1 and 7.

Saturday, April 11 (Moon in Libra)   The full moon forms in your eleventh house and illuminates friendships, group membership and participation matters, and the possibility of rating some special bonus or stipend. Are you overlooking some advantage and financial opportunity? Copper and bronze are your colors. Lucky lottery: 3, 12, 21, 30, 39, 48.

Sunday, April 12 (Moon in Libra to Scorpio 10:56 a.m.) Spend time with kindred spirits. Get away from the usual and familiar, to take a walk in the park and trace the advance of spring or browse in boutiques and bookstores. Peach is your color; your lucky number is 5.

Monday, April 13 (Moon in Scorpio)   Fine trends exist for finishing up odd chores, making evaluations, producing summaries, filing important documents away, and mailing business reports. You want to stretch and yawn after some hard work. You would love to change your scene, but this may not be possible, except in the privacy of your own mind. Purple is your color; your number is 9.

Tuesday, April 14 (Moon in Scorpio to Sagittarius 10:52 p.m.)   Scorpio and Pisces point the way. Your awareness is growing and you can surmise what is happening behind the scenes, and other matters that will influence the turn of some events. Good trends exist for sorting, sifting, and making decisions and evaluations. Hot combination numbers: 2 and 6.

Wednesday, April 15 (Moon in Sagittarius)   Today, tomorrow, and the next day, you will be in your lunar-cycle high, a very fortuitous cycle for cashing in on your skills, talents, and lucky stars. Seize and hold the initiative, take the lead, be quick to zero in on advantages and opportunities, and demonstrate self-reliance. Old rose and rust are your colors. Lucky lottery: 4, 13, 22, 31, 40, 49.

Thursday, April 16 (Moon in Sagittarius) Continue to push for first place. Go after the prizes and seize all opportunities and shake them empty. Take advantage of the goodwill you have spread in the past, speak up for yourself, and let others know that you have ambitions to fulfill. Another Sagittarius and a Leo are helpful. Your number is 6.

Friday, April 17 (Moon in Sagittarius to Capricorn 9:05 a.m.) Be positive, affirmative, and sure of yourself. Self-realization is more than probable if you stay in the lead and let others know that you intend to win big. Lessons you learned long ago can now pay off. You can depend on some gratitude and much appreciation. Hot combination numbers: 8 and 2.

Saturday, April 18 (Moon in Capricorn) Capricorn shows up and this can mean more money for you. Does the government owe you something you have not taken then pains to collect? Watch what is taking place at cash registers of life, because mistakes can be made. Senior citizens tend to be on your side in any competition at this time. Lucky lottery: 1, 10, 19, 28, 37, 46.

Sunday, April 19 (Moon in Capricorn to Aquarius 4:41 p.m.) Consider ways to increase your earning power and income. The possessions in your home may be worth more than you realize. What about family keepsakes and what you jokingly refer to as heirlooms? Know their true worth. Your color is silver; your number is 3.

Monday, April 20 (Moon in Aquarius) There is more spontaneity today, and you can inject it into your partying and socializing. The affairs of your children may be chaotic; so look into them. Your beloved may want you to be more demonstrative and affectionate. Your lucky number is 7.

Tuesday, April 21 (Moon in Aquarius to Pisces 9:06 p.m.) Aquarius has questions but may hesitate butting in. The usual, familiar, and expected will demand some part of your time. Everyday matters are favored, and you tend to handle them well. Siblings and neighbors are present at every turn. You can communicate effectively over the afternoon. Try the number 9.

Wednesday, April 22 (Moon in Pisces)   Pisces offers good advice on family situations. Good trends exist for inspecting your house and workplace. Know what deterioration has taken place over winter and early spring. Renovation now can save higher expenses later. Lucky lottery: 2, 11, 20, 29, 38, 47.

Thursday, April 23 (Moon in Pisces to Aries 10:31 p.m.)   Discuss future plans with members of your household. Know what children have in mind concerning travel and spring breaks. This is a fine day for addressing community, property, and ownership matters. You may find some catering and other local services unsatisfactory. Hot combination numbers: 4 and 7.

Friday, April 24 (Moon in Aries)   Aries has some impressive and courageous ideas. You respond warmly as the moon stimulates your love zone. You will enjoy romantic interludes as you are entirely positive, warmhearted, and endearing. There is much approval and appreciation coming your way. Venetian gold is your color; Your lucky number is 6.

Saturday, April 25 (Moon in Aries to Taurus 10:09 p.m.)   Today is fine for spontaneous partying and entertainment. Reach out to those who need your love and understanding. You have it in your power now to make your beloved, your children, and your parents very happy. There is special creativity and imagination in your lovemaking. Lucky lottery: 8, 17, 26, 35, 44, 2.

Sunday, April 26 (Moon in Taurus)   The new moon is born in your sixth house and illuminates health, new preventive-medicine ideas, and wiser approaches toward diet, weight, and exercise regimens. Keep things simple. Tawny orange is your color; your lucky number is 1.

Monday, April 27 (Moon in Taurus to Gemini 9:55 p.m.)   Taurus and Virgo have key roles. You can do a lot of dull chores if you rise early and get to work before the others. Tackle what you have been ignoring. Perserverance will pay handsome dividends under the prevailing aspects. Cherry is your color; your lucky number is 5.

Tuesday, April 28 (Moon in Gemini)   Gemini enters with the gift of gab. Joint endeavors and investments offer good potential. It's a day when your learning processes are strongly stimulated and you can benefit from advice of your mate, in-laws, the associates of your mate, and your business partners. Ivory and silver are your colors; try the number 7.

Wednesday, April 29 (Moon in Gemini to Cancer 11:57 p.m.)   Today is fine for pillow talk and heart-to-heart conversation, and for reaching a genuine understanding with your beloved. It's a day for zealous and stringent honoring of all contracts. An in-law may mean well, but still deal in unwholesome gossip. Burgundy is your color. Lucky lottery: 9, 18, 27, 36, 45, 6.

Thursday, April 30 (Moon in Cancer)   Cancer and Scorpio are sympathetic and will do you an impressive favor if asked. You can improve the security system in and around your home and workplace at a time when auto thefts are common. Hot combination numbers: 2 and 4.

MAY 1998

Friday, May 1 (Moon in Cancer)   Consider a new savings program as the month begins. Anticipate some increased expenses as you move closer to summer. The water signs (Cancer, Scorpio, and Pisces) and the matters they rule in your horoscope are dominant. Security, swingover from one project to another, and family values are favored. Your number is 2.

244

Saturday, May 2 (Moon in Cancer to Leo 5:49 a.m.) The day and the season conspire to bring on a desire for travel. You are looking far head and your sense of expectancy is strong. Recycling happy travel ventures may not suffice, and you could take off for a long weekend at a resort not too far from home. Leo and Aries are in your corner. Lucky lottery: 4, 13, 22, 31, 40, 49.

Sunday, May 3 (Moon in Leo) Today is fine for relaxation and for morale-boosting ventures away from home. Dining out, sightseeing, and enjoying the companionship of other guests are all indicated. Long-range and long distance interests get top billing. Your winning colors are amber and earth; your lucky number is 6. Another Sagittarius can be helpful.

Monday, May 4 (Moon in Leo to Virgo 3:47 p.m.) You are in the mood for love as Venus moves into your fifth house. Romance is easily identified in the music you hear and the scenes you witness. Entertainments and parties do well and you can bond more closely with your beloved and with difficult young people. Your lucky number is 1.

Tuesday, May 5 (Moon in Virgo) You can begin some project or job all over again in a more purposeful, practical way. Virgo and Capricorn are prominent. It's a day for career potential and resulting advancement. Volunteer for an extra assignment and discuss your salary with those in power. Your number is 3.

Wednesday, May 6 (Moon in Virgo) Apply your top talents and skills to the jobs that have to be done. If you give your best shot, top-flight success is bound to follow as the element of luck is serving you. Those who remember the good work you have done in the past may expect near perfection from you now. Your winning color is gold. Lucky lottery: 5, 14, 23, 32, 41, 50.

Thursday, May 7 (Moon in Virgo to Libra 4:19 a.m.) Friendships can become stronger under the prevailing

245

aspects. You are very much at home at the center of a group, club, or clique. Others look to you for leadership, ideas, and explanations. You have handy suggestions. Hot combination numbers: 7 and 3.

Friday, May 8 (Moon in Libra) There is a strong sense of togetherness among you and your dear friends. Libra and Aquarius have key roles. There are excellent trends for using available cash more wisely and for running down a new source of income. It's one of those days when you consider self-employment. Your lucky number is 9.

Saturday, May 9 (Moon in Libra to Scorpio 5:10 p.m.) Today is perfect for spending time with the right companions. A walk around the downtown squares, through a park where the flowers are budding, and also through a busy mall for a little window shopping are all possibilities on today's agenda. With Venus in your fifth house, you are loving, kind, cheerful, and outgoing. Lucky lottery: 2, 11, 20, 29, 38, 47.

Sunday, May 10 (Moon in Scorpio) Scorpio takes over as the physical side of love becomes strongly important. You engineer relationships now, doing what you know another person wants you to do. You are full of favors, generosity, and compliments as you finish up odd chores that bother you. Pastels are right; try the number 4.

Monday, May 11 (Moon in Scorpio) The full moon forms in your twelfth house, which illuminates the past and extracts additional gains from former successes. You surmise, suspect, and intuitively know what is transpiring out of view. You are reading difficult people as you would a well-plotted book. Try the number 8.

Tuesday, May 12 (Moon in Scorpio to Sagittarius 4:48 a.m.) Hurrah! You have arrived at your lunar-cycle high, when things tend to go your way. If you hold the initiative and demonstrate the highest self-confidence and self-reliance, nothing will stop you from arriving at the rainbow of happiness. Your number is 1.

Wednesday, May 13 (Moon in Sagittarius)   Go for it! You are favored, preferred, and intent on first place. You can serve your career, professional, and authority interests wisely, and sparkle and scintillate socially. You can have the exciting feeling that the world is on your side. Lucky lottery: 3, 12, 21, 30, 39, 48.

Thursday, May 14 (Moon in Sagittarius to Capricorn 2:39 p.m.)   Anther Sagittarius and a Gemini are helpful in unusual and even peculiar ways. You can strike wonderful bargains on a day such as this. Today is also fine for signing new and improved contracts and agreements. Speak up, air your aspirations and ambitions, and invite more investment capital your way. Silver is your color. Hot combination numbers: 5 and 3.

Friday, May 15 (Moon in Capricorn)   Love triumphs (Venus in Aries); work goes well and fast (Mercury in Taurus); and money is earmarked for you (Moon in Capricorn). With your fifth, sixth, and second houses strongly activated, you can make this a day of gain, joy, delight, and inner pleasure. Keep active, see people, and declare your intentions. Your number is 7.

Saturday, May 16 (Moon in Capricorn to Aquarius 10:30 a.m.)   Money can be earned and saved in special ways. What about a garage or patio sale or some bargain hunting, where you can hit those shopping lines early. You may uncover a source of income. Your winning colors are wheat and sand. Lucky lottery: 9, 18, 27, 36, 45, 6.

Sunday, May 17 (Moon in Aquarius)   Aquarius and Gemini and the matters they rule will impact your day. Local, immediate, and pressing matters, as well as studies, hobbies, and the fine art of sharing and cooperating, are all indicated. You may move about your own community more than usual, and chat at length with a neighbor or two. Lime and lemon are your colors; your lucky number is 2.

Monday, May 18 (Moon in Aquarius)   Stick to what you know and what you can do under the prevailing aspects. Don't attempt anything too new and unfamiliar. The little things of life also matter, so concentrate and fend off distractions over the busy afternoon. If you show patience, another will answer the question that is bothering you. Your number is 6.

Tuesday, May 19 (Moon in Aquarius to Pisces 4:03 a.m.)   Consult Pisces on a family or property matter. Excellent trends exist for sprucing up the appearance of your lawn, and for transferring seedling plants outdoors. A strong accent falls on the local scene and brings out the best qualities of neighbors in their relationships with one another. Pinks and blues are right; try the number 8.

Wednesday, May 20 (Moon in Pisces)   Family values, household renovation, and changing schedules are high on your agenda. Cancer and Scorpio, and the matters those signs rule, are activated. Pay attention to security matters and permit past experiences to come full circle to serve the present. Yellows are right. Lucky lottery: 1, 10, 19, 28, 37, 46.

Thursday, May 21 (Moon in Pisces to Aries 7:06 a.m.)   Aries and Gemini have front seats. It's a fine day for love, romance, adventure, and excitement, and for bonding more closely with your beloved. Love and marriage go together like two peas in a pod. You can make headway in your social life today and come into a better understanding of your children. Your number is 3.

Friday, May 22 (Moon in Aries)   Closeness with your beloved makes this a perfect day. Today is fine for sharing, cooperating, and reciprocating. You can improve relationships with your spouse's family and friends. You want to please under these aspects, and you will succeed beyond your highest aims. Canary is your color. Hot combination numbers: 5 and 2.

Saturday, May 23 (Moon in Aries to Taurus 8:06 a.m.)   Let love come first and the day will belong to you and yours. The romance and adventure potential of the season are with you. Today is fine for dining on your balcony or on your patio, and excellent for bringing the family into closer harmony. Parties and entertainment will go well this evening. Taupe is your color. Lucky lottery: 7, 16, 25, 34, 43, 5.

Sunday, May 24 (Moon in Taurus)   Don't attempt too much in the way of grueling tasks. Just relax, enjoying the peace of soul and mind that belongs to you today. Project a cheerful, positive attitude toward people. Don't bother to organize your hours; be spontaneous, welcoming what comes your way. Aquamarine is your color; your lucky number is 9.

Monday, May 25 (Moon in Taurus to Gemini 8:25 a.m.) Taurus and Virgo have key roles. Pursue personal and family security goals. Fine trends exist for dealing in changes, improvements, and corrections. The day calls for looking situations straight in the eye and doing something about them. Olive and emerald are your colors; try the number 4.

Tuesday, May 26 (Moon in Gemini)   Gemini comes calling and tells the entire story. Intimate little tidbits of gossip are enjoyed fully. Even the minor guilt that you and Gemini can share seems exciting. You cover a lot of territory in your chatter, and in the end, you know plenty. Your number is 6.

Wednesday, May 27 (Moon in Gemini to Cancer 9:58 a.m.)   Sharing, communications on some difficult subjects, and cooperating more fully—even if a little reluctantly—are indicated. Your marital state and business partnerships can be fair topics. You may feel very much the complete individual, but at the same time are willing to compromise. Cerulean blue is your color. Lucky lottery: 8, 17, 26, 35, 44, 2.

Thursday, May 28 (Moon in Cancer)   Trust what Pisces and Cancer are telling you. Now you can implement some of the changes you made recently, refine and define them, and forge forward along new paths. It's a good day to handle accumulated funds, investing in property, government bonds, and hotel and motel chains. Apricot is your color. Hot combination numbers: 1 and 7.

Friday, May 29 (Moon in Cancer to Leo 2:38 p.m.)   Fine trends exist in security, savings, and investment matters. Discussions with your banker and broker can prove wise and helpful, and joint investments with a family member are possible under current aspects. Changes, improvements, and corrections do well. Hot combination numbers: 3 and 6.

Saturday, May 30 (Moon in Leo)   You warm up to health and work improvements, as Venus enters your sixth house. Leo has unusual but promising suggestions for you. Information arrives even before it was due and can impact your thinking. Long-range and long-distance matters require attention. Pea green is right. Lucky lottery: 5, 14, 23, 32, 41, 50.

Sunday, May 31 (Moon in Leo to Virgo 11:21 p.m.)   Today is fine for moving about close to home. Visit, drop in, and see somebody you have been neglecting. You want dramatic episodes to dot the day, and to be with exciting people with whom you once were closer than you are today. Travel, sharing, sightseeing, and dining out are indicated. Your lucky number is 7.

JUNE 1998

Monday, June 1 (Moon in Virgo)   You make excellent headway in a career, professional, or authority matter. Virgo and Capricorn are on stage. A practical,

250

logical, and simple approach will prove wise. You tend to dig in for the long haul under these aspects. Tawny beige is your color; your lucky number is 8.

Tuesday, June 2 (Moon in Virgo) If you keep your nose to that grindstone, you can make today count in the work you are doing. You excel in encouraging, guiding, and inspiring assistants and apprentices. You exude self-confidence, and many little vocational skills tend to buttress the mental. Hot combination numbers: 1 and 7.

Wednesday, June 3 (Moon in Virgo to Libra 11:17 a.m.) It's the kind of day when you could be rewarded with more than a smile from your supervisor or your employer. The way you have taken hold of a changing project is doing you a lot of good where effort and deportment are at stake. The pastels are your colors. Lucky lottery: 3, 12, 21, 30, 39, 48.

Thursday, June 4 (Moon in Libra) Spend some time with kindred spirits—those with whom you can let your hair down. Brain-to-brain talk is going to accomplish the day's mission. Libra and Gemini can impact your thinking and physical activities. Lemon and lime are your colors; your lucky number is 5.

Friday, June 5 (Moon in Libra) It's a fine day to be with people. You're popular and can be the center of attention. Group activities produce many happy moments and advance your goals, such as funding charitable and humanitarian projects. Keep good records and steer clear of gossips. Light blue is your color. Hot combination numbers: 7 and 3.

Saturday, June 6 (Moon in Libra to Scorpio 12:06 a.m.) You can get a lot of work done around the grounds of your home today. Beautification is your primary goal. Today is for landscaping, using bricks and plants, and decorating your patio and deck. Good effort also will be put forth by a Scorpio. Your winning colors are off-white and lilac. Lucky lottery: 9, 18, 27, 36, 45, 3.

Sunday, June 7 (Moon in Scorpio) Your awareness of what can be corrected and improved is strong. Extra-sensory perception also is marked where you are anticipating a relative's next move. You can win at games today and a sports stadium or card table could be in the picture. Winning colors are browns and cream; your lucky number is 2.

Monday, June 8 (Moon in Scorpio to Sagittarius 11:34 a.m.) There's success where you rise early, get to work before the mob, and pounce on an opportunity that is right in line with your special talents and skills. If you volunteer to take on additional work, you'll profit enormously later in the year. Alabaster is your color; your lucky number is 6.

Tuesday, June 9 (Moon in Sagittarius) Now you are in your lunar-cycle high, and can maneuver and turn things to your own advantage. You have the drive and the motivation, as well as the courage of your convictions. Stay in the lead, showing the right direction, and look, act, and speak with considerable authority. Hot combination numbers: 8 and 2.

Wednesday, June 10 (Moon in Sagittarius to Capricorn 8:50 p.m.) The full moon forms in your sun sign, which makes this a doubly good day for you. You can court Lady Luck and hold the initiative; what you want from life and how to get it will be illuminated. The prizes are there waiting for you. Cardinal is your color. Lucky lottery: 1, 10, 19, 28, 37, 46.

Thursday, June 11 (Moon in Capricorn) Push for higher earning power and income. If it's additional cash you require, look around and create your own job, doing odd chores for senior citizens, using your vehicle as a taxi for older people who have many errands. An outdoor secondary job will suit you fine. Your number is 3.

Friday, June 12 (Moon in Capricorn) Capricorn has some good financial and investment tips for you. Big business and government can serve your needs through printing and publishing. Make allowances for an assistant who has yet to learn the ropes. If it's a matter of lack of self-confidence, do what you can to boost this person's ego. Hot combination numbers: 5 and 2.

Saturday, June 13 (Moon in Capricorn to Aquarius 4:03 a.m.)   Narrow your sights, concentrate, and pay attention to all immediate and pressing matters. The usual, familiar, and expected can be served well today. Studies, hobbies, communications, and transportation matters get top billing. A discussion with an older person should produce good results. Pink is right. Lucky lottery: 7, 16, 25, 34, 43, 5.

Sunday, June 14 (Moon in Aquarius)   You do well in your contacts with relatives and neighbors. You are especially articulate and have much to say, and there are many who want to listen. You communicate effectively with both older and younger people—in some ways, you may feel you are a bridge that links others together. Your lucky number is 9.

Monday, June 15 (Moon in Aquarius to Pisces 9:31 a.m.)   You can do plenty with accumulations of time, money, and energy, as Mercury moves into your eighth house. You handle immediate and pressing matters perfectly and enjoy the feeling of finally getting some old chores out of the way for good. Libra and Gemini are responsive to your wishes. Your number is 4.

Tuesday, June 16 (Moon in Pisces)   Pisces and Scorpio have key roles as family and home matters top your agenda. Summer plans of older and younger relatives require greater absorption by you. Time seems to steal up on you where your children are concerned. It's a good day for moving around your own community. Hot combination numbers: 6 and 1.

Wednesday, June 17 (Moon in Pisces to Aries 1:23 p.m.)   Domestic changes are brewing. Teenagers are lobbying for a later curfew now that summer is here. Older loved ones may desire more attention from you and may not appreciate how busy you are. Household routines and schedules are slipping away from you. Lucky lottery: 8, 17, 26, 35, 44, 1.

Thursday, June 18 (Moon in Aries)   Aries stimulates your thinking, and you are apt to see possibilities where yesterday all was confusion. It's a fine day to make love, to be close to your beloved, and to come to grips with some outside affairs of your offspring. A little home entertaining might help. Carmine is your color; your number is 1.

Friday, June 19 (Moon in Aries to Taurus 3:47 p.m.)   You see romance where others may not. You are reaching out for a more adventurous weekend. Spending quality time with your beloved can do a lot for your ego and morale. It may be the time to spend a little money to court good times and special memories. Your number is 3.

Saturday, June 20 (Moon in Taurus)   Taurus and Virgo figure prominently. Work that you thought was easy and quick can backfire and prove much more time consuming. Children may complain about not feeling well; watch this. Orange and flame are winning colors. Dressing up can boost your morale. Lucky lottery: 5, 14, 23, 32, 41, 50.

Sunday, June 21 (Moon in Taurus to Gemini 5:26 p.m.)   Jobs you schedule for yourself tend to slip out of reach, or be overlooked or forgotten in the press of some surprise events. You are exposed to whining and complaining over matters that you consider trivial. Pink and baby blue are your colors; your number is 7.

Monday, June 22 (Moon in Gemini)   The longest day of the year gives you support in marriage, other partnerships, contracts, agreements, promises. There is a strong effort to live up to what has been agreed to, but there may be interference and the best of intentions fall short of the mark. Gemini and Cancer are involved. Try the number 2.

Tuesday, June 23 (Moon in Gemini to Cancer 7:39 p.m.) Good trends exist to make up for lost time. Sharing, cooperation, and wise compromise, are all represented. Feuding factions can arrive at a wise consensus. The air signs (Gemini, Libra, and Aquarius) give an intellectual and flexible dimension to the day. Hot combination numbers: 4 and 3.

Wednesday, June 24 (Moon in Cancer) The new moon is born in your eighth house, which illuminates budgeting, bargain hunting, savings, investments, and insurance matters. You tap in on some good financial advice. There are sudden opportunities to get in on the ground floor of a good investment. Lucky lottery: 6, 15, 24, 33, 42, 51.

Thursday, June 25 (Moon in Cancer) As Venus enters Gemini, you can bond more closely with your beloved. Meanwhile, all financial accumulations are sensitized, and some good investment decisions can be made jointly. The new season brings a sense of change, improvement, and correction. This is the time to plan and organize. Ultramarine is your color; your number is 8.

Friday, June 26 (Moon in Cancer to Leo 12:06 a.m.) All things being equal, it would be a good idea to relax a bit today when travel, change, and long-range and long-distance thinking and planning top your agenda. Privacy will help you arrive at the right decisions. Scorpio and Cancer are in your corner. Hot combination numbers: 1 and 7.

Saturday, June 27 (Moon in Leo) Leo can inspire and guide you to make some reasonable improvements and corrections in organizational matters. You see your way clear now to spend a little more money. Self-confidence and the feeling that all will turn out right are big assists on this busy day. Azure blue is your color. Lucky lottery: 3, 12, 21, 30, 39, 48.

Sunday, June 28 (Moon in Leo to Virgo 7:54 a.m.) It's an earthy very practical day, which can put your self-reliance to good work. Virgo and Capricorn have key roles. Pay attention to a possible career change or some improved and more interesting assignments. Sapphire is your color; your number is 5. You tend to dress down rather than up.

Monday, June 29 (Moon in Virgo) Today is fine for sticking with the job that has to be done before the month slips away. Keep checking with the big boss to make sure you are right on track. Discount rumors and gossip that are making the rounds at your workplace. Fine trends exist in gardening, and the lawn can be improved, too. Fuchsia is your color; your number is 9.

Tuesday, June 30 (Moon in Virgo to Libra 7:05 p.m.) Taurus and Capricorn can impact your day. A strongly self-disciplined approach will serve you well today, when you have more duties, obligations, and responsibilities than usual. Avoid interruptions and other distractions to work up to par. A conservative attitude will work well. Hot combination numbers: 2 and 6.

JULY 1998

Wednesday, July 1 (Moon in Libra) You begin this month in a friendly, charming, outgoing mood. Friendships, group activities, prizes, a bonus and the promise of a financial stipend all top your agenda. You enjoy considerable privileges now because of the popularity you have earned. Rainbow is your color. Lucky lottery: 2, 11, 20, 29, 38, 47.

Thursday, July 2 (Moon in Libra) Today is much like yesterday, as you reach out to others and they meet you more than halfway. You ability to get along with others, including difficult coworkers, gives you an important advantage in your career and in the way those in power view you. Off-white is your color; your number is 4.

Friday, July 3 (Moon in Libra to Scorpio 7:45 a.m.) Scorpio and Pisces are helpful. Prepare for Independence Day, issuing invitations by phone to those you want to share the day with you. Shop for food and drinks for a picnic. The great outdoors is beckoning to you. Amber and canary are your colors. Hot combination numbers: 6 and 1.

Saturday, July 4 (Moon in Scorpio)   You tend to be more organized than others and excel in bringing loved ones and friend together. You are able to delve into two matters at once and perform chores in various departments of life. Your energy endears you to those who lack it. Lucky lottery: 8, 17, 26, 35, 44, 2.

Sunday, July 5 (Moon in Scorpio to Sagittarius 7:24 p.m.)   Looking ahead, you may feel overwhelmed with the demands of this month, but this is a good day to take care of the little details and for knocking big jobs down to handling size. Also, be sure to enlist the efforts of other members of your household. Saffron yellow is your color; your lucky number is 1.

Monday, July 6 (Moon in Sagittarius)   You can rise to all challenges now that you are in your lunar-cycle high. You can take over, gain, or regain control, and you can lead others to important goals. You can shift the emphasis, maneuver, and turn your life the way you want it to go. Your lucky number is 5.

Tuesday, July 7 (Moon in Sagittarius)   Air your personal aspirations and ambitions for best results. Work beyond par during the morning and afternoon, warding off all interruptions and distractions and totally applying

257

yourself to the job. This evening is for genuine rest and relaxation. Hot combination numbers: 7 and 3.

Wednesday, July 8 (Moon in Sagittarius to Capricorn 4:27 a.m.)   Push your earning power and income matters. Stick to budgets and enlist the support of your immediate family to do the same. Acquaint children with the facts of financial and economic life. Capricorn can be of considerable help here. Your winning colors are aquamarine and emerald. Lucky lottery: 9, 18, 27, 36, 45, 6.

Thursday, July 9 (Moon in Capricorn)   The full moon in your second house illuminates all worrisome money matters and directs your attention to new ways of saving and better ways of investing money, time, and personal efforts. Ask questions liberally. Read up on the current economy and the ways it differs from the usual economic trends. Cherry is your color; your lucky number is 2.

Friday, July 10 (Moon in Capricorn to Aquarius 10:52 a.m.)   You are still in an advantageous financial period, when many bargains can be located. There is good potential for running down new possible sources of capital. You budget more wisely and can see where improvements can be engineered. Your winning color is red. Hot combination numbers: 4 and 7.

Saturday, July 11 (Moon in Aquarius)   Aquarius will help you take care of little pressing jobs around your home, lawn, and yard. Note where deterioration has set in on trees and shrubbery. Special care of precious bushes may be a must. A neighbor can lend benefit of experience in rearing an exotic plant. Ask questions. Lucky lottery: 6, 15, 24, 33, 42, 51.

Sunday, July 12 (Moon in Aquarius to Pisces 3:22 p.m.)   Hobbies, answering the demands of your own creativity and imagination, and stepped-up communications with a somewhat silent person are all represented in your chart. Siblings and neighbors want to know all about your plans. You tend to find peace of mind more easily now. Beige and taupe are your colors; your number is 8.

Monday, July 13 (Moon in Pisces)   Pisces and Cancer figure prominently. Good trends exist for beach and water activities, enjoying a day at the shore with young people. You can be quite conscious of the value of your property today and somewhat concerned about keeping what you own in excellent condition. Grey is your color; your number is 3.

Tuesday, July 14 (Moon in Pisces to Aries 6:45 p.m.)   Family traditions and conventions top your agenda. There may be a need for brain-to-brain talks with children, rather than the usual heart-to-heart talks. What kids aren't told, they often don't know. Ward off the possibility of future excuse making. Hot combination numbers: 5 and 2.

Wednesday, July 15 (Moon in Aries)   Listen to what Aries is saying, then evaluate your own conclusions. Your love department is strongly stimulated and romantic overtures and interludes are indicated. It's a good day for parties, entertainment, spontaneous socializing, and administering to the needs of children and parents. Lucky lottery: 7, 16, 25, 34, 43, 3.

Thursday, July 16 (Moon in Aries to Taurus 9:33 p.m.)   Make love, bonding more closely with your beloved. A difficult youngster requires special understanding and assistance, and some school problems can best be met during vacation time. Another Sagittarius and a Gemini will have pertinent advice. Your lucky number is 9.

Friday, July 17 (Moon in Taurus)   Know when too much is too much, where you and your growing children are concerned. If a day of rest and staying out of the sun is what you believe is required, then by all means honor this feeling. Theater, museums, and libraries may offer the right escape. Strawberry is your color; your number is 2.

Saturday, July 18 (Moon in Taurus)   Taurus, Virgo and the matters they rule in your horoscope are activated. The special needs of health and work can top this list. Also, career demands that can be met by you personally in your own home, or at least away from the job, will all respond to your attention. Lucky lottery: 4, 13, 22, 31, 40, 49.

Sunday, July 19 (Moon in Taurus to Gemini 12:18 a.m.) Don't try to do it all alone—be willing to accept usual as well as unusual assistance. Gemini has many of the creative and intellectual information you may require. Sharing, cooperating with partners, and listening to what is being said in your presence will make this day go easier. Try the number 6.

Monday, July 20 (Moon in Gemini)   Your preference in colors today are light blue, pink, and canary yellow. The day calls for honoring yourself, by answering some personal needs that your mate and others will approve of. Outdoor chats, as well as sports observation and participation, are going to be pleasant. Your number is 1.

Tuesday, July 21 (Moon in Gemini to Cancer 3:43 a.m.) Pisces and Cancer make good companions. Fine trends exist for paying attention to accumulations of time and money. Talks with your broker, banker, and other financial advisers will all go well. If you have not subscribed to a helpful money magazine, this is a good time to order it. Your number is 3.

Wednesday, July 22 (Moon in Cancer)   Pay attention to security matters, locks, and bolts. Make sure you aren't overlooking certain keys. Also, this is a fine day for implementing changes, improvements, and corrections in the way children and others handle their financial allowances. Raspberry is your color. Lucky lottery: 5, 14, 23, 32, 41, 50.

Thursday, July 23 (Moon in Cancer to Leo 8:48 a.m.) The new moon in your ninth house illuminates travel plans, long-range gains or losses, and long-distance advantages and opportunities. Keep in close touch with loved ones near and far away. Talk to a travel bureau and gather brochures and folders. France and Italy, both Leo-ruled nations, may beckon. Henna and auburn are your colors; your number is 7.

Friday, July 24 (Moon in Leo) Keep on the go, traveling or at least recycling trips made earlier in life. Your memory is strongly sensitized in all long-distance matters, including special memories. Discussions of travel plans and travel memories will make the day all the more pleasant. Wheat is your color; try the number 9.

Saturday, July 25 (Moon in Leo to Virgo 4:34 p.m.) It may be difficult to stop long enough to gather your wits under prevailing aspects. You're so busy. You can accomplish a great deal from keeping on the go. You're positive, cheerful, and willing to take a risk and even gamble a little. Your self-confidence is masterful. Lucky lottery: 2, 11, 20, 29, 38, 47.

Sunday, July 26 (Moon in Virgo) Virgo helps you catch up through improved organizational skills. You pull all high-blown ideas down to Earth and take a realistic look at them. Fine trends exist for thriftiness and for figuring out if anything has gone wrong in your approach toward your career. Foxy orange is your color; your number is 4.

Monday, July 27 (Moon in Virgo) At home or abroad, your career won't go away. What you see or hear can remind you of some career advantages and opportunities that are within your scope and abilities. As usual, there is a very self-disciplined and practical approach to what you are thinking along professional and authority lines. Your number is 8.

Tuesday, July 28 (Moon in Virgo to Libra 3:14 a.m.)   It's a good day for relaxation and for spending quality time doing what comes naturally to you. Libra is in your corner and the potential in close or newer friendships is enormous. A wonderful lasting relationship can begin under these aspects. Lemon is your color. Hot combination numbers: 1 and 7.

Wednesday, July 29 (Moon in Libra)   There are things you can and want to do during this peak of high summer, and this day is ideal for doing them. Spend time with kindred spirits, who know and appreciate the real you. Group activities give you a chance to really shine. Socializing, rather than work, is the trend. Lucky lottery: 3, 12, 21, 30, 39, 48.

Thursday, July 30 (Moon in Libra to Scorpio 3:44 p.m.)   Libra and Gemini make good companions, but it is not wise to compete with Gemini to any great extent. This is a good socializing day. You will enjoy meeting with some clubmates you haven't seen lately, because of summer involvements. Cerulean blue and purple are your colors. Hot combination numbers: 5 and 2.

Friday, July 31 (Moon in Scorpio)   Travel is blocked, as Mercury turns retrograde in your ninth house. But you can finish up all the odd chores and tasks of this month and be ready for August. Pay bills, settle accounts, and file important papers away. You may have some difficulty in figuring out what is happening behind the scenes. Blue is your color; your lucky number is 7.

AUGUST 1998

Saturday, August 1 (Moon in Scorpio)   Today constitutes a period of grace for getting last month's business taken care of immediately. What spills over from July can take considerable effort now. Travel is slow, facing obstacles. Looking ahead, the future may be somewhat foggy. What you have developing at a distance seems temporarily blacked out. Lucky lottery: 6, 15, 24, 33, 42, 51.

Sunday, August 2 (Moon in Scorpio to Sagittarius 3:48 a.m.) How lucky can you be! After yesterday's involvement with the past, today brings you completely up to date, so you can tackle your weight in wildcats. You are in your lunar-cycle high and can turn the day's hours to good accounting. Self-realization is your goal. Promote yourself. Tan and tawny brown are your colors; your lucky number is 8.

Monday, August 3 (Moon in Sagittarius) Still in your lunar-cycle high, be sure you are holding the initiative and demonstrating the highest in self-confidence. Others interfere less with your plans and you can make magnificent progress in personal affairs. Look the part of a winner and dress to the hilt—no bluejeans or gingham! Be sharp and svelte. Your lucky number is 3.

Tuesday, August 4 (Moon in Sagittarius to Capricorn 1:18 p.m.) Go for the prizes, looking rich and royal and speaking out in your own behalf. Be proud of your ambitions and aspirations. An Aries and a Leo are rooting for you, and another Sagittarius also wants to see you win. Beige and mauve are your winning colors. Hot combination numbers: 5 and 2.

Wednesday, August 5 (Moon in Capricorn) There is money earmarked for you, if you become more fully aware of your personal financial potential. Push your earning power in more than one area. Make sure you are using your talents, skills, available cash, effort, and time to good advantage. Primrose is your color. Lucky lottery: 7, 16, 25, 34, 43, 3.

Thursday, August 6 (Moon in Capricorn to Aquarius 7:31 p.m.) Capricorn and Taurus have key roles.

Good trends exist for comparing prices before making a major purchase. Comparison shopping could net good bargains. There are times when you should buy some items in quantity and this is one of them. Your number is 9.

Friday, August 7 (Moon in Aquarius)   Concentrate on the work that can be gotten out of the way. Organize your time well and take shortcuts where feasible. Don't neglect any hobby that ultimately can be put on a money-making basis. Discuss your chances of success with an interested relative. Try the number 2.

Saturday, August 8 (Moon in Aquarius to Pisces 11:04 p.m.)   The full moon in your third house illuminates studies, learning processes, intellectual ideas, hobbies, local matters, and all communications and transportation potential. Today is fine for buying a new telephone or alarm system, and for making sure that an elderly loved one has a lifeline installed. Lucky lottery: 4, 13, 22, 31, 40, 49.

Sunday, August 9 (Moon in Pisces)   Give first attention to your family. It's a good at-home day when loved ones can drop in and feel welcome. Phone somebody you would like to see and invite this person over for lunch or an early-evening meal. Fish should be on the menu and it should be prepared in an interesting way. Seaweed green is your color; your lucky number is 6.

Monday, August 10 (Moon in Pisces)   Pisces and Scorpio figure prominently. Property and ownership matters can top your agenda. Community problems can be discussed fruitfully. Problems in running the metropolis that are hidden in colder weather can stand out today. Are you expecting too much of your mate? Your lucky number is 1.

Tuesday, August 11 (Moon in Pisces to Aries 1:10 a.m.) Today is perfect for lovemaking, bonding more closely with your beloved, giving quality time to soothe the anxieties of your children, and entertaining. You are warm-hearted, anxious to please, and equally desirous to see or hear from somebody at a distance. Phone and write letters. Hot combination numbers: 3 and 9.

Wednesday, August 12 (Moon in Aries)   Aries and Leo understand each other, but under prevailing aspects you may consider them both and daring, or even aggressive. You are not the one to let others encroach on your personal and private thinking and decision making. It's a good day to be close to your beloved and your children. Claret is your color. Lucky lottery: 5, 14, 23, 32, 41, 50.

Thursday, August 13 (Moon in Aries to Taurus 3:04 a.m.)   You warm up to the idea of travel as Venus enters Leo. You may be considered extremely possessive of your children. Realize there comes a time when kids have to grow up and learn to make some decisions on their own. Taurus and Leo have parts to play. Amber is your color; your lucky number is 7.

Friday, August 14 (Moon in Taurus)   Don't press too much work on yourself today. Health, proper diet, adequate rest and relaxation, and preventive-medicine routines are of vital importance under existing aspects. Avoid worrying about tasks that can be done another time. Umber is your color. Hot combination numbers: 9 and 6.

Saturday, August 15 (Moon in Taurus to Gemini 5:46 a.m.)   Gemini and the matters it rules are strongly in evidence. Two heads are better than one, so you'll gain from listening to your mate and business partners. You could be dissatisfied with some contracts and agreements, and with the way you purchase supplies. You can speak up under these trends. Lucky lottery: 2, 11, 20, 29, 38, 47.

Sunday, August 16 (Moon in Gemini)   Communications are stepped up and important topics are discussed.

Teamwork is the idea, rather than attempting to do everything by yourself. Joint efforts and joint investments get the green light. It's a fine day for figuring out where the family should go from here. Blue is your color; your number is 4.

Monday, August 17 (Moon in Gemini to Cancer 9:55 a.m.) Cooperate with your mate and other partners for best results. Honor all contracts on a day when you could be faulted for ignoring the same. Gemini and Libra are present, and there can be gains, if you are pleasant to your in-laws and the friends and business associates of your spouse. Your number is 8.

Tuesday, August 18 (Moon in Cancer) Cancer and Scorpio can impact your financial thinking. It's a fine day to work on budgeting, bargain hunting, bartering operations, savings, and investments. You are open to novel concepts of loved ones and others. You give support where your feel there is promise. Ultramarine is your color. Hot combination numbers: 1 and 7.

Wednesday, August 19 (Moon in Cancer to Leo 4:01 p.m.) You adjust well to the changes imposed on you, and there can be a big payoff for the flexibility you are demonstrating under current aspects. Pisces approves and appreciates your personal values and the way you rise to all challenges. Purple is your color. Lucky lottery: 3, 12, 21, 30, 39, 48.

Thursday, August 20 (Moon in Leo) Today is fine for taking off like a big bird, doing your own thing in travel, sightseeing, and living it up. You succeed, if you look ahead to the future and if you handle matters at a distance. Buying imports—lovely items from France and Italy—may be on your agenda. Hot combination numbers: 5 and 2.

Friday, August 21 (Moon in Leo) Aries and another Sagittarius can impact your thinking. You feel very much at home with people you are meeting for the first time.

You have decided to be positive and more aggressive, and these approaches and attitudes win much approval. Brown is your color; your number is 7.

Saturday, August 22 (Moon in Leo to Virgo 12:21 a.m.)   The eclipsed sun can present obstacles. If traveling, there can be pesky pressures, and perhaps something lost, delayed, or postponed. Information may be held back or be unavailable altogether. Try to laugh at the ridiculous excuses clerks are making. Pinecone is your color. Lucky lottery: 9, 18, 27, 36, 45, 6.

Sunday, August 23 (Moon in Virgo)   It's a career, professional, and authority day both on and off the job. You may want to shut your phone off and refuse to answer doorbells. There is a great deal of selfishness permeating the day and some guilt when people don't have their nose to the grindstone. Your number is 2.

Monday, August 24 (Moon in Virgo to Libra 11:02 a.m.)   Mercury resumes direct movement in your ninth house, so what was delayed or postponed can arrive now, as information begins to flow freely again. Invitations that didn't materialize when you wanted them can now be yours. You may change your evaluation of what is going on at a distance. Try the number 6.

Tuesday, August 25 (Moon in Libra)   Wonderful trends exist in your social life. Friendships, group activities, and the social side of your job, are all perking favorably. You and your assistants, supervisors, and coworkers generally are in a good mood and, as a result, work is more enjoyable. The more positive and cheerful you are, the more popular you will be. Light browns are your colors. Hot combination numbers: 8 and 2.

Wednesday, August 26 (Moon in Libra to Scorpio 11:25 p.m.)   A kindred spirit, with whom you can let down your hair, will have the information and explanations you are seeking. You are not quite ready to pick up the threads of church and club work that was canceled over

267

the summer months, but there is somebody trying to goad you into this. Lucky lottery: 1, 10, 19, 28, 37, 46.

Thursday, August 27 (Moon in Scorpio)   It's an excellent day to close out the month, tackling projects that are supposed to be finished before the start of September. You can count on the help of a Scorpio and a Pisces. Still, you can have the feeling that there is something subtle in the nuances of this day, something mysterious. Try the number 3.

Friday, August 28 (Moon in Scorpio)   You may surprise yourself by getting more work done today than you thought possible. Today is fine for filing papers away, presenting work for approval, editing, proofreading, and getting the show on the road. Work you do now will prove enduring and lead to a salary increase. Flaxen gold is your color. Hot combination numbers: 5 and 2.

Saturday, August 29 (Moon in Scorpio to Sagittarius 11:55 a.m.)   Today is fine for completions, finishing up the odd chores of August and preparing for the end of summer. It may not be easy to pinpoint what is going on, but suspicions and surmises are generated in your twelfth house. Get in touch with those who feel you owe them a favor. Lucky lottery: 7, 16, 25, 34, 43, 3.

Sunday, August 30 (Moon in Sagittarius)   You have everything going for you today, since you are in your second lunar-cycle high. You can complete the advantages and opportunities that worked so well for you at the beginning of August. You can build on this month and carry off the resulting prizes. Maroon is your color; your number is 9.

Monday, August 31 (Moon in Sagittarius to Capricorn 10:23 p.m.)   Air aspirations as you hold the initiative and lead the big race for important goals in your life. The entire month is paying off for you. Your Pluto-induced awareness gives you enormous extrasensory perception, so accept it and cash in on it. Your colors are tangerine and orange, your lucky number is 4.

SEPTEMBER 1998

Tuesday, September 1 (Moon in Capricorn)   It's a money day, the aspects favoring earning power, income, and the creation of wealth. Persist in attaining special money that you feel is due you. Attending sales and wise bargain hunting are part of the scenario. You could learn that some of your possessions are more valuable than realized. Try the number 3.

Wednesday, September 2 (Moon in Capricorn)   Capricorn and Virgo have practical financial advice for you. Is it time to press forward in your career for better assignments that ultimately will mean increased income? The financial decisions that you make now can impact your future. Ruby is your color. Lucky lottery: 5, 14, 23, 32, 41, 50.

Thursday, September 3 (Moon in Capricorn to Aquarius 5:21 a.m.)   Fine trends exist for handling usual, everyday, and expected schedules and routines in an admirable and productive way. It's time to conserve your energies and direct them where they will show the most good. Don't waste any time, money, or effort. Keep plodding. Your lucky number is 7.

Friday, September 4 (Moon in Aquarius)   Aquarius and Libra are on stage. Studies, hobbies, communications skills, and movement in your own locality are of vital importance. You know when to work alone and when to invite cooperation and teamwork. This potpourri can set the stage for the weekend ahead. Blue is your color. Hot combination numbers: 9 and 6.

Saturday, September 5 (Moon in Aquarius to Pisces 8:48 a.m.)   An Aquarian will make your day pleasant and profitable. Your studies, creative hobbies, and spirit

269

of independence in everyday matters are all accented and worthy of effort. You articulate your opinions well. Lucky lottery: 2, 11, 20, 29, 38, 47.

Sunday, September 6 (Moon in Pisces) The full moon forms in your fourth house which illuminates family and residential matters. Fine trends exist for taking care of what you own, and community interests are also represented. Concerted action on the part of locals can deal successfully with any worries and problems. Your number is 4.

Monday, September 7 (Moon in Pisces to Aries 9:53 a.m.) You warm up to your career potential as Venus enters Virgo. You are really looking forward to a new season of opportunity at work. Establish improved relationships with supervisors and coworkers. There could be minor conflicts between your public and private lives. Mocha is your color; your number is 8.

Tuesday, September 8 (Moon in Aries) Your love life is strongly stimulated. You relate well to your mate and all demonstrations of love will be reciprocated fully. A romantic glow settles on you and any courtship is going to make amazing progress. Also, you can improve your understanding of your children. Russet is your color. Hot combination numbers: 1 and 7.

Wednesday, September 9 (Moon in Aries to Taurus 10:16 a.m.) It's a fine day for spontaneous entertaining and socializing with mixed company. You excel in reaching out to others and assuring them of your concern and affection. It's a fine day also for improving relationships with in-laws and with the working associates of your spouse. Lucky lottery: 3, 12, 21, 30, 39, 48.

Thursday, September 10 (Moon in Taurus) Push health and work improvements. The fall season may call for a different approach to preventive-medicine routines. Some of your favorite fruits and vegetables may no longer be available. Taurus and Virgo have the answers

270

you are seeking. Beige is your color. Hot combination numbers: 5 and 2.

Friday, September 11 (Moon in Taurus to Gemini 11:40 a.m.)　You may have the feeling that an assistant or co-worker is showing antipathy toward your ideas, but don't press your objections. This person is not apt to listen to reason anyway. Be diplomatic, and you'll win the desired approval. Mauve is your color; your number is 7.

Saturday, September 12 (Moon in Gemini)　It's an altogether different day, with an airy, intellectual atmosphere permeating your environment. Gemini and Libra make ideal companions. You are tops at sharing and cooperating, and some good decisions can be made. Your marital state and other partnerships get top billing. Lucky lottery: 9, 18, 27, 36, 45, 3.

Sunday, September 13 (Moon in Gemini to Cancer 3:20 p.m.)　You will want to spend time with loved ones on a good day for talking things over quietly and recognizing valid points of disagreement. People are not all alike; rather there are twelve distinct solar groups, and within these are millions of individual types. Your lucky number is 2.

Monday, September 14 (Moon in Cancer)　Today is excellent for improving your personal financial worth. Savings, investments, insurance, and tax matters are strongly supported. Cancer and Virgo are on your side as you respond well to changes and corrections. Titian gold is your color; your number is 6.

Tuesday, September 15 (Moon in Cancer to Leo 9:48 p.m.)　Push for decisions, especially joint ones in marriage and other partnerships. Design changes that you feel ought to be made before autumn. You use accumulations of money, time, and energy wisely. Scorpio and Pisces can be consulted with confidence. Your colors are khaki and olive. Hot combination numbers: 8 and 1.

Wednesday, September 16 (Moon in Leo)   It may be time to get away from the job and change your scene, even if only for a few days. Travel, visiting, sightseeing, and dining in unusual places are all well represented in your chart. You are looking forward, solving problems before they grow bigger. Apricot and plum are your colors. Lucky lottery: 1, 10, 19, 28, 37, 46.

Thursday, September 17 (Moon in Leo)   Leo gives good directions and information, and will answer your unusual questions. What you have perking for yourself at a distance is expanding and becoming more promising. It's a day for anticipating, looking far ahead, and not limiting yourself to the present. Salmon is your color. Hot combination numbers: 3 and 9.

Friday, September 18 (Moon in Leo to Virgo 6:52 a.m.)   You can make valuable contributions to your job, whether you are at work or away. Just enjoying a conversation with somebody involved in your profession or vocation may engender ideas on which you can build your future career. Authority comes easily to you today. Pearl gray is your color; your number is 5.

Saturday, September 19 (Moon in Virgo)   Listen to Virgo. Your economic and social level are inching up jointly, and there is new promise to your career potential. In many ways, it becomes a matter of relating to your supervisors and employers. Invite a coworker you like to dinner. Cardinal red is your color. Lucky lottery: 7, 16, 25, 34, 43, 3.

Sunday, September 20 (Moon in Virgo to Libra 5:57 p.m.)   The new moon in your tenth house illuminates where you want to go from here, how you can make achievements in your career more recognizable. You want to be complimented by loved ones and professional associates. Be patient; people may not know how to express their admiration. Try the number 9.

Monday, September 21 (Moon in Libra)   Court approval, appreciation, and popularity for the best results under these aspects. Friendships, group activities, and the expansion of your social involvements are all indicated, and church and club volunteer effort will also bring a strong response in your favor. Alabaster and cream are your colors; your lucky number is 4.

Tuesday, September 22 (Moon in Libra)   You can be the center of attention today, as others want to be in your company. Invitations are coming your way. This type of popularity is more than a bubble and you can use it to open important doors. Your outgoing, cheerful ways, and your positive thinking, are endearing you even to former critics. Your number is 6.

Wednesday, September 23 (Moon in Libra to Scorpio 6:22 a.m.)   Libra and Scorpio and the matters they rule in your chart top your agenda. Your ability to spread goodwill and to be fair in all your decisions, and the way you can extract additional gains from the past, are all going to work to your advantage. Today is fine for completing a project. Lucky lottery: 8, 17, 26, 35, 44, 2.

Thursday, September 24 (Moon in Scorpio)   Your social life is stepped up as Mercury enters Libra. What has been hidden and transpiring behind the scenes can suddenly burst forth and actually rebound to your advantage. You can count on strong extrasensory perception under these Pluto trends. Bay green is your color; your lucky number is 1.

Friday, September 25 (Moon in Scorpio to Sagittarius 7:05 p.m.)   You encourage others to stick to what they are doing and, as a result, important projects can be completed today. Don't hurry or complain, just inspire and guide with patience and perseverance. Top management will realize that success began with your attitude and approach. Chestnut is your color; your lucky number is 3.

Saturday, September 26 (Moon in Sagittarius)   Now in your lunar-cycle high, you can accomplish miracles, working rings around others. You are especially effective where you are working overtime. It is important that you speak out, airing your ambitions and letting others sense the force of your self-confidence. Lucky lottery: 5, 14, 23, 32, 41, 50.

Sunday, September 27 (Moon in Sagittarius)   Continue yesterday's march to success. Out in the open or indoors, you tend to stand out in a physical and mental way. What you say carries a big wallop. Others are impressed with your determination and ability to both participate and observe. Indigo is your color; your number is 7.

Monday, September 28 (Moon in Sagittarius to Capricorn 6:30 a.m.)   You can realize financial gains under the prevailing aspects. Go for the prizes, taking advantage of all that you have learned lately, and invest it well. Your earning power and income may be more important than your credit rating. Move power speedily from income you can count on into a mutual fund investment. Try the number 2.

Tuesday, September 29 (Moon in Capricorn)   Pay all bills that are due or about to become due. Know what money you have to spend and how much should be put away for the expensive month ahead. Your children will require new clothes and additional allowances as their social life expands. Claret is your color; your lucky number is 4.

Wednesday, September 30 (Moon in Capricorn to Aquarius 2:53 p.m.)   Capricorn and Virgo can give you good banking and investment advice under the prevailing aspects. There is a growing possibility that somebody may request a loan from you. You may feel uncertain about your own financial prospects and react accordingly. Mocha and white are your colors. Lucky lottery: 6, 15, 24, 33, 42, 51

Thursday, October 1 (Moon in Aquarius)   Give local, immediate, and pressing problems your best shot. Siblings and neighbors are interested in your plans. You communicate effectively and can gain from moving around your own neighborhood, checking things out with merchants, shopping a little, and getting the real lay of the land. Hot combination numbers: 6 and 1.

Friday, October 2 (Moon in Aquarius to Pisces 7:23 p.m.)   Aquarius and Gemini and the matters they rule are impacted by the day's aspects. Togetherness, rather than an independent attitude, will prove to be the best approach. Friendships give you a great deal of self-confidence with the sun, Venus, and Mercury all stimulating your eleventh house. Violet is your color; your lucky number is 8.

Saturday, October 3 (Moon in Pisces)   Domestic, community, ownership, and property matters are high on your agenda. You can enjoy closeness with your family, and there is a tendency for unusual communications. What may not have been told as recently as a week ago can be mentioned today as secrets are revealed. There are subtle situations. Lucky lottery: 1, 10, 19, 28, 37, 46.

Sunday, October 4 (Moon in Pisces to Aries 8:32 p.m.)   Pisces and Cancer figure prominently. It's a good at-home day with elders and younger persons in the picture. Family values and traditions are in evidence and there is a special sense of satisfaction where loved ones are in almost total agreement. Contact distant relatives by phone. Your lucky number is 3.

Monday, October 5 (Moon in Aries)   The full moon forms in our fifth house of love, romance, courtship, spontaneous socializing, and the affairs of children. All of these will be illuminated for you and, as a result, you can make good decisions regarding them. You are

275

happy, cheerful, and looking forward with a strongly loving and positive mood. Your number is 7.

Tuesday, October 6 (Moon in Aries to Taurus 7:57 p.m.)   Bond more closely with your beloved, children, and parents. You build a bridge between the younger and older generations. The great outdoors is beckoning and you and your dear one will enjoy a brisk walk in your own neighborhood. Laughter is the prologue to rewarding lovemaking. Your colors are flesh and ivory. Hot combination numbers: 9 and 6.

Wednesday, October 7 (Moon in Taurus)   Taurus understands the mechanics of the job you are about to do. Blue-collar rather than white-collar workers are more sympathetic and helpful under the prevailing aspects. There is some hard work that will prove therapeutic today. You could hear many health complaints now. Lucky lottery: 2, 11, 20, 29, 38, 47.

Thursday, October 8 (Moon in Taurus to Gemini 7:44 p.m.)   Organizational interests, the rights of workers, and improved relationships between management and labor are all showing good potential. Meetings, discussions, investigations, estimations, and voting are all favored. It's a day for solving problems so that important work can proceed. Silvery white is your color. Hot combination numbers: 4 and 7.

Friday, October 9 (Moon in Gemini)   Set up a program for an exciting weekend, keeping on the go in the great outdoors, hiking, checking the advance of autumn, raking leaves, and appreciating the glorious colors and those clear October skies. Gemini and Aquarius are your ideal companions. Electric blue is your color; your number is 6.

Saturday, October 10 (Moon in Gemini to Cancer 9:48 p.m.)   Your marital state and other partnerships, as well as joint endeavors and investments, are all favored. Don't attempt to go it alone; rather, listen to what partners have to say and make a joint decision. Today is fine for working on the designs for new contracts, agreements, and purchasing plans. Lucky lottery: 8, 17, 26, 35, 44, 2.

Sunday, October 11 (Moon in Cancer)   The water signs (Cancer, Scorpio, and Pisces) have the upper hand. Accumulations of money, time, and energy are indicated and can be put to good use. You can weed out some no-win ideas and projects and put in their place plans with potential for success. Your color is ecru; your lucky number is 1.

Monday, October 12 (Moon in Cancer)   You can predict some of your present plans on past successful results, now that Mercury has made its Scorpio ingress. You are tops at reevaluating former involvements, successes, and failures, and extricating what you can from them as the basis for some new important project. Earth is your color; your number is 5.

Tuesday, October 13 (Moon in Cancer to Leo 3:25 a.m.)   You can change your scene now; take on a futuristic project; and learn more about computers, E-Mail, and the Internet. You can't stand still on a day such as this. All around you people are maneuvering, shifting the emphasis, and deciding that they must know more about this electronic era. Pumpkin and melon are your colors; your number is 7.

Wednesday, October 14 (Moon in Leo)   It's go, go and go—all switches are pushed forward and new ideas and new ways are crowding into your life. Long-range and long-distance interests get top billing. Leo and Aquarius will help you open new doors and strive for gain along new paths. Partners may have to be won over to your innovations. Lucky lottery: 9, 18, 27, 36, 45, 3.

Thursday, October 15 (Moon in Leo to Virgo 12:32 p.m.)   If the mountain will not come to you, then you must go to the mountain. Your powers of persuasion are good, with the moon and Venus in favorable alignment, so persuade others to look ahead and not into the past. Coffee is your color; your number is 2.

Friday, October 16 (Moon in Virgo) Virgo is helpful in a career, professional, or authority matter. Some social conservation and thrift will be a good idea. It's not a day for being too independent in the clinches or taking your professional status for granted. Orange is your color. Hot combination numbers: 4 and 7.

Saturday, October 17 (Moon in Virgo) Shop for items that might help you perform career assignments better. It's also a good day for buying fall garments and wardrobe accessories. Capricorn and Taurus can be depended on in any emergency. A new approach to weight reduction could be a topic of conversation. Brown is your color. Lucky lottery: 6, 15, 24, 33, 42, 51.

Sunday, October 18 (Moon in Virgo to Libra 12:02 a.m.) You are into a wonderful social cycle, so issue and accept invitations for today and the next several days. Libra and Gemini are available for any pointers you may need. Introducing a new friend to older acquaintances makes this a pleasant time. Coral is your color; your lucky number is 8.

Monday, October 19 (Moon in Libra) Spend time with members of your club, group, or clique, for your popularity is assured. You know how to cash in on such high levels of approval and acceptance, so entertaining in your home or favorite intimate restaurant won't go wrong. Your lucky colors are tawny brown and canary; your lucky number is 3.

Tuesday, October 20 (Moon in Libra to Scorpio 12:36 p.m.) It's another wonderful social day, when you will enjoy the company of those whom destiny has put in your corner. You have the wonderful knack of brightening their lives and providing them with a new positive vision of what they can achieve at this time. Azure and baby blue are your colors. Hot combination numbers: 5 and 2.

Wednesday, October 21 (Moon in Scorpio) It's time to consider what you want to do between now and the end of the month. You are empowered by the moon, Mars, and Mercury to close out no-win projects, to muster your forces for a final showdown, and to direct your power into making the field of competition less threatening. Lucky lottery: 7, 16, 25, 34, 43, 3.

Thursday, October 22 (Moon in Scorpio) You are tops at surmising what is being hidden from you, at figuring out what the competition has in mind, and generally suspecting what is happening behind the scenes. You could learn that opposing forces have a shocking way of conspiring together. Yellows are your colors; your lucky number is 9.

Friday, October 23 (Moon in Scorpio to Sagittarius 1:16 a.m.) In your lunar high cycle today, you can change all things for the better. It's a case of green lights and high opportunities. It's important that you believe in yourself and in your lucky star, Jupiter. What you tackle now, you can bring to a successful conclusion. Blue is your color. Hot combination numbers: 2 and 6.

Saturday, October 24 (Moon in Sagittarius) Seize and hold the initiative in all things. Lead, arising early and getting all the wheels turning. Your self-reliance puts you in an enviable position for getting your own way. You compete and challenge, confidently airing your aspirations and extracting new gains from past experiences. Lucky lottery: 4, 13, 22, 31, 40, 49.

Sunday, October 25—Daylight Saving Time ends (Moon in Sagittarius to Capricorn 12:05 p.m.) You warm up to past experiences and tend to view them in more gentle lights. You could find yourself thinking of an old flame, as Venus enters Scorpio. This is an aspect related to all the women and men, who "got away," as

279

the saying goes. Phone or send a warm note to some unforgettable former friend. Your color is red; your number is 6.

Monday, October 26 (Moon in Capricorn)   Upgrade finances now that the moon is illuminating your second house and your earning power and income will respond to the attention you give them. Take care of expensive possessions and make certain that your valuables are secure and insured. Cinnamon is your color; your lucky number is 1.

Tuesday, October 27 (Moon in Capricorn to Aquarius 9:44 p.m.)   It's an excellent day for collecting what is owed you. A dutiful and obligatory approach in all money matters will produce good results. You have a responsibility to those who need financial advice and instructions, so assist one who has little understanding or appreciation of money. Hot combination numbers: 3 and 6.

Wednesday, October 28 (Moon in Aquarius)   Aquarius and Libra give approval and appreciation. You gain from localizing and concentrating, from dealing in usual routines and schedules, and from handling everyday matters with self-confidence. Talks with relatives and neighbors can restore the flow of information. Your winning colors are pumpkin and canary. Lucky lottery: 5, 14, 23, 32, 41, 50.

Thursday, October 29 (Moon in Aquarius)   Pay attention to household maintenance and some possible renovation. If storm windows and doors are not in place, then this is a good cycle for getting them up. Trees, bushes, and shrubbery may be demanding special attention and care now. Neighbors have much to tell you. Your lucky number is 7.

Friday, October 30 (Moon in Aquarius to Pisces 3:58 a.m.)   A loved one may be hoarding some complaint and feel that this is not the time to air it, but you tend to suspect and surmise rather accurately and it would be well to arrange a comfortable setting for confidences to be shared. Family spirituality can be counted on to offset any argument. Old rose is your color. Hot combination numbers: 9 and 6.

Saturday, October 31 (Moon in Pisces)   Give quality time to members of your immediate family. Asking questions in a quiet, uncritical, nonjudgemental way. Goodwill and empathy will run interference for you. Much can be gotten out into the open, and problems or threatening problems can be solved or even nipped in the bud. Lucky lottery: 2, 11, 20, 29, 38, 47.

NOVEMBER 1998

Sunday, November 1 (Moon in Pisces to Aries 6:27 a.m.)   It's a great day for making love, letting yourself go as you and your beloved demonstrate the joys and force of your commitment. It's a romantic day, when courtships will flourish. You can bond more closely with your children and with younger folk generally. Celebrations go well. Your number is 1.

Monday, November 2 (Moon in Aries)   Aries and another Sagittarius figure prominently. Spontaneity marks your social and physical involvements. Parties and other entertainment go well. What you organize and arrange is bound to succeed beyond your highest hopes. Reddish-yellows are complimentary to your appearance; your number is 5.

Tuesday, November 3 (Moon in Aries to Taurus 6:12 a.m.)   Taurus and Virgo and the matters they rule in your horoscope are favored. Work goes smoothly and you advance in your career more through hard effort than preferment. The health of aging loved ones requires closer checking under the existing aspects. Chestnut is your color. Hot combination numbers: 7 and 3.

Wednesday, November 4 (Moon in Taurus) The full moon forms in your sixth house and illuminates health, dietary, nutritional, preventive-medicine, and allied matters. The right work, including some earthy physical effort, will give you a pleasant sense of well-being. You spread goodwill at work. Lucky lottery: 9, 18, 27, 36, 45, 6.

Thursday, November 5 (Moon in Taurus to Gemini 5:11 a.m.) You will achieve more by working in close harmony with partners, including your spouse, than by attempting to go it alone. Discussions, compromises, reconciliations are favored. Be on guard against anyone who tends to divide you against a partner. Your winning color is beige. Hot combination numbers: 2 and 6.

Friday, November 6 (Moon in Gemini) Gemini and Libra have front seats. Contracts can be improved, so review and discuss them with partners, and make sure you are purchasing business supplies and any outside assistance in the right way and the right place. Olive green and Earth brown are your colors; your number is 4.

Saturday, November 7 (Moon in Gemini to Cancer 5:39 a.m.) Cancer and Scorpio figure prominently. Good trends exist for bargain hunting, budgeting, discussing allowances with children, and encouraging members of your household to be thrifty. Your yen to save more is increasing and becoming more compelling. Lucky lottery: 6, 15, 24, 33, 42, 51.

Sunday, November 8 (Moon in Cancer) Discussions about savings and investments can go well. You feel that it is time to deal in impressive changes in standard and cost of living matters. The idea is to secure the support of others involved in these joint efforts. Improvements and corrections are knocking at your door. Try the number 8.

Monday, November 9 (Moon in Cancer to Leo 9:33 a.m.) It's time to ask you banker and broker for required advice. Go to the authorities before making any vital decision. What is coming at you from a distance may be difficult to absorb. Investments in items important to a family, to family values, seem good. Your number is 3.

Tuesday, November 10 (Moon in Leo)   Long-range and long-distance interests get top billing, and travel does well. You tend to personalize whatever you do now, since both Venus and Mercury are moving in your sign. You will make travel decisions yourself, going where you want to go and pursuing the goals that mean most to you. Hot combination numbers: 5 and 2.

Wednesday, November 11 (Moon in Leo to Virgo 5:37 p.m.)   At home or away from home, you are good at anticipating, surmising, suspecting, and increasing your awareness of what is happening behind the scenes. You are in a better position than most to make the right decisions. You want stability in your love life to be more assured. Pumpkin is you color. Lucky lottery: 7, 16, 25, 34, 43, 3.

Thursday, November 12 (Moon in Virgo)   Virgo and Taurus have key roles. You give more to your career, professional, and authority interests than those around you. You are willing to make personal sacrifices for your career, and to put up with many annoyances in order to keep on top of things. Carmine and black are your colors; your number is 9.

Friday, November 13 (Moon in Virgo)   The usual superstitions connected with this day and date are surfacing again. Your horoscope shows power to advance in your career and to endear yourself to many coworkers. Impress top management with your willingness, self-discipline, and attention to responsibilities. Your color is orange; your number is 2.

Saturday, November 14 (Moon in Virgo to Libra 4:58 a.m.)   It's a day for catching up on your social life.

Friends will be glad to hear from you. Scurry up some joint endeavors if possible, getting into the great outdoors, tracking the advance of autumn, and collecting a few colorful leaves for decorative use. Lucky lottery: 4, 13, 22, 31, 40, 49.

Sunday, November 15 (Moon in Libra)   Libra and Gemini are in the picture. Group activities, church and club membership and participation matters, and opportunities for spending some time with a kindred spirit, can make this a rewarding day. You are well disposed toward people generally. Amber is your color; your lucky number is 6.

Monday, November 16 (Moon in Libra to Scorpio 5:41 p.m.)   Begin the week with a word of cheer to supervisors and coworkers, especially those who seem to be under the weather for one reason or another. You are recognized as the prime spreader of goodwill today. Your ruling orb, Jupiter, endows you with availability. You see the humor as well as the pathos of life. Your number is 1.

Tuesday, November 17 (Moon in Scorpio)   Good opportunities for closing out, finishing up, and preparing for new deals. Discuss the possibility of finishing up some no-win project. There are personal interests to be sacrificed in favor of progress. Yellow is your color; your number is 3.

Wednesday, November 18 (Moon in Scorpio)   You are dressing up your top personality and character assets as Venus moves into Sagittarius, and clearing the decks for important upcoming actions. Your personal interests are coming over the horizon and you want to be ready to cash in on your special abilities. Lucky lottery: 5, 14, 23, 32, 41, 50.

Thursday, November 19 (Moon in Scorpio to Sagittarius 6:13 a.m.)   The new moon illuminates past involvements, permitting you to extract additional gains from matters you believed finished and closed. Your personal power is enormous, and you sense many ways for using it successfully. Turquoise is your color. Hot combination numbers: 7 and 3.

Friday, November 20 (Moon in Sagittarius) Pounce on opportunities as soon as you recognize them. This is your day to achieve, to advance all personal causes, for you are in your lunar-cycle high. Stake your claims, inviting favorable attention by dressing to the hilt and standing tall. Lead, rather than follow. Accept all responsibilities. Try the number 9.

Saturday, November 21 (Moon in Sagittarius to Capricorn 5:45 p.m.) Take a breather as Mercury goes retrograde in your sign, but know your personal worth and stand on your convictions where required. Spruce up your personal appearance while Venus is in your sign. Examine your ledgers and your bookkeeping records, and evaluate financial conditions. Lucky lottery: 2, 11, 20, 29, 38, 47.

Sunday, November 22 (Moon in Capricorn) Push your earning power and income matters. Decide how much you have to spend on entertainment and celebrations, and issue invitations to distant relatives you want to see before the year ends. Preparation work for social expansion will go well under the prevailing aspects. White and black are your colors; your number is 4.

Monday, November 23 (Moon in Capricorn) The sun enters Sagittarius and you can take a more personal role in realizing financial stability. The cost and standard of maintaining your family and home can be reviewed wisely and successfully. Some unexpected cash can suddenly come into the picture. Foxy orange is your color; your lucky number is 8.

Tuesday, November 24 (Moon in Capricorn to Aquarius 3:43 a.m.) Concentrate on what can be done right away, and know what siblings and neighbors expect of you in the way of family and community stability. You communicate well, although some of your decisions seem ultra-independent. You are very much interested in securing agreements and will compromise if necessary. Hot combination numbers: 1 and 7.

Wednesday, November 25 (Moon in Aquarius) Aquarius and Libra can be counted on today. You are good at narrowing your sights and zeroing in on that squeaky wheel that needs oiling in many departments of your life. You investigate well. You surmise, suspect, and spread your amazing awareness and intuition far and wide. Lucky lottery: 3, 12, 21, 30, 39, 48.

Thursday, November 26 (Moon in Aquarius to Pisces 11:14 a.m.) Immediate and pressing obligations demand personal attention. You explain things well, but there are those who expect more than explanations. Short-distance travel gets green lights. You could have a sudden revelation that you need to study more to keep up with the changes in society. Saffron yellow is your color; your lucky number is 5.

Friday, November 27 (Moon in Pisces) Pisces brings a spiritual dimension to the day. Family, residential, property, and ownership matters require special attention. Some complaints may be coming at you and, if you look closely, you could spot some mark of physical deterioration in the construction of your home or other dwelling that you may own. Yellows and reds are right; your lucky number is 7.

Saturday, November 28 (Moon in Pisces to Aries 3:34 p.m.) There are many annoyances and much criticism going on in your community. People are more inclined to speak out now than they would have been in the "olden days." Neighbors do not appreciate the one who neglects lawn, leaves, and other matters. Be above this trend. Lucky lottery: 9, 18, 27, 36, 45, 6.

Sunday, November 29 (Moon in Aries) This month began with you in a loving and cheerful disposition and

286

it will end on this same note. Aries gives you more self-confidence. Demonstrative love, romantic interludes, and a little flirtation. A strong sense of being "fit as a fiddle and ready for love" permeates your day. Your lucky number is 2.

Monday, November 30 (Moon in Aries to Taurus 4:53 p.m.) You are in an extremely positive mood and can count on great popularity with loved ones and others. This is a fine day to entertain in your home, and to make a spontaneous lunch date with a kindred spirit, or perhaps an old flame. Russet is your color; your lucky number is 6.

DECEMBER 1998

Tuesday, December 1 (Moon in Taurus) Dress appropriately at a time when common colds and sore throats are spreading. You may not feel like working beyond your available energy over the late afternoon, but there are others who want to press on and complete a project or two. Pinecone is your color; your number is 6.

Wednesday, December 2 (Moon in Taurus to Gemini 4:30 p.m.) Taurus and Capricorn have key roles. You may feel that work is piling up and should be attended to even, though reserves of energy can be a little lower than usual. People want to do their work in their own way and this tends to annoy you when you realize they are not performing up to par. Lucky lottery: 8, 17, 26, 35, 44, 2.

Thursday, December 3 (Moon in Gemini) The full moon in your seventh house and illuminates all partnerships, including marriage, as well as sharing, cooperation, and the need to abide by contracts, standards, and conventions. Steer clear of petty arguments. Your winning color is ruby. Hot combination numbers: 1 and 7.

Friday, December 4 (Moon in Gemini to Cancer 4:28 p.m.)   Share and cooperate for the best results. Listen to what a Gemini has to say about the day's potential. It's not too early to consider, review, and evaluate the committee, charitable, and humanitarian work you will be asked to involve yourself in during this month. Mauve is your color; your number is 3.

Saturday, December 5 (Moon in Cancer)   Pisces and Cancer can impact your day. Fine trends exist for figuring out your holiday expenses, and for deciding just how much you can spend on gifts, greeting cards, and social involvements. Remember there are service personnel who will expect a financial gratuity—mailman, paperboy, and other delivery people. Lucky lottery: 5, 14, 23, 32, 41, 50.

Sunday, December 6 (Moon in Cancer to Leo 6:55 p.m.)   Today is fine for putting up holiday decorations and outdoor and indoor lights. You warm to making your lawn and the rest of the front of your home look splendid, and there are aspects that will encourage your creativity. You may exceed your budget despite resolutions to the contrary. Wear light greens; try the number 7.

Monday, December 7 (Moon in Leo)   Leo brings news and so does the postman. You have a warm feeling for old friends who now live far away. Today is fine for mailing gifts that have a long way to travel. You will be remembering places where you used to live when you were much younger and a tear of nostalgia might fall. Your color is beige; your number is 2.

Tuesday, December 8 (Moon in Leo)   Mail greeting cards that have a distance to go. Phone somebody who has meant a great deal to you through the years. Your children may be interested in what they call your "olden times." Sorting and sifting ideas and plans will move along well. Carmen is your color. Hot combination numbers: 4 and 3.

Wednesday, December 9 (Moon in Leo to Virgo 1:21 a.m.)   Virgo introduces method and thoroughness. You make these contributions to your career, professional, and authority matters. It's an excellent evening for holiday shopping in the company of a relative or close friend. The practical applications of your basic talents make this a good day. Lucky lottery: 6, 15, 24, 33, 42, 51.

Thursday, December 10 (Moon in Virgo)   Push your career potential on a day when you can advance through logic and practicality. The more self-disciplined you are, the more favorable the attention you attract. Taurus will stick with you. The plans you make now will have staying power. Copper and maroon are your colors; your lucky number is 8.

Friday, December 11 (Moon in Virgo to Libra 11:43 a.m.)   Point your questions toward Capricorn. You use authority wisely today and this will reflect great credit on you when the rewards are handed out. Fine trends exist for annual parties, church and club banquets, money-raising charitable sales, and humanitarian causes in general. Hot combination numbers: 1 and 7.

Saturday, December 12 (Moon in Libra)   You see beautiful things and wish you could buy them as Venus transits your second house of possessions and expensive tastes. Friendships are of great importance under current trends, and it would be wise to accept all invitations you receive for local, friendly get-togethers. Lucky lottery: 3, 12, 21, 30, 39, 48.

Sunday, December 13 (Moon in Libra)   Entertain friends, or bring them up to date with letters or phone calls. Group efforts can raise money and be fun. There may be a sudden unexpected call on your sympathy and generosity, so do what you can to provide holiday food for the homeless. Forest green is your color; your number is 5.

Monday, December 14 (Moon in Libra to Scorpio 12:16 a.m.) Put the finishing touches on holiday plans. Scorpio can give you fine directions and advice. There is increased awareness of how to handle something challenging and perhaps embarrassing. Get your home in order for future entertaining and guests. It's a fine evening for shopping wisely. Hot combination numbers: 9 and 3.

Tuesday, December 15 (Moon in Scorpio) It's an excellent time to tap into what is hidden, being kept secret, and transpiring behind the scenes. The past has a way of coming around full circle. You may be disgusted with an associate who never seems able to put it all together and wise up. Avoid imposing unwanted views. Hot combination numbers: 2 and 6.

Wednesday, December 16 (Moon in Scorpio to Sagittarius 12:46 p.m.) Awareness is strong and good decisions about the rest of the month can be made. As President Truman said, "Some people need more sex than others." Be tolerant of them. A lot of previously hidden tales are coming to light concerning friends and family members. Cream and magenta are your colors. Lucky lottery: 4, 13, 22, 31, 40, 49.

Thursday, December 17 (Moon in Sagittarius) Hurrah! You are now in your lunar-cycle high, where you can take control. You know what you're doing. Air your aspirations and ambitions as you hold the initiative and show the highest in self-confidence. Another Sagittarius and a Gemini are applauding. Auburn and scarlet are your colors. Hot combination numbers: 6 and 1.

Friday, December 18 (Moon in Sagittarius to Capricorn 11:55 p.m.) The new moon in your sun sign illuminates what you're all about, what you want out of life, and how you can get it. You're doubly favored, with the moon in Sagittarius, along with the sun and newly direct Mercury. In short, it's your day to get what you want. Hot combination numbers: 8 and 1.

Saturday, December 19 (Moon in Capricorn)   This is a fine money day. Look for bargains and special sales, and buy some little gifts in quantity. You can find elegant items that are also priced reasonably if you look for them in the right places. Discuss this shopping venture with a friend who is known for his or her good taste. Lucky lottery: 1, 10, 19, 28, 37, 46.

Sunday, December 20 (Moon in Capricorn)   You handle money well today, and you could even discover you have more available spending money than you realized. Ways of increasing your earning power and income can occur to you under these aspects. Capricorn and Virgo are in your corner. Stick to the game plan. Old rose and ivory are your colors; your number is 3.

Monday, December 21 (Moon in Capricorn to Aquarius 9:15 a.m.)   Pounce on work that has to be done before the holiday spirit interferes. Try to keep coworkers and assistants on the ball, despite all the shopping they are trying to get in during work hours. The self-discipline you can muster will be strongly appreciated by your employer. Beige and hazel are your colors; your number is 7.

Tuesday, December 22 (Moon in Aquarius)   Take care of what is pressing. Studies, hobbies, communications, and short-distance travel get the stellar nod. Siblings and neighbors have favors to ask. You cannot take too independent an attitude, for others are accustomed to a little more effort on your part. Have you spoiled them? Hot combination numbers: 9 and 3.

Wednesday, December 23 (Moon in Aquarius to Pisces 4:45 p.m.)   Aquarius and Libra have key roles. You would appreciate a little time to yourself, to put the finishing touches on house chores that are your special province. Nevertheless, the group, the family, and friends will call on you for decisions or opinions. Primrose and saffron yellow are your colors. Lucky lottery: 2, 11, 20, 29, 38, 47.

Thursday, December 24 (Moon in Pisces)   The moon in transiting your fourth house of domestic interests. Your family and your values top your agenda. Pisces, a strongly spiritual sign, is of vital importance in your life at this time. Hot combination numbers: 4 and 3.

Friday, December 25 (Moon in Pisces to Aries 10:04 p.m.)   The spiritual meaning of the day comes into its own, despite all the tinsel and commercialism that has preceded it. You feel especially close to your family now and will want as many of them as possible around your home. Rest, peace, joy, and meaningful delight are evident, along with a little Pisces–Neptune-ruled sloth. Try the number 6.

Saturday, December 26 (Moon in Aries)   Some of the items you wanted and thought too expensive are on sale today. If you are really interested, get to the stores right after they open. Aries will make a wonderful and adventurous partner on this search for bargains. You feel love, approval, and appreciation all around you. Casual clothing is right. Wear something plaid. Lucky lottery: 8, 17, 26, 35, 44, 2.

Sunday, December 27 (Moon in Aries)   Make love, enjoy the romance of the season, visit people. Bond more closely with children and with your beloved. It's a fine day for trying out something new, and inviting others to drop by for a pot of hot tea. Complement the tea with scrumptious cookies. Try the number 1.

Monday, December 28 (Moon in Aries to Taurus 1:05 a.m.)   Taurus and Capricorn are in this picture. Don't attempt to work at a time when you and coworkers want to relax a bit. It may be difficult to get the holidays out of your system. There is an effort to possess all the good memories that were built up this month. Still, neglecting duties and obligations can bring a sense of guilt. Salmon is your color; your lucky number is 5.

Tuesday, December 29 (Moon in Taurus)   Today is good for abiding by schedules and routines. The work that must get done somehow gets accomplished. There can be a sense of letdown at parties and other entertainments. Be careful what you eat and drink, avoiding anything overly stale or left out of the refrigerator too long. Hot combination numbers: 7 and 3.

Wednesday, December 30 (Moon in Taurus to Gemini 2:22 a.m.)   Today is fine for sharing, cooperating, and working in tandem. What wasn't done yesterday or last week can be accomplished now. There is some good catching up on activities. Gemini and Libra have key roles. Discussions make the atmosphere more peaceful on a day when compromise is acceptable. Lucky lottery: 9, 18, 27, 36, 45, 3.

Thursday, December 31 (Moon in Gemini)   With Gemini present, the discussions, partying, and entertaining will go well, but it will be all the better if you attend a celebration in your own neighborhood. An intellectual atmosphere, perhaps unexpected, can take over. Everybody has a lot to say. Gray is your color; your number is 2.

HAPPY NEW YEAR!

ABOUT THE AUTHOR

Born on August 5, 1926, in Philadelphia, Omarr was the only person ever given full-time duty in the U.S. Army as an astrologer. He also is regarded as the most erudite astrologer of our time and the best known, through his syndicated column (300 newspapers) and his radio and television programs (he is Merv Griffin's "resident astrologer"). Omarr has been called the most "knowledgeable astrologer since Evangeline Adams." His forecasts of Nixon's downfall, the end of World War II in mid-August of 1945, the assassination of John F. Kennedy, Roosevelt's election to the fourth term and his death in office . . . these and many others are on the record and quoted enough to be considered "legendary."

FREE
Love
Advice

Does he really love me?
Will I ever get married?
Is he being faithful?

FREE
sample
psychic reading
answers any
question!

1-800-
743-6130

18+. For Ent. Purposes Only.

WIN A PERSONALIZED HOROSCOPE FROM SYDNEY OMARR!
ENTER THE SYDNEY OMARR HOROSCOPE SWEEPSTAKES!

No purchase necessary. Details below.

Name_____

Address_____

City_____State_____Zip_____

Mail to:
SYDNEY OMARR HOROSCOPE SWEEPSTAKES
P.O. Box 9232
Medford, NY, 11763-9232

Offer expires September 30, 1997.

OFFICIAL RULES

1. NO PURCHASE NECESSARY TO ENTER OR WIN A PRIZE. To enter the SYDNEY OMARR HOROSCOPE SWEEPSTAKES, complete this official entry form (original or photocopy), or, on a 3" x 5" piece of paper, print your name and complete address. Mail your entry to: SYDNEY OMARR HOROSCOPE SWEEPSTAKES, P.O. Box 9232, Medford, NY, 11763-9232. Enter as often as you wish, but mail each entry in a separate envelope. All entries must be received by September 30, 1997, to be eligible. Not responsible for illegible entries, lost or misdirected mail.

2. Winners will be selected from all valid entries in a random drawing on or about October 15, 1997, by Marden-Kane, Inc., an independent judging organization whose decisions are final and binding. Odds of winning are dependent upon the number of entries received. Winners will be notified by mail and may be required to execute an affidavit of eligibility and release which must be returned within 14 days of notification or an alternate winner will be selected.

3. One (1) Grand Prize winner will receive a personalized prediction for one (1) year from Sydney Omarr. One (1) Second Prize winner will receive a personalized prediction for one (1) month from Sydney Omarr. Twenty-five (25) Third Prize winners will receive a free phone call to Sydney Omarr's 1-900 number to hear a personal prediction. No transfer or substitution for prize offered. Estimated value of all prizes: $250.

4. Sweepstakes open to residents of the U.S. and Canada 18 years of age or older, except employees and the immediate families of Penguin Putnam, Inc., its affiliated companies, advertising and promotion agencies. Void in the Province of Quebec and wherever else prohibited by law. All Federal, State, Local, and Provincial laws apply. Taxes, if any, are the sole responsibility of the prize winners. Canadian winners will be required to answer an arithmetical skill testing question administered by mail. Winners consent to the use of their name and/or photos or likenesses for advertising purposes without additional compensation (except where prohibited).

5. For the names of the major prize winners, send a self-addressed, stamped envelope after October 15, 1997, to: SYDNEY OMARR HOROSCOPE SWEEPSTAKES WINNERS, P.O. Box 4320, Manhasset, NY, 11030-4320.

Ⓢ Signet

Penguin Putnam, Inc. ✳ Mass Market